College Caesar

Latin Text with Facing Vocabulary and Commentary

Geoffrey Steadman

College Caesar
Latin Text with Facing Vocabulary and Commentary

First Edition

© 2011 by Geoffrey D. Steadman

ISBN-13: 978-0-9843065-7-2
ISBN-10: 0-9843065-7-9

Published by Geoffrey Steadman
Cover Design: David Steadman

Fonts: Times New Roman

geoffreysteadman@gmail.com

Table of Contents

Selections from Caesar's *Commentāriī dē Bellō Gallicō*

35 Lessons by Title

Preface to the Series

The aim of this commentary is to make selections from Julius Caesar's *Gallic War* as accessible as possible to intermediate-level Latin readers so that they may experience the joy, insight, and lasting influence that comes from reading one of greatest works in classical antiquity in the original Latin. To accomplish this goal, I have decided to eschew the traditional commentary format and adopt the best features of Clyde Pharr's *Aeneid*.

Beneath each of the 35 sections, hereafter called "lessons," of the Latin text are all the corresponding vocabulary words that occur four or fewer times in the commentary, arranged alphabetically in two columns. On the page facing the Latin text and vocabulary is a single page of grammar commentary, which is organized according to line numbers and likewise arranged into two columns. This format allows me to include as much information as possible and yet insure that the entries are distinct and immediately accessible to readers. To complement the vocabulary within the commentary, I have added a running core vocabulary list at the beginning of this commentary that includes all words occurring five or more times arranged according to the lesson in which readers first encounter them. An alphabetized form of this list can be found in the glossary. Together, this book has been designed in such a way that, once readers have mastered the running core list, they will be able to rely solely on the Latin text and facing notes and not need to turn a page or consult outside dictionaries.

The grammatical notes are designed to help beginning readers read the text, and so I have passed over detailed literary and historical explanations in favor of short, concise, and frequent entries that focus exclusively on grammar and morphology. Assuming that readers complete their initial study of Latin with varying levels of ability, I draw attention to almost all subjunctive and accusative-infinitive constructions, identify unusual verbs forms and noun constructions, and in general explain aspects of the Latin that they should have encountered in their elementary review of Latin grammar but perhaps forgotten. As a rule, I prefer to offer too much assistance rather than too little.

For instructors, I have intentionally placed the readings in Book VI before those in Book V. This arrangement conveniently breaks the book into halves of 17 and 18 lessons so that those reading in college may complete one lesson per class and have a midterm after L. 17. For those reading in a high school block schedule (90 90-minute classes), the order allows teachers to complete one lesson per day and administer several tests by the end of the 4.5-

week (22-day) interim and to finish all 35 lessons by the 9-week (45 day) interim. Year-long Latin programs can devote two days to each lesson and finish well within a 90-day semester.

Better Vocabulary-Building Strategies

One of the virtues of this commentary is that it eliminates time-consuming dictionary work. While there are occasions where a dictionary is necessary for developing a nuanced reading of the Latin, in most instances any advantage that may come from looking up a word is outweighed by the time and effort spent in the process. Many continue to defend this practice, but I am convinced that such work has little pedagogical value for intermediate and advanced students and that the time saved can be better spent reading more Latin, memorizing vocabulary, mastering principal parts, and reading advanced-level commentaries and secondary literature.

As an alternative to dictionary work, I recommend that readers review the running core vocabulary list (5 or more times) as soon as possible. Once they have mastered these words, I encourage them to single out, drill, and memorize the words that occur 3-4 times as they encounter them in the reading and devote comparatively little attention to words that occur once or twice. Altogether, I am confident that readers who follow this regimen will learn the vocabulary more efficiently and develop fluency more quickly than with traditional methods.

Print on Demand Books

This volume is a self-published, print-on-demand (POD) book, and as such it gives its author distinct freedoms not available in traditional publications. Since this book is no more than a pdf file waiting to be printed, I am able to respond very quickly to readers' recommended changes and create an revised edition that is available online or in retail within 24 hours. If you would like to suggest changes or download a free .pdf copy of this commentary, please see one of the addresses below. All criticisms are welcome, and I would be very grateful for your help.

Finally, I would like to thank Christopher Lauber at the Fordham Preparatory School and Jim Westcot at Blue Ridge High School for reading through the text and commentary and saving readers from innumerable errors, both great and small. I am very grateful for their sound judgment and keen observations.

Geoffrey Steadman Ph.D.
geoffreysteadman@gmail.com
http://www.geoffreysteadman.com

Introduction to Caesar's *Commentāriī dē Bellō Gallicō*

Gaius Julius Caesar was a ruthless killer and consummate writer. He did not come to Gaul to rescue the people from themselves; he came to conquer, and his commentaries on the *Bellum Gallicum* were a vehicle to magnify his reputation among the Roman people. Nowhere are these two traits of Caesar better illustrated than in the passage below from Book I.12. In an effort to stop the 368,000 Helvetians from migrating to Western Gaul, Caesar pursues with three legions and intercepts one-fourth of the Helvetians (up to 92,000) as they are about to cross the Arar river and rejoin those who have already crossed. What ensues is a slaughter:

> I.12 Flūmen est Arar, quod per fīnēs Haeduōrum et Sēquanōrum in Rhodānum īnfluit, incredibilī lenitāte, ita ut oculīs in utram partem fluat iudicārī nōn possit. Id 1 Helvetiī rātibus ac lintribus iunctīs transībant. Ubi per explōrātōrēs Caesar certiōr factus est trēs iam partēs cōpiārum Helvetiōs id flūmen tradūxisse, quārtam vērō partem citrā flūmen Ararim reliquam esse, dē tertiā vigiliā cum legiōnibus tribus ē castrīs profectus ad eam partem pervēnit quae nondum flūmen transīerat. 5
>
> Eōs impedītōs et inopinantēs aggressus, magnam partem eōrum concidit; reliquī sēsē fugae mandāvērunt atque in proximās silvās abdidērunt. Is pagus appellābātur Tigurīnus; nam omnis cīvitās Helvētia in quattuor pāgōs dīvīsa est. Hic pāgus ūnus, cum domō exīsset, patrum nostrōrum memoriā L. Cassium consulem interfēcerat et eius exercitum sub iugum mīserat. Ita sīve cāsū sive cōnsiliō deōrum immortālium 10 quae pars civitātis Helvetiae īnsignem calamitātem populō Romanō intulerat, ea prīnceps poenam persolvit. Quā in rē Caesar nōn sōlum pūblicās, sed etiam prīvātās iniūriās ultus est, quod eius socerī L. Pīsōnis avum, L. Pīsōnem lēgātum, Tigurinī eōdem proeliō quō Cassium interfēcerant. 15

The passage is rich in rhetorical devices which Caesar employs to dehumanize the enemy, downplay the loss of life, and yet magnify his image as a Roman general. First, Caesar does not depict the Helvetians as human beings worthy of sympathy. In lines 4-7 he refers to the enemy with the banal term "partem," and in line 7, the only line which depicts the attack itself, he employs nondescript pronouns and adjectives such as "eōs," "eōrum," and "reliquī" which suggest that Caesar is attacking a faceless enemy rather than an entire community. In line 4, when he refers to the Helvetians as "copiārum," his word choice is not simply vague but misleading, The word *cōpiae* can refer to "supplies" or "baggage" and rightly describe the long train of Helvetians travelling with their possessions, but throughout Caesar's writings, the word denotes "troops;" and so, when Caesar uses this word to describe the Helvetians, he perhaps intentionally suggests that he is facing armed men rather than unarmed innocents.

Since in lines 8-9 Caesar refers to the group which he attacks as a *pagus*, one of the four political districts of Helvetia, we can conclude that Caesar in fact attacked men and women of all ages. Thus, when Caesar describes those whom he attacked as "those weighed down and unsuspecting" (*eōs impedītōs et inopināntēs*, l. 7), though the passage may lead us to believe that these are *cōpiae*, troops, hindered by their packs, they are more likely men and women of all ages weighed down not by weapons but by the young, by the sick, and by the elderly.

Besides word choice, another rhetorical strategy that Caesar employs involves the relative size and arrangement of passages in his narrative. Elsewhere, Caesar is very detailed in his descriptions of battles. Here, he devotes only two lines (7-8) to the attack itself, but six (1-6) to an introduction and another nine (8-16) to his justification. In doing so, Caesar not only minimizes the importance of an attack on 92,000 but also stresses the lengthier justification—making his defense rather than the slaughter the most memorable passage in the account.

Not surprisingly, even Caesar's justification strains credulity. Caesar claims that "in the memory of our fathers" (*patrum nostrōrum memoriā*, 10) the same part of Helvetia that he attacked had killed the consul Cassius and enslaved his soldiers. Caesar's portrayal makes the consul's death seem recent and Caesar's action a timely response, but from other sources we know that Cassius was killed in 107 BC, 50 years before Caesar's attack. Caesar's dating appears intentionally vague. Caesar is likewise misleading when he says that his encounter with the district which killed Cassius was "either by chance or by the plan of the immortal gods" (*sīve cāsū sive cōnsiliō deōrum*, 11): he not so subtly suggests that the gods approve his action and therefore readers should look upon Caesar as both just and favored by the gods.

Caesar's ploys do not stop there. In addition to referring to himself in the third person, which makes his account seem objective rather than biased, he asserts in lines 14-16 that he is avenging not only a public injustice but a private wrong: the grandfather of Caesar's father-in-law was killed along with Cassius. Even if the Romans found such a claim on behalf of a distant relative credible, the fact that Caesar did not know he was attacking this particular *pagus* shows that, whatever the outcome, vengeance was not among his primary motives.

As readers, therefore, we should view Caesar's *Bellum Gallicum* not as a boring rehash of war but, just as the passage above, a lively attempt to depict events in a way that deflects blame and increases Caesar's reputation among the Romans. Whether Caesar is vilifying the enemy (Book 1, 6) or drawing attention away from his haste and lack of preparation (Book 4, 5), we should be sceptical of Caesar's account and ever vigilant to distingiush fact from bias.

Outline of the *Bellum Gallicum*

Scholars debate when Caesar wrote his *Commentaries*. One appealing theory is that he—perhaps with the help of staff—wrote and published each book individually while settled in winter-quarters. Such timing would have allowed Caesar to report his campaigns to the Senate and, more importantly, respond immediately to less favorable or accusatory reports spread by his political enemies.

Book 1 (58 BC): Campaign against the Helvetians. Campaign against Ariovistus.
Caesar departs from the province of Transalpine Gaul, where he is currently governor, to stop the migration of 368,000 Helvetians from Helvetia, modern Switzerland, to western Gaul. Caesar then turns his forces against Ariovistus and the Germans in Eastern Gaul and drives them across the Rhine river, the customary boundary between the Gauls and Germans.

Book 2 (57 BC): Campaign against the Belgians.
The Belgian Gauls amass forces to resist the Romans, and Caesar marches toward them. The Remi, a Belgic tribe, agree to assist Caesar. The fighting that ensues, particularly with the Belgian Nervii, is among the fiercest in the entire Gallic War. The Romans emerge victorious.

Book 3 (56 BC): Campaign against the Veneti
As troops under Servius Galba fend off attacks by Gauls in the Alps, the Veneti, a tribe in northwest Gaul on the coast of the Atlantic, seize and imprison Roman envoys. Caesar's response is to fight the seaworthy Veneti on the Atlantic ocean, capture their fortresses, and execute their leaders for seizing the Roman envoys. In the meantime, the quaestor Marcus Crassus defeats the Aquitani to the south.

Book 4 (55 BC): Caesar Bridges the Rhine. First Expedition to Britain
The Suebi along with other Germanic tribes, the Usipetes and Tencteri, venture west across the Rhine into Belgian territory to avoid the fierce Germanic Suevi. After negotiations, Caesar repulses the Germans, builds a bridge to span the Rhine within ten days, and after brief skirmishes returns to Gaul. In late August, Caesar makes his initial expedition to Britain.

Book 5 (54 BC): Second Expedition to Britain.
After landing in Britain unopposed, he proceeds inland and fights with Britons under the leadership of Cassivellaunus. After Caesar subdues Cassivellaunus at Kent , he returns to Gaul. On account of low grain supplies, the Romans settle into scattered winter-quarters, which are subsequently attacked by the Gauls. While the forces under the the legates Titurius and Cotta are overwhelmed by the leader Ambiorix, those under Cicero and Labienus prevail over the Nervii and Treveri respectively.

Book 6 (53 BC): Expedition to Germany. Customs among the Gauls and Germans.
As Labienus defeats the Treveri, Caesar assists Cicero's camp and pursues Ambiorix and the Eburones. He briefly crosses the Rhine river to prevent Ambiorix from receiving assistance from the Germans, but Amborix continues to elude the Romans. Caesar describes the organization and customs of the Gauls, the religion and warfare among the Germans, and the animals found in the Hercynian forest in Germania.

Book 7 (52 BC): The Gauls Rally and Fall under Vercingetorix
The Gauls rally under the leader Vercingetorix. After several sieges and battles, Caesar besieges Vercengetorix and the main Gaul force at Alesia. When the Gauls eventually surrender, Vercgetorix is led to Rome, where he will eventually be led in chains and executed to celebrate Caesar's triumph.

Book 8 (51 BC): Written by Aulus Hirtius, a legate of Caesar, possibly after Julius Caesar's death, the book details how Caesars quells small uprisings and rewards loyal Romans and Gauls with gifts.

The Life of Julius Caesar

B.C.

100   Caesar is born on July 12th

87   Flamen Dialis, selected to priesthood

83   Marries Cornelia, daughter of Cinna

80-78   Serves in the army in Asia Minor

76-75   Studies oratory in Rhodes

68   Quaestor, elected

67   Marries Pompeia

65   Aedile, elected

63   Pontifex Maximus, elected

62   Praetor, elected

61   Propraetor, serves in Spain

60   Forms First Triumvirate with Pompey, Crassus

59   Consul, marries Calpurnia

58-49   Proconsul in Gaul

56   Triumvirate renewed at Luca

50   Openly breaks with Pompey

49   Crosses the Rubicon, civil war begins

48   Battle of Pharsalia in Greece, defeats Pompey's forces

47   Subdues Egypt

46   Battle of Thapsus in North Africa, defeats Cato and senators, Dictator for 10 years

45   Battle of Munda in Spain, defeats sons of Pompey, Imperator for life

44   Assasinated by a conspiracy on March 15th

_____

43   Grand-nephew Gaius Octavius made heir, renamed Gaius Julius Caesar Octavianus
       Second Triumvirate formed by Octavian, Mark Antony, and Lepidus

31   Battle of Actium, Octavian defeats Mark Antony and Cleopatra, becomes sole ruler

31-AD 14   Octavian receives the cognomen "Augustus," becomes the first Emperor

How to Use this Commentary

Research shows that, as we learn how to read in a second language, a combination of reading and direct vocabulary instruction is statistically superior to reading alone. One of the purposes of this book is to help readers identify the most frequent words and encourage active acquisition of vocabulary.

1. Skim through the book and familiarize yourself with every grammar box and the appendix.

2. Master the core vocabulary list as soon as possible.

A. Develop a daily regimen for memorizing vocabulary and forms before you begin reading. Start with an intensive review of the running core list on the next page. Although a substantial number of core vocabulary words come within the first few lessons of the commentary, readers have already reviewed most of these words in first year Latin and can devote their efforts to mastering the handful of words in the initial lessons that they have never encountered.

B. Download and use the core list flashcards available online (ppt or jpg format). Research has shown that you must review new words at least seven to nine times before you are able to commit them to long-term memory. Flashcards are particularly efficient at promoting repetition. As you work, delete flashcards that you have mastered and focus your efforts on the remaining words.

Digital flashcards for less frequent vocabulary (occurring 3-4 times) will appear online in time.

3. Read actively and make lots of educated guesses

A. Persistence counts. Caesar is very consistent in his use of vocabulary and grammar, and so while the readings will maintain the same level of difficulty, you will become a much better reader with time. The more earnestly you learn vocabulary and new grammar in the early readings, the more fluently you will be able to read later passages without much preparation.

B. Read in Latin word order. Initially, readers have a tendency both (i) to scan through the entire Latin sentence quickly to order to attain a sense of the constructions and (ii) to treat the sentence as a puzzle and jump around the passage from subject to verb to object and so forth. Ideally, you should read in Latin word order. Whatever method you use, always review the sentence which you have just translated in Latin word order. Over time, as you acquire more vocabulary and your comfort with Caesar increases, make reading in Latin word order your primary method of reading. It is a lot of fun, and with persistence it is very satisfying.

4. Reread a passage or lesson immediately after you have completed it.

Repeated readings not only help you commit Latin to memory but also increase your ability to read the Latin as Latin. Caesar's consistent use of vocabulary and grammar makes it possible for readers to develop reading proficiency very quickly. Always read the words out loud (or at least whisper them to yourself). While you may be inclined to translate the text into English as you reread, develop the habit of reading Latin as Latin and acquiring meaning without using English.

5. Reread the most recent passage or lesson immediately before you begin a new one.

This additional repetition will strengthen your ability to recognize vocabulary, forms, and syntax quickly, bolster your confidence, and most importantly provide you with much-needed context as you begin the next selection in the text.

Caesar Running Core Vocabulary (5 or more times)

The following list includes all words in the Latin selections that occur five or more times arranged in a running vocabulary list. The number in the left column indicates in which lesson the word first occurs. The author tabulated the frequency lists by collating all of Caesar's words into a single list and counting them. Flashcards (.ppt and .jpg) are available online. For an alphabetized list of the core words, readers should consult the glossary.

1 **ā, ab:** (away) from; by, 80
1 **absum, -esse, āfuī:** be absent, lack, 6
1 **ad:** to, toward; near, at 110
1 **alius, -a, -ud:** other, another, else, 13
1 **animus, -ī m:** mind, spirit; *pl.* courage, 6
1 **appellō (1):** to call, call by name, 5
1 **atque:** and, and also, and even, 60
1 **aut:** or (aut...aut – either...or), 32
1 **Belgae, -ārum m.:** Belgians, 6
1 **bellum, -ī, n.:** war, 16
1 **capiō, -ere, cēpī, captum:** to take, capture, seize, 11
1 **causa, -ae f.:** reason, cause; case, 21
1 **contineō, -ēre, -nuī, -tentum:** to hold or keep together, 6
1 **cum:** with (+ abl.); when, since, although, 86
1 **dē:** (down) from; about, concerning, 41
1 **dīcō, -ere, dīxī, dictus:** to say, speak, tell, call, name, 18
1 **et:** and, also, even, 167
1 **etiam:** also, even, besides, 8
1 **ferē:** almost, nearly, closely, 7
1 **fīnis, -is m./f.:** end, border; territory, 17
1 **flūmen, -inis n.:** river, stream, 9
1 **fortis, -e:** strong, brave, valiant, 7
1 **Gallia, -ae f.:** Gaul, 17
1 **Gallus, -a, -um:** Gallic; *subst.* a Gaul, 15
1 **Germānus, -a, -um:** German, 9
1 **gerō, -ere, gessī, gestus:** to carry (on), wage, 8
1 **Helvētius, -a, -um:** Helvetian; *subst.* a Helvetian 16
1 **hic, haec, hoc:** this, these, 92
1 **in:** in, on (abl.), into, to (acc.) 173
1 **initium, -ī n.:** beginning, entrance, 6
1 **inter:** between, among (+ acc.), 15
1 **ipse, ipsa, ipsum:** -self; the very, 17
1 **is, ea, id:** this, that; he, she, it, 133
1 **longē:** far, at a distant, 6
1 **noster, nostra, nostrum:** our, 36
1 **obtineō, -ēre, -uī, -tentum:** hold, maintain, 6
1 **omnis, omne:** every, all, 72
1 **pars, partis, f.:** part, share, side 43
1 **pertineō, -ēre, -tinuī:** to stretch out, reach, extend to, 7
1 **proelium, -iī n.:** battle, combat, 15
1 **prohibeō, -ēre, -uī, -itus:** keep off, prohibit, 6
1 **prōvincia, -ae f.:** province, 7

1 **proximus, -a, -um:** nearest, very close, 12
1 **-que:** and, 108
1 **quī, quae, quod (quis? quid?):** who, which, that, 225
1 **reliquus, -a, um:** remaining, the rest of, 28
1 **Rhēnus, -ī m.:** Rhine River, 9
1 **Rhodanus, -a, -um:** Rhone, 5
1 **sē:** himself, herself, itself, themselves, 74
1 **Sēquanus, -a, -um:** Sequanian, 5
1 **sum, esse, fuī, futūrum:** to be, 165
1 **suus, -a, -um:** his, her, its, their own, 54
1 **tertius, -a, -um:** third, 8
1 **trēs, tria:** three, 7
1 **ūnus, -a, -um:** one, 29
1 **virtūs, -ūtis f.:** valor, manhood, excellence, 11
2 **ager, agrī m.:** field, land; farm, 8
2 **alter, -era, -erum:** other (of two), 12
2 **altus, -a, -um:** high, lofty, tall, 5
2 **amīcitia, -ae, f.:** friendship, 12
2 **annus, -ī m.:** year, 11
2 **apud:** among, at the house of (acc.), 7
2 **arbitror, arbitrārī, arbitrātus sum:** to judge, think, 10
2 **autem:** however, moreover, 5
2 **cīvitās cīvitātis, f.:** state, citizenship, 20
2 **confirmō (1):** make strong, confirm strengthen, 5
2 **constituō, -ere, -uī, -ūtus:** decide, establish, resolve, 14
2 **copia, -ae f.:** abundance, supply; troops, 12
2 **dūcō, -ere, dūxī, ductus:** lead, draw; consider, 7
2 **ē, ex:** out from, from, out of (+ abl.), 72
2 **facilis, -e:** easy; adv. facile, easily, 10
2 **faciō, -ere, fēcī, factum:** do, make, perform; grant, 40
2 **fīnitimus, -a, -um:** neighboring; subst. neighbors, 6
2 **frūmentum, -ī n.:** grain, 10
2 **habeō, -ēre, habuī, -itus:** have, hold; consider, 32
2 **homō, -inis m./f.:** man, mortal, human, 15
2 **imperium, -ī n.:** command, power, 7
2 **inferō, -ferre, -tulī, illātum:** wage, carry on, 7
2 **iter, itineris n.:** way, road, route, journey, 17
2 **locus, -ī m.:** place, region, location, 31
2 **magnus, -a, -um:** great, large; mighty, important, 29
2 **maximus, -a, -um:** greatest, largest, 15
2 **mīlle pl. mīlia, ium n.:** thousand, 9
2 **minor, minus:** less, smaller, 7
2 **multitūdo, inis f.:** multitude, population, people, 11
2 **numerus, -ī m.:** number, multitude, 13
2 **Orgetorix, -is m.:** Orgetorix, 6
2 **passus, -ūs:** pace, step, 7
2 **pāx, pācis f.:** peace, quiet, rest, 6
2 **permoveō, -ēre:** to move deeply, trouble, excite, agitate, 5

2 **persuādeō, -ēre, -suāsī, -suāsum:** persuade, convince, 12
2 **possum, posse, potuī:** be able, can, avail, 40
2 **praestō, -āre, -stitī, -stitus:** perform, show, be better, 6
2 **prō:** before, for, in behalf of (abl.), 16
2 **profectio, -ōnis f.:** departure, 5
2 **proficīscor, -ī, -fectus:** set out, depart, 23
2 **regnum, -ī n.:** royal power, kingdom, realm, 8
2 **rēs, reī, f.:** thing, matter, affair, business, 64
2 **tōtus -a, -um:** whole, entire, 7
2 **undīque:** (from) everywhere, from or on all sides, 5
2 **ut:** as, just as, when (+ ind.); (so) that, in order that, 59
3 **ac:** and, and also, and even, 24
3 **accipiō:** to take without effort, receive, get, accept, 10
3 **arma, -ōrum n.:** arms, equipment, tools, 7
3 **cōgō, cōgere, coēgī, coāctum:** to collect; compel, 11
3 **cōnor, cōnārī, cōnātus sum:** to try, 6
3 **diēs, -ēī m./f.:** day, time, season, 33
3 **dō, dare, dedī, datum:** give; grant, 18
3 **īdem, eadem, idem:** the same, 14
3 **exercitus, -ūs m.:** (trained) army, 9
3 **fīlius, -iī m.:** son, 5
3 **ille, illa, illud:** that, those, 22
3 **incitō (1):** put into motion, urge on, 5
3 **maximē:** exceedingly, especially, 6
3 **mors, mortis, f.:** death, 9
3 **multus, -a, -um:** much, many, 11
3 **nē:** lest, that not, no, not, 13
3 **neque:** and not, nor (neque…neque = neither…nor), 27
3 **nōn:** not, by no means, not at all, 36
3 **ob:** on account of, because of (acc.), 5
3 **ōrātio, -ionis f.:** speaking, speech, 8
3 **per:** through, across (acc) 18
3 **populus, -ī m.:** people, nation, 9
3 **probō (1):** approve, commend, 5
3 **Rōmānus, -a, -um:** of Rome, Roman, 15
3 **spērō (1):** hope (for), expect, 6
3 **tempus, temporis, n.:** time, occasion, 11
4 **cōnsilium, -iī n.:** plan, counsel, 12
4 **conveniō, -īre, -vēnī, -ventus:** come together, assemble, 9
4 **duo, duae, duo:** two, 8
4 **existimō (1):** judge, consider, think, 9
4 **iubeō, iubēre, iussī, iussum:** to order, command, 17
4 **nihil:** nothing, 10
4 **nūllus, -a, -um:** none, no, no one, 9
4 **oppugnō (1):** capture by assault, attack, 6
4 **perīculum, -ī n.:** risk, danger, peril, 14
4 **post:** after, behind (+ acc.); afterward, next, 5
4 **prīvō (1):** deprive of, rob, strip from (abl), 5

4 **quisque, quidque:** each one, each person, 9
4 **recipiō, -ere, -cēpī, -ceptum:** take back, recover, 10
4 **singulus, -a, -um:** one by one, separate, 5
4 **spēs, -ēī f.:** hope, expectation, 6
4 **trānseō, -īre, -iī (īvī), itus:** pass (by), 6
4 **ūtor, -ī, ūsus sum:** use, employ (abl.), 5
4 **videō, vidēre, vīdī, vīsum:** to see, 14
5 **adventus, -ūs m.:** arrival, approach, 7
5 **Caesar, -aris m.:** Caesar, 40
5 **certus, -a, -um:** definite, sure, certain, reliable, 8
5 **dum:** while, as long as, until, 6
5 **facultās, -tātis f.:** opportunity, power, skill, ability, 5
5 **imperō (1):** command, order, bid, 7
5 **lēgātus, -ī m.:** an envoy, legate, 16
5 **legio, -ōnis f.:** legion, (~4200 soldiers), 32
5 **licet:** impersonal, it is allowed or permitted, 5
5 **mīles, mīlitis, m.:** soldier, 33
5 **mittō, -ere, mīsī, missus:** send, hurl, dismiss, 20
5 **perveniō, -īre, -vēnī, -ventum:** arrive, 8
5 **sī:** if (only), whether, in case that, 30
5 **sine:** without (abl.), 8
5 **sub:** under, below, beneath, underneath, 5
5 **tamen:** however, nevertheless, 14
5 **teneō, tenēre, tenuī, tentum:** to hold, keep, 6
5 **ūllus, -a, -um:** any, 5
5 **volō, velle, voluī:** will, wish, be willing, 13
6 **animadvertō, -ere, -vertī, -versum:** turn mind to, notice 5
6 **at:** but; mind you; but, you say, 7
6 **barbarus, -a, -um:** foreign, savage, 5
6 **cognōscō, -ere, -nōvī, -nitum:** to learn, come to know, pf. know, 14
6 **co(n)iciō, -ere, -iēcī:** throw together, throw, take oneself, 10
6 **cōnsuescō, -ere, cōnsuē(v)ī, -suētum:** to be accustomed, 8
6 **ēgredior, -ī, -gressus:** go out, disembark, 5
6 **equitātus, -ūs m.:** cavalry, 5
6 **genus, generis, n.:** origin, kind, sort, 10
6 **gravis, -e:** heavy, serious, severe; venerable, 9
6 **hostis, -is m./f.:** stranger, enemy, foe, 43
6 **longus -a, -um:** long, 8
6 **magnitūdo, -inis f.:** greatness, size, 5
6 **manus, manūs, f.:** hand; group, 9
6 **nam:** for, 9
6 **nāvis, nāvis, f.:** ship, boat, 23
6 **nisi:** if not, unless 6
6 **paulus, -a, -um:** little, small, 9
6 **pēs, pedis m.:** foot, 5
6 **plērumque:** for the most part, mostly, commonly, 5
6 **propter:** on account of, because of, 5
6 **pugna, -ae f.:** battle, fight, 7

6 **pugnō** (1): to fight, 9

6 **subsequor, -ī, secūtus sum:** follow after or behind, 7

6 **summus, -a, -um:** top of, highest (part of) 10

6 **telum, -ī n.:** projective, weapon, blow, 9

6 **ūsus, -ūs m.:** use, practice, application, 10

7 **aliquī, -qua, -quod:** some, any, definite, 8

7 **coepī, coepisse, coeptum:** to begin, 9

7 **compleō, -ēre, -ēvī, -ētum:** fill up, fill, 6

7 **conspiciō, -ere, -spexī, -spectus:** see, behold, 5

7 **dēsum, -esse, -fuī, -futūrum:** be lacking, lack, fail, 6

7 **eques, equitis m.:** horseman, rider, 12

7 **ferō, ferre, tulī, lātus:** carry, bear, endure, 7

7 **impetus, -ūs m.: attack, assault, onset,** 7

7 **ordō, -inis m.:** order, line, array; status, 6

7 **perturbō** (1): confuse, disturb, throw into confusion, 6

7 **prīmus -a -um:** first, 15

7 **pūblicus, -a, -um:** public, common, 11

7 **signum -ī, n.:** sign, signal; gesture, seal, 5

7 **subsidium, iī n.:** reserve troops; third line of battle, 5

7 **tantus, -a, -um:** so great, so large, 10

7 **tum:** then, at that time, 12

7 **uterque, utraque, utrumque:** each (of two) 8

8 **Britannia, -ae f.:** Britain, 6

8 **castra, -ōrum n.:** camp, encampment, 23

8 **dēferō, -ferre, -tulī, -lātum:** report, offer 8

8 **dēmonstrō** (1): to show, demonstrate, 5

8 **nox, noctis, f.:** night, 9

8 **obsēs, obsidis m./f.:** hostage, 5

8 **petō, petere, petīvī, petītum:** seek, aim at, 7

8 **sed: but, moreover,** however, 13

8 **sēsē:** emphatic form of reflexive sē, 14

8 **subitō:** suddenly, 5

8 **superō** (1): surpass, overcome, 6

8 **superus, -a, -um:** upper, higher, above, 9

8 **veniō, -īre, vēnī, ventus:** come, go, 14

9 **accidō, -ere, accidī:** to happen, fall to, 13

9 **complūres n.:** several, 5

9 **discēdō, -ere, -cessī, -cessum:** to go away, depart, 9

9 **efficiō, -ere, -fēcī, -fectus:** make, form, 5

9 **impedīmentum, -ī n.:** baggage, impediment, 6

9 **ita:** so, thus, 7

9 **itaque:** and so, 6

10 **casus, -ūs m.:** misfortune, mishap; fall 5

10 **consuētūdo, -inis f.:** custom, habit, 5

10 **etsī:** even if, although, though, 5

10 **intermittō, -ere:** interrupt, discontinue, leave off, 5

10 **maior, maius:** greater, 6

11 **cohors, cohortis f.:** cohort, company, troop 14

11 **interficiō, -ere, -fēcī, -fectum:** kill, slay, destroy, 14
11 **interim:** meanwhile, in the meantime, 5
11 **premō, -ere, pressī, pressus:** check, pursue, control, 7
11 **sustineō, -ēre, -uī:** hold up, sustain, 8
12 **celeritās, -tātis f.:** quickness, swiftness, speed, 5
12 **celeriter:** quickly, swiftly, speedily, 6
12 **circiter:** (round) about, not far from, 7
12 **nuntius, -iī m.:** messenger, 6
12 **quantus, -a, -um:** how great, much, many, 6
13 **contrōversia, -ae f.:** dispute, debate, 7
13 **disciplīna, -ae f.:** training, instruction, 5
13 **Druidēs, -um m.:** Druids, 6
13 **praemium, -ī n.:** reward, prize, 5
14 **ibi:** there, in that place, 5
14 **littera, -ae f.:** letter of the alphabet, letter, literature, 12
14 **ratio, ratiōnis, f.:** calculation, account, method, 5
15 **circumveniō, -īre:** to come around, encircle, 6
15 **vīta, -ae, f.:** life, 5
16 **pōnō, ponere, posuī, positum:** to put, place, 6
17 **concilium, -iī n.:** meeting, rendezvous, 6
18 **Ambiorix, -rigis m.:** Ambiorix, 15
18 **Cicero, Cicerōnis m.:** Cicero 14
18 **Cotta, -ae m.:** Cotta, 10
18 **Crassus, -ī m.:** Crassus, 5
18 **Eburōnēs, -um m.:** Eburones (German), 5
18 **hīberna, -ōrum n.:** winter-quarters, 26
18 **Labiēnus, ī m.:** Labienus, 5
18 **Lucius, -ī m.:** Lucius, 10
18 **Nerviī, -iōrum m.:** Nervii (Belgic Gauls) 9
18 **Quintus, -ī m.:** Quintus, 6
18 **Sabīnus, ī m.:** Sabinus, 7
18 **Titurius, -ī m.:** Titurius, 8
19 **ascendō, -ere, -ī, -ēnsus:** ascend, mount 2
19 **oppugnātio, -tiōnis f.:** an assault, 6
19 **resistō, -ere, -stitī:** stand still, halt; oppose, 5
19 **vallum, -ī n.:** wall, fortification, palisade, 11
20 **Aduātucī, -ōrum m.:** Aduatuci (in Belgae), 5
20 **commūnis, -e:** common, 6
21 **salūs, -ūtis f.:** safety, refuge; health, 10
21 **tūtus, -a, -um:** safe, secure, guarded, 7
22 **calamitās, -tātis f.:** loss, misfortune, calamity, disaster, 5
22 **quidem:** indeed, in fact, certainly, 6
22 **victoria, -ae f.:** victory, 7
23 **relinquō, -ere, -līquī, -lictum:** to leave behind, 7
25 **accēdō, -ere, -cessī, -cessus:** approach, 5
28 **mūnītio, -iōnis f.:** fortification, paving, 7
28 **turris, turris f.:** tower, walled tower, 7
32 **Pullo, Pullōnis, m.:** Pullo, 6 and **Vorēnus, -ī m.:** Vorenus, 5

Abbreviations

abs.	absolute		m.	masculine
acc.	accusative		n.	neuter
act.	active		nom.	nominative
adj.	adjective		obj.	object
adv.	adverb		PPP	Perfect passive participle
app.	appositive		pple.	participle
comp.	comparative		pass	passive
dat.	dative		pf.	perfect
dep.	deponent		pl.	plural
d.o.	direct object		plpf.	pluperfect
f.	feminine		pred.	predicate
fut.	future		prep.	preposition
gen.	genitive		pres.	present
imp.	imperative		pron.	pronoun
impf.	imperfect		reflex.	reflexive
impers.	impersonal		rel.	relative
indic.	indicative		seq.	sequence
i.o.	indirect object		sg.	singular
inf.	infinitive		subj.	subject or subjunctive
inter.	interrogative		superl.	superlative
l.	line		voc.	vocative
ll.	lines			

Citations in Caesar

The universal method for referring to pages in any edition of Caesar's *Commentarii dē Bellō Gallicō* is through a sequence of two or even three numbers: e.g. IV.24.2 or 4.24. The first number denotes the book in *dē Bellō Gallicō*; the second number, the paragraph; and the third number, if it is included, a subsection about the length of one sentence. Throughout this commentary I have chosen to use Roman numerals to indicate the book number (eg. IV), but it is not uncommon for scholars to use Arabic numerals (e.g. 4). The paragraph number is always an Arabic numeral and is uniform from one edition of Caesar to the next (e.g. IV.24, 4.24). In this book I place the paragraph number in boldface at the beginning of each paragraph. This system allows readers to pick up any edition of Caesar in English or Latin and, regardless of the page numbering of that edition, locate a particular passage in Caesar.

Each paragraph in *dē Bellō Gallicō* can also be divided into subsections, which may be included or left out of citations (e.g 4.24.1 or simply 4.24). In this commentary I have chosen for pedagogical reasons to include the numbers of these subsections within the text itself. In a classroom setting, teachers can conveniently ask individual students to recite and translate by subsection and not have to refer awkwardly to the initial words in each sentence.

Line numbers, located in the inside margin of the text, are peculiar to this commentary. I have included them so that I can efficiently refer to words and phrases in the grammar and readers can easily locate those words and phrases. While you can refer to the line numbers in class discussions, use only the book, paragraph, and subsection numbers when you cite Caesar in written work.

I'm going to spare the defeated, I'm going to speak to the crowd.
I'm going to spare the defeated, 'cause I'm going to speak to the crowd.
I'm going to teach peace to the conquered, I'm going to tame the proud.

- Bob Dylan

To make the ancients speak, we must feed them with our own blood.

- von Wilamowitz-Moellendorff

1.1 Gallia est omnis dīvīsa in partēs trēs, quārum ūnam incolunt Belgae,   1
aliam Aquītānī, tertiam quī ipsōrum linguā Celtae, nostrā Gallī appellantur.
2. Hī omnēs linguā, īnstitūtīs, legibus inter sē differunt. Gallōs ab Aquītānīs
Garumna flūmen, ā Belgīs Matrona et Sēquana dīvidit.

3. Hōrum omnium fortissimī sunt Belgae, proptereā quod ā cultū atque   5
hūmānitāte Prōvinciae longissimē absunt, minimēque ad eōs mercātōrēs
saepe commeant atque ea quae ad effēminandōs animōs pertinent
important, 4. Proximīque sunt Germānīs, quī trāns Rhēnum incolunt,
quibuscum continenter bellum gerunt. Quā de causā Helvetiī quoque reliquōs
Gallōs virtūte praecedunt, quod ferē cotīdiānīs proeliīs cum Germānīs   10
contendunt, cum aut suīs finibus eōs prohibent aut ipsī in eōrum finibus
bellum gerunt.

5. Eōrum ūna pars, quam Gallōs obtinēre dictum est, initium capit ā
flūmine Rhodanō, continētur Garumnā flūmine, Ōceanō, fīnibus Belgārum,
attingit etiam ab Sēquanīs et Helvētiīs flūmen Rhēnum, vergit ad   15
septentriōnēs. 6. Belgae ab extrēmīs Galliae fīnibus oriuntur, pertinent ad
inferiōrem partem flūminis Rhēnī, spectant in septentriōnem et orientem
sōlem. 7. Aquitania ā Garumnā flūmine ad Pyrenaeōs montēs et eam partem
Ōceanī quae est ad Hispāniam pertinet; spectat inter occāsum sōlis et
septentriōnēs.   20

Aquitānī, -ōrum m.: Aquitani, 2
Aquitania, -ae f.: Aquitania, 1
attingō, -ere, tigī, tāctum: touch to, border, 1
Celtae, -ārum m.: Celts, 1
commeō (1): to travel, go to and fro, 1
contendō, -ere, -ī, -ntus: strive; hasten, 4
continenter: continuously, incessantly, 1
cotidiānus, -a, -um: daily, of every day, 3
cultus, -ūs m.: culture, refinement, 2
differō, -ferre,: differ, carry different ways, 2
dīvidō, -ere, -vīsī, -vīsus: divide, distribute, 4
effēminō (1): soften, make into women, 1
extrēmus, -a, -um: farthest, outermost, 2
Garumna, -āe f.: Garumna river, 4
Hispania, -ae f.: Spain, 2
hūmānitās, -tātis f.: humanity, nature, 1
importō (1): bring in, introduce, import, 1
incolō, -ere, -uī: inhabit, dwell on, 3
inferus, -a, -um: below, lower, 3
institum, ī n.: institution, practice, custom, 2

lēx, -lēgis f.: law, regulation, decree, 3
lingua, ae f.: tongue, language, 2
Mātrōna, -ae f.: Matrona (Marne) river, 1
mercātor, -ōris m.: merchant, trader, 1
minimē: least of all, least, 1
mons, montis m.: mountain, mount, 4
occāsus, -ūs m.: fall, destruction, 2
Oceānus, ī m.: Oceanus, 3
orior, -īrī, ortus: arise, rise, spring, 3
praecēdō, -ere, cessī, -cessum: surpass, 1
proptereā: on this account, therefore, 4
Pyrenaeus, -a, -um: of the Pyrenees, 1
quoque: also, 2
saepe: often, 3
septentriōnēs, -um m.: north, (7 stars), 3
Sēquana, -ae: Sequana (Seine) River, 1
sōl, sōlis m.: sun, 3
spectō (1): watch, observe, behold, inspect, 3
trans; over, across (+ acc.), 3
vergō, -ere, versī: turn, bend, 1

1 **est...dīvīsa**: *is divided*; dīvīsa is a predicate adjective and not part of a perfect pass. verb
quārum ūnam...aliam...tertiam: *of which (parts) one (part)...another (part)...a third (part)*; a genitive at the beginning of the clause is often, as here, a partitive gen. (gen. of whole)

2 **Aquītānī**: *Aquitanians (inhabit)*; add incolunt which is missing through ellipsis (omission)
Tertiam (incolunt) quī...: *(those) who.... (inhabit) the third*; the missing antecedent of the relative clause is subject of missing incolunt
ipsōrum linguā: *in the language of (these) very ones*; i.e. of the Gauls, ipse usually modifies a noun, which is missing and must be supplied; linguā is an ablative of respect (in respect to..)
nostrā: *in our (language)*; supply linguā
Celtae...Gallī: nom. predicates of appellantur

3 **linguā, īnstitūtīs, lēgibus**: *in...in...in...*; "in respect to...," all three are abl. of respect

4 **Garumna flūmen (dīvidit)**: subject, add verb
Matrona et Sēquana: nom. pl. with a 3rd sg. verb because the rivers form a single boundary; supply Gallōs as acc. direct object

5 **Hōrum omnium**: *of all these*; or "among all these," partitive gen., as in line 1, Caesar often uses a a genitive at the beginning of a clause and then specifies the parts within the clause
proptereā quod: *because*; lit. "on this account because," which is a pleonasm (redundancy)

6 **Prōvinciae**: *of the Province*; i.e. Gallia Transalpina, the area in southern France controlled by the Romans. Although the word prōvincia is a general term, the Romans referred to this province as "the Province". This edition uses the capital "P" to distinguish it from other provinces.

6 **longissimē**: *very far*; superlative adverb longē
ad eōs *to those...*; eōs is demonstrative

7 **ea quae** *those things which...*; neut. pl.

ad effēminandōs...: *for softening...*; lit. "for courage going to be softened" ad + gerundive (fut. pass. pple) often expresses purpose; when translating, readers should employ a gerund-gerundive flip: translate the gerundive as a gerund (e.g. softening) and the noun modified by the gerundive as an object of the gerund

8 **Germānīs**: dat. with special adj. proximī

9 **quibuscum**: cum quibus
Quā dē causā: *for which reason*; "concerning which reason" quā modifies causā; as often, Caesar places the adjective, here a relative adj., before the preposition

10 **virtūte**: *in (respect to) valor*; abl. respect
quod: *because*
cum...prohibent...gerunt: *when...*; cum + indicative, not a preposition with suīs fīnibus.

11 **suīs fīnibus**: *from their borders*; abl. of separation (a construction which includes but is not limited to place from which), governed by prohibent, "(Helvetians) keep"
suīs: *their*; Helvetians', reflexive possessive
eōs: *them*; i.e. Germans, personal pronoun
ipsī: *(they) themselves*; Helvetians

12 **eōrum**: *their*; i.e. Germans

13 **eōrum**: *of these (three parts)*; partitive gen.
obtinēre: ind. discourse (that clause), Gallōs is acc. subj. and quam is acc. d.o.
dictum est: *it has been said*; as in line 2 above

14 **continētur**: governs all three abl. of means, which are missing conjunctions, asyndeton

15 **ab Sēquānīs...**: *from (the side of)...*

16 **oriuntur**: *rise*; pres. deponent, orior

17 **spectant in septentriōnem**: *looks to the northern...*; i.e. opens up to the northeast
orientem: *eastern*; "rising" sun; pres. pple.

18 **eam partem**: *that part*; demonstrative

19 **ad Hispāniam**: *near Hispania*; with est
spectat: *looks to...*; i.e. opens up to...

Gerund-Gerundive Flip

A gerundive (effeminandus,-a,-um, line 7) is a future passive participle. It is a verbal adjective which agrees with a noun in case, number, and gender. Because it is awkward to translate (e.g. going to be softened), readers should often employ a "gerund-gerundive flip" and translate the gerundive as a gerund, a verbal noun (e.g. softening), and the noun modified by the gerundive as the gerund's object. Ad + gerund + object is in fact uncommon in Latin but it is an easy way to translate ad + noun + gerundive into suitable English. This is a popular construction in Caesar. So, be prepared.

Flip

Ad animōs effēminandōs   →   ad effēminandum animōs
for courage (going) to be softened   *for softening courage*

2.₁ Apud Helvētiōs longē nōbilissimus fuit et ditissimus Orgetorīx. Is, M.   1
Messālā, et M. Pīsōne cōnsulibus, regnī cupiditāte inductus coniūrātiōnem
nōbilitātis fēcit et civitātī persuāsit ut dē fīnibus suīs cum omnibus copiīs
exīrent: 2. perfacile esse, cum virtūte omnibus praestārent, tōtīus Galliae
imperiō potīrī.   5

3. Id hōc facilius eīs persuāsit, quod undique locī nātūrā Helvetiī
continentur: ūnā ex parte flūmine Rhēno lātissimō atque altissimō, quī
agrum Helvētium ā Germānīs divīdit; alterā ex parte monte Iūrā altissimō,
quī est inter Sēquanōs et Helvētiōs; tertiā lacū Lemannō et flūmine Rhodānō,
quī provinciam nostram ab Helvetiīs divīdit. 4. Hīs rēbus fīēbat ut et minus   10
lātē vagārentur et minus facile fīnitimīs bellum īnferre possent; 5. Quā ex
parte hominēs bellandī cupidī magnō dolōre afficiēbantur. 6. Prō multitūdine
autem hominum et prō glōriā bellī atque fortitūdinis angustōs sē fīnēs habēre
arbitrābantur, quī in longitūdinem mīlia passuum CCXL, in lātitūdinem
CLXXX patēbant.   15

3.₁ Hīs rēbus adductī et auctōritāte Orgetorīgis permōtī cōnstituērunt ea
quae ad proficīscendum pertinērent comparāre, iumentōrum et carrōrum
quam maximum numerum coemere, sementēs quam maximās facere, ut in
itinere cōpia frumentī suppeteret, cum proximīs cīvitātibus pācem et
amīcitiam cōnfirmāre. 2. Ad eās rēs cōnficiendās biennium sibi satis esse   20
dūxērunt; in tertium annum profectiōnem lēge cōnfirmant.

---

addūcō, -ere, duxī, ductum: draw/lead to, 4
adficiō, -ere, -fēcī, -fectum: affect, afflict, 3
angustus, -a, -um: narrow, confined, 4
auctōritās, -tātis f.: influence, clout, 3
bellō (1): to wage war, fight, 1
biennium, -ī n.: a period of two years, 1
carrus, -ī m.: wagon for, baggage, wagon, 2
coemō, -ere, -ēmī, -emptum: buy up, 1
comparō (1): prepare, get ready, provide, 4
cōnficiō, -ere: to exhaust, finish, 4
coniūrātio, -ōnis f.: pact, union, conspiracy 3
cōnsul, -is m.: consul, 3
cupiditās, -tātis f.: desire, eagerness for, 1
cupidus, -a, -um: desirous, eager, keen, 2
dīs, dītis adj: rich, wealthy, 2
dīvidō, -ere, -vīsī, -vīsus: divide, distribute, 4
dolor, -ōris m.: pain, grief, anger, passion, 2
exeō, -īre, -iī (īvī), -itus: go out, 4
fiō, fierī, factus: become, be made, 3
fortitūdō, -dinis f.: strength, courage, 1
glōria, -ae, f.: glory, fame, 2
indūcō, -ere, duxī, ductum: draw/lead in, 1
iūmentum, -ī n.: beast of burden, 1

Iūra, -ae f.: Iura (a mountain range), 3
lacus, -ūs m.: lake, pond, pool, 2
latē: widely, far and wide, 2
lātitūdo, -dinis f.: breadth, width, 1
latus, -a, -um: wide, 1
Lemannus, -ī m.: (w/ lacus) Lake Geneva, 1
lēx, -lēgis f.: law, regulation, decree, 3
longitūdo, -inis f.: length, width, 2
M.: Marcus, 3
Messāla, -ae f.: Messala, 1
mons, montis m.: mountain, mount, 4
nātūra, -ae. f.: nature, 3
nōbilis, -e: noble, renowned, 3
nōbilitās, -tātis f.: nobility, renown, 1
pateō, -ēre, -uī: lie open, extend, 1
perfacilis, -e: very easy; *adv.* very easily 2
Pīsō, Pīsōnis m.: Piso, 2
potior, -īrī, -ītus: gain, win (*abl.*), 2
satis: enough, sufficient, 2
sementis, -is f.: sowing, planting, 1
suppetō, -ere, īvī, ītum: suffice, be at hand 2
vagor, -ārī: wander, roam, go to and fro, 1

1 **nōbilissimus, ditisissimus**: superlative adjs.
fuit: pf. sum, esse
M. Messālā et M. Pīsōne cōnsulibus: *when Marcus Messala and Marcus (Pupius) Piso were consuls*; "with Messala and Piso (being) consuls" abl. abs. i.e. 61 BC, Romans named the year after their annually elected consuls; since there is no pple. for sum, esse, the subject and predicate are the abl. abs.

2 **regnī**: *for the kingship*; objective gen. governed by cupiditāte, equivalent to "he desires kingship

3 **persuāsit ut…**: *persuaded* (dative) *that…*; this common verb in Caesar governs an indirect command (ut + impf. subj. in secondary seq.)

4 **exīrent**: *they come out*; impf. subjunctive, exeō, exīre in an ind. command, which can often be translated as an inf.: "persuaded…to come out"
perfacile esse…: *(and) that it is very easy…*; ind. discourse also governed by persuāsit above; asyndeton, supply a conjuction between the ind. command above and perfacile esse
cum…praestārent: *since they excelled*; causal with impf. subjunctive governing abl. respect
tōtius: gen. sg. (-ius) modifying Galliae

5 **potīrī**: *to possess*; dep. inf. potior governs an ablative object

6 **id…persuāsit**: *he persuaded them (to do) this*
hōc…quod: *by this (reason)…because*; abl. of cause
facilius: comparative adv. facilis, facile

7 **ūnā ex parte**: *on one side*; "from one part"
flūmine Rhēnō: abl. means; supply the verb "continentur," an example of ellipsis

8 **agrum Helvētium**: *Helvetian land*
alterā ex parte: *on another side*; see line 7
monte Iūrā: *by Iura range*; add "continentur"

9 **tertiā (ex parte)**: parallel with line 7 and 8
lacū Lemannō: abl. means, add "continentur"

10 **hīs rēbus**: *because of…*; abl. of cause
fiēbat ut: *it happened that…*; fiō governs ut + impf. subjunctive (noun result clause); the subjunctives are impf. in secondary sequence because the main verb is impf.

11 **vagārentur, possent**: impf. subj. vagor and possum; in result clauses these are translated

as normal impf. indicatives; vagor is deponent
minus: comparative adverb; minor, minus

11 **facile**: *easily*; irreg. adverb from facilis, facile
fīnitimīs: *on neighbors*; dat. of compound verb (the infinitive inferre)
quā ex parte: *for which reason*; "from which respect"

12 **bellandī**: *of waging war*; gerund, gen. sg. with the adj. cupidī which in turn modifies hominēs
Prō…prō: *because of…*; "in proportion to" or "according to," prō is causal in force

13 **sē habēre**: *that they had*; ind. discourse in secondary sequence: angustōs fīnēs is acc. d.o.

14 **milia passuum**: *miles*; "thousands of paces," a mile is 1000 steps; subject of patēbant

16 **adductī…permōtī**: *Helvetians influenced… and moved;* the participles are nom. pl. agreeing with a missing subject
ea quae: *those (things) which*; ea is object of comparāre and is translated as a demonstrative

17 **ea quae…pertinērent**: *those (things) which pertain/would pertain;* a relative clause of characteristic clarifies what sort of thing the antecedent is (i.e. ea) and can be translated here with or without modal "would"
ad proficiscendum: *for setting out*; gerund (verbal noun) + ad expresses purpose
comparāre, coemere, facere, cōnfirmāre: complementary infinitives with cōnstituērunt, supply the missing conjunction "et"

18 **quam maximum**: *as great…as possible*; quam + superlative is frequently translated "as X as possible," here it modifies numerum
quam maximās: see above, with sementēs
ut…suppeteret: *so that… might suffice;* ut + impf. subj., purpose clause in secondary seq.
ad…conficiendās: *for accomplishing…;* "for those things going to be accomplished" ad + gerundive (fut. pass. pple modifying rēs) often expresses purpose; when translating, employ a gerund-gerundive flip: translate as a gerund and eās rēs as the object of the gerund
biennium…esse: *that…;* ind. discourse
sibi: *for themselves*; dat. of interest/advantage

21 **in…annum**: *into the…;* i.e. "during," 58 BC

Translating Subjunctives

With the exception of purpose clauses (*may, might*), conditional sentences (*if should, would; if were, would; if had, would have*), and some relative clauses of characteristic (*would*), almost all the subjunctive constructions that readers will encounter do not require a special translation in English. Readers should simply identify the tense and translate the subjunctive as one would an indicative. Imperfect and pluperfect subjunctives are the most common tenses in secondary sequence.

3.3 Ad eās rēs conficiendās Orgetorīx dēligitur. Is sibi lēgātiōnem ad   1
cīvitātēs suscēpit. In eō itinere persuādet Casticō, Catamantaloedis fīliō,
Sēquanō, cuius pater rēgnum in Sēquanīs multōs annōs obtinuerat et ā
senātū populī Rōmānī amicus appellātus erat, ut rēgnum in cīvitāte suā
occupāret, quod pater ante habuerit; 4. itemque Dumnorigī Haeduō, fratrī   5
Dīviciācī, quī eō tempore principātum in cīvitāte obtinēbat ac maximē plebī
acceptus erat, ut idem cōnārētur persuādet eīque fīliam suam in
matrimōnium dat. 5. Perfacile factū esse illīs probat cōnāta perficere,
proptereā quod ipse suae civitātis imperium obtentūrus esset: 6. nōn esse
dūbium quin tōtīus Galliae plūrimum Helvetiī possent; sē suīs copiīs suōque   10
exercitū illīs regna conciliātūrum cōnfirmat. 7. Hāc ōrātiōne adductī inter sē
fīdem et iusiūrandum dant et regnō occupātō per trēs potentissimōs ac
firmissimōs populōs tōtīus Galliae sēsē potīrī posse sperant.

4.1 Ea rēs est Helvētiīs per indicium ēnūntiāta. Mōribus suīs Orgetorīgem
ex vinculīs causam dīcere coēgērunt; damnātum poenam sequī oportēbat, ut   15
ignī cremārētur.

2. Diē cōnstitūtā causae dictiōnis Orgetorīx ad iudicium omnem suam
familiam, ad hominum mīlia decem, undique coēgit, et omnēs clientēs
obaeratōsque suōs, quōrum magnum numerum habēbat, eōdem condūxit;
per eōs nē causam dīceret sē ēripuit. 3. Cum cīvitās ob eam rem incitāta armis   20
iūs suum exsequī cōnārētur multitūdinemque hominum ex agrīs magistrātūs
cōgerent, Orgetorīx mortuus est; 4. neque abest suspiciō, ut Helvetiī
arbitrantur, quin ipse sibi mortem conscīverit.

---

addūcō, -ere, duxī, ductum: draw/lead to, 4
amīcus, -a, -um: friendly, 1
ante: before, in front of (acc); *adv.* before, 4
Casticus, -ī m.: Casticus, 1
Catamantāloedis, -is m.: Catamantaloedis, 1
cliens, -entis m.: client, dependent, 4
conciliō (1): win over, unite, 1
condūcō, -ere: bring together, gather, 2
cōnficiō, -ere: to exhaust, finish, 4
conscīscō, -īre: to resolve, decree; bring on oneself, 1
cremō (1): burn, consumed by fire, 2
damnō (1): condemn, punish, convict, 1
decem: ten, 1
dēligō, -ere, -lēgī, -lectum: choose, elect, select, 2
dictio, -ōnis m.: pleading, saying; speech, 1
Diviciācus, -ī m.: Diviciacus, 1
dubius, -a, -um: doubtful, wavering, 1
Dumnorīx, -īgis m.: Dumnorix, 1
ēnuntiō (1): announce, speak out, divulge, 1
ēripiō, -ere, -uī, reptus: rescue, take from, 4
exsequor, sequī, secūtum: follow/carry out 1

factū: to do (supine), 2
familia, -ae f.: family, household, 1
fīdēs, eī f.: faith, honor, 4
fīlia, -iae f.: daughter, 1
firmus, -a, -um: strong, steadfast, 1
frāter, -tris m.: brother, 2
Haeduus, -a, -um: Haeduan, Aeduan, 1
ignis, ignis, m.: fire, 4
indicium, -iī n.: information, evidence, 1
item: also, likewise, in like manner, 3
iudicium, -ī n.: decision, judgment; trial 3
iūs, iūris n.: justice, law, right, 2
ius-iūrandum, iūrisiūrandī n.: sworn oath, 2
lēgātio, -ōnis f.: embassy, envoy, 2
magistratus, -ūs m.: magistrate, officer, 3
mātrimōnium, -iī n.: wedlock, marriage, 1
morior, morī, mortuus sum: die, 2
mōs, mōris m.: custom, manner, law, 4
obaerātus, -a, -um: indebted, 1
occupō (1): seize, occupy, 4
oportet: it is proper, fitting, necessary, 2

pater, patris, m.: father, 4
perfacilis, -e: very easy; *adv.* very easily2
perficiō, -ere: complete, accomplish, 3
plebs, plēbis, f.: common people, masses, 2
plūrimus, -a, -um: most, very many, 4
poena, poenae, f.: punishment, penalty, 3
potēns, -entis: powerful, ruling (*gen.*), 2
potior, -īrī, -ītus: gain, win (*abl.*), 2

principātus, -ūs m.: leadership, rule, 2
proptereā: on this account, therefore, 4
quīn: (but) that, who (not), 2
senātus, -ūs m.: senate, council of elders, 1
sequor, -ī, secūtus: follow, pursue, 4
suscipiō, -ere, -cēpī, -ceptum: undertake, receive, 1
suspīcio, -ciōnis f.: mistrust, suspicion, 4
vinculum, -ī n.: bond, chain, 2

---

1 **ad...conficiendās**: *for accomplishing...;* "for those things going to be accomplished" ad + gerundive (fut. pass. pple modifying rēs) often expresses purpose; when translating, employ a gerund-gerundive flip: translate as a gerund and eās rēs as the object of the gerund
sibi: *for himself;* dat. of interest/advantage

2 **eō**: *this;* demonstrative pronoun
persuādet Casticō...ut: *persuades Casticus... that;* verb governs dat. and ind. command

3 **cuius**: *whose;* gen. sg. relative pronoun
multōs annōs: *for...;* acc. of duration

4 **appellātus erat**: *had been named;* + predicate nominative; the verb behaves as a linking verb
ut...occupāret: *that he occupy;* ind. command with persuādet can often, but not always, be translated as an infinitive: "to occupy..."

5 **quod...habuerit**: *which....had...;* pf. subj., relative clause of characteristic
Dumnorīgī Haeduō: *(he persuades) Dumnorix the Aeduan;* dat. i.o. of missing persuādet in a construction parallel to Casticō above

6 **eō tempore**: *at...* ; abl. of time when
maximē...acceptus erat: *had been especially (well) received;* governs a dative of agent (by...)

7 **ut...cōnārētur**: *that...*: ind. command governed by persuādet; impf. deponent cōnor
idem: *the same thing;* id-dem, neuter acc. d.o., referring to ut...occupāret in ll. 4-5 above
eī: *to him;* dat. sg. indirect object with dat

8 **perfacile...esse...perficere**: *that it is very easy to...;* ind. disc. governed by probat; perficere is inf. subject and perfacile is the pred. adj.
factū: *to do;* "in doing" abl. sg. supine (PPP stem + ū), an abl. of respect limiting perfacile
illīs: *for those (men);* dat. interest
cōnāta: *the things attempted;* PPP, neuter pl.

9 **proptereā quod**: *because;* lit. "on this account because" which is a pleonasm (redundancy)
ipse: *(he) himself;* i.e. Orgetorix
obtentūrus esset: *would attain;* "was going to attain," fut. pple + sum (here impf. subj.) is a periphrastic fut.; verbs in subordinate clauses in

ind. disc. are placed in the subjunctive mood
nōn esse dūbium: *that he did not doubt*

10 **quin...plūrimum possent**: *that...they would have very much power;* a common idiom; quin + subj. following a verb of doubt or hindering

11 **conciliātūrum (esse)**: *that they will win over;* fut. infinitive; ind. disc., sē is acc. subj.

12 **ius-iurandum**: *a sworn oath;* as one or two words; both decline; gerundive iurō , -āre

13 **tōtīus**: *of the entire;* gen. sg. with Galliae
sēsē: *that they;* acc. subject of posse
potīrī: *to possess;* dep. inf., regnō as abl. obj.

14 **Ea rēs**: *this matter;* i.e. Orgetorix's conspiracy
est....ēnūntiāta: ēnūntiāta est; pf. passive
per indicium: i.e. through spies and informers
mōribus suīs: *according to their customs;* "from their customs," often with "ex" denotes a source of action (separation) not abl. cause

15 **causam dīcere**: *to plead the case;* idiom
damnātum...sequī: *that (he) if condemned follow...;* deponent inf., PPP is conditional
oportēbat: *it was necessary that;* impersonal
ut...cremārētur: *that...;* ind. command
ignī: ablative of means; i-stem 3rd decl. noun

17 **diē cōnstitūtā**: *on the...;* abl. of time when
causae dictiōnis: *for the pleading of the case*
ad...mīlia decem: *around;* ad means "up to" or "nearly" throughout this passage

18 **coēgit**: *gathered;* cōgō (co-agō) means (a) compel or (b) drive together; cf. ll. 15 and 22

19 **eōdem**: *in the same (place);* abl. place where

20 **nē...dīceret**: *so that...not;* neg. purpose. cf. 15
cum...conārētur...cōgerent: *after...;* cum clause with two impf. subjunctives
exsequī: pres. dep. infinitive, exsequor
ob eam rem: *on account of this matter*

22 **mortuus est**: *died;* pf. deponent, morior
neque abest suspīcio: i.e. "there is a suspicion that..." litotes; equiv. to "there is no doubt..."
ut...: *as;* common meaning with indicative

23 **quin sibi...cōnscīverit**: *that he brought...on himself;* quin + pf. subj. cōnscīscō, after a verb of doubting or hindering; cf. line 9 above

5.1 Post eius mortem nihilō minus Helvētiī id quod cōnstituerant facere   1
cōnantur, ut ē fīnibus suīs exeant. 2. Ubi iam sē ad eam rem parātōs esse
arbitrātī sunt, oppida sua omnia, numerō ad duodecim, vīcōs ad
quadringentōs, reliqua prīvāta aedificia incendunt; 3. frūmentum omne,
praeter quod sēcum portātūrī erant, combūrunt, ut domum redītiōnis spē   5
sublātā parātiōrēs ad omnia perīcula subeunda essent; trium mensum molita
cibāria sibi quemque domō efferre iubent. Persuādent Rauracīs et Tulingīs et
Latobrīgīs fīnitimīs utī, eōdem ūsī cōnsiliō, oppidīs suīs vīcīsque exustīs ūnā
cum eīs proficīscantur, Boiōsque, quī trāns Rhēnum incoluerant et in agrum
Noricum transīerant Noreiamque oppugnābant, receptōs ad sē sociōs sibi   10
adsciscunt.

6.1 Erant omnīnō itinera duo, quibus itineribus domō exīre possent: ūnum
per Sēquanōs, angustum et difficile, inter montem Iūram et flūmen
Rhodanum, vix quā singulī carrī dūcerentur, mōns autem altissimus
impendēbat, ut facile perpaucī prohibēre possent; 2. alterum per provinciam   15
nostram, multō facilius atque expedītius, proptereā quod inter fīnēs
Helvētiōrum et Allobrogum, quī nūper pācātī erant, Rhodanus fluit isque
nōnnūllis locīs vadō trānsītur.

3. Extrēmum oppidum Allobrogum est proximumque Helvētiōrum fīnibus
Genava. Ex eō oppidō pōns ad Helvētiōs pertinet. Allobrogibus sēsē vel   20
persuāsūrōs, quod nōndum bonō animō in populum Rōmānum vidērentur,
existimābant vel vī coactūrōs ut per suōs fīnēs eōs īre paterentur. Omnibus
rēbus ad profectiōnem comparātis diem dīcunt, quā diē ad rīpam Rhodanī
omnēs conveniant. Is diēs erat a. d. V. Kal. Apr. L. Pīsōne, A. Gabīniō
cōnsulibus.   25

a(d)sciscō, -ere, -scīvī: receive, admit, adopt, 1
aedificium, -iī n.: building, edifice, 2
Allobrogēs, -um: Allobroges, 3
angustus, -a, -um: narrow, confined, 4
April, Aprilis m.: April, 2
Boii, -ōrum m.: Boians (Bohemia) 1
bonus, -a, -um: good, kind(ly), useful 2
carrus, -ī m.: wagon for baggage, wagon, 2
cibāria, -ōrum n.: rations, rationed food, 1
comburō, -ere, -ussī, -ustum: burn up, 1
comparō (1): prepare, get ready, provide, 4
cōnsul, -is m.: consul, 3
d.: diem; day, 1
difficilis, difficile: hard, difficult, 1
domus, -ūs f.: house, home, dwelling, 3
duodecim: twelve, 1
efferō, -ferre, -tulī, ēlātus: raise, lift up 4

eō, īre, īvī: to go, come, 4
exeō, -īre, -iī (īvī), -itus: go out, 4
expedītus, -a, -um: unimpeded, fast, 4
extrēmus, -a, -um: farthest, outermost, 2
exūrō, -ere, -ussī, -ustum: burn up, 1
fluō, -ere, flūxī, flūxus: flow, 1
Gabinius, -ī m.: Gabinius, 1
Genava, -ae f.: Geneva, 3
iam: now, already, soon, 4
impendeō, -ēre: hang over, threaten, 1
incendō, -ere, -ī, -ēnsus: kindle, burn, 2
incolō, -ere, -uī: inhabit, dwell on, 3
Iūra, -ae f.: Iura (a mountain range), 3
Kal.: Kalends, 1
L.: Lucius, 2
Latobrīgī, -ōrum m.: Latobrigians (Latovici) 1
mensis, -is m.: month, 2

molō, -ere, moluī, molitum: grind (in a mill), mill, 1
mons, montis m.: mountain, mount, 4
nondum: not yet, 3
nōnnullus, -a, -um: some, not none, 2
Noreia, -ae f.: Noreia, 1
Noricum, -ī m.: Noricum (modern Austria) 1
nūper: recently, lately, newly, 1
omnīnō: altogether, wholly, entirely, 2
oppidum, -ī n.: town, 4
pācō (1): make peaceful, pacify, 1
parō (1): prepare, make ready, 3
patior, -ī, passus: suffer, endure; allow, 2
perpaucī, -ae, -a: very few, 1
Pīsō, Pīsōnis m.: Piso, 2
pons, pontis m.; a bridge, 2
portō (1): carry, bear, bring, 2
praeter: beyond, past (+ acc.), 2

proptereā: on this account, therefore, 4
quadringenti: four hundred, 2
Raurācī, -ōrum: Rauraci, 1
reditiō, -ōnis f.: return, going back, 1
rīpa, -ae f.: bank, shore, 1
socius, -ī m.: comrade, ally, companion, 2
subeō, -īre, -iī, -itum: approach, undergo, 1
tollō, -ere, sustulī, sublātum: destroy, raise, 2
trans; over, across (+ acc.), 3
Tulingī, -ōrum m.: Tulingi, 1
ubi: where, when, 4
vadum, -ī n.: shallow, shoal, ford, 2
vel: or, **vel...vel**, either...or, 2
vīcus, -ī m.: village, neighborhood, district, 2
vīs, vīs, f., pl. **virēs**: force, power, violence, 4
vix: with difficulty, with effort, scarcely, 2

---

1 **eius**: *his*; i.e. Orgetorix, gen. sg.
  nihilō minus: *no less*; "less by nothing," comp. adverb; nihilō is abl. degree of difference
  id quod: *that which*; id is object of facere
2 **ut...exeant**: *(namely) that...*; pres. subj. exeō, in a noun purpose clause in apposition to id
  ad eam rem: *for this matter*; expresses purpose
  sē: *that they*; acc. subject of parātōs esse
3 **arbitrātī sunt**: pf. deponent
  numerō: *in number*; abl. of respect
  ad: *around*; "up to" or "nearly"
5 **praeter quod**: *except (that) which...*
  sēcum: *cum sē*
  portātūrī erant: *were going to carry*; periphrastic fut. (fut. act. pple + impf. sum)
  ut...essent: *so that...*; result, impf. sum
  spē sublātā: *with hope having been carried off*; abl. absolute, pf. pass. pple from tollō
6 **ad...subeunda**: *for approaching...*; "for all dangers going to be approached," a gerundive subeō + ad expresses purpose and is best translated through a gerund-gerundive flip as a gerund + object: "for approaching all dangers"
  molīta: *ground*; i.e flour, PPP "set in motion"
8 **utī...proficiscantur**: *that...*; an alternative spelling for ut (note: the pres. inf. for ūtor is ūtī with an initial long-u); introducing an ind. command with pres. subj.
  ūsī: *having employed*; nom. pl. PPP, deponent ūtor governs an ablative object
  ūnā: *altogether*; adverb formed from an abl.
10 **trānsīerant**: pluperfect of trānseō
  sōciōs: *(as) allies*; in apposition to Boiōsque
12 **erant**: *there were*

itinera: *routes*
quibus...possent: *by which...*; rel. clause of characteristic; impf. subj. of possum, quibus is a relative adj. with itineribus, which is redundant and may be left untranslated
domō: *from home*; place from which
ūnum: *one (route)*; in apposition to itinera
14 **quā**: *by which (way)*; or "where," abl. as adv.
  quā...dūcerentur: *by which...*; relative of characteristic with impf. subjunctive, the path is so narrow that carts must pass one at a time
15 **ut...possent**: *so that*; result clause, impf. subj.
  facile: *easily*; irregular 3rd decl. adv. facilis, -e
  alterum (iter): *the other (route)*; in apposition to itinera (line 12) and parallel to "ūnum"
16 **multō**: *much*; lit. "by much", abl. degree of difference modifies comparative adjectives
  facīlius atque expedītius: comparative adjs., neuter singular modifying "alterum (iter)"
  proptereā quod: *because*; 3rd instance so far
18 **vadō**: *in the shallows*; "in a ford"; place where
20 **sēsē...persuāsūrōs (esse)...coāctūrōs (esse)**: *that they would persuade or compel*; fut. inf.
21 **bonō animō**: *seemed not yet of good will to...*; abl. of quality in the predicative position
22 **vī**: irregular ablative of means, vīs
  paterentur: *they (Allobrogēs) allow*; impf. subj. of the deponent patior (3rd-io)
23 **diem dīcunt quā diē**: *they name the day on which (day)...*; ablative time when
24 **a(nte) d(iem) V. Kal(ends) Apr(ilis)**: *5th day before the Kalends of April*; March 28th, 58
  L. Pīsōne...cōnsulibus: abl. abs; add "being"

7.1 Caesarī cum id nūntiātum esset, eōs per prōvinciam nostram iter facere 1
cōnārī, mātūrat ab urbe proficīscī et quam maximīs potest itineribus in
Galliam ulteriōrem contendit et ad Genavam pervenit. 2. Prōvinciae tōtī
quam maximum potest mīlitum numerum imperat (erat omnīnō in Galliā
ulteriōre legiō ūna), pontem, quī erat ad Genavam, iubet rescindī.   5

   3. Ubi dē eius adventū Helvētiī certiōrēs factī sunt, legātōs ad eum mittunt
nobilīssimōs civitātis, cuius legātiōnis Nammeius et Verucloetius principem
locum obtinēbant, quī dīcerent sibi esse in animō sine ūllō maleficiō iter per
prōvinciam facere, proptereā quod aliud iter habērent nūllum: rogāre ut eius
voluntāte id sibi facere liceat. Caesar, quod memoriā tenēbat L. Cassium   10
consulem occīsum exercitumque eius ab Helvētiīs pulsum et sub iugum
missum, cōncēdendum nōn putābat; 4. neque hōminēs inimīcō animō, datā
facultāte per provinciam itineris faciendī, temperātūrōs ab iniūriā et
maleficiō existimābat. 5. Tamen, ut spatium intercēdere posset dum mīlitēs
quōs imperāverat convenīrent, lēgātīs respondit diem se ad dēlīberandum   15
sūmptūrum: sī quid vellent, ad Id. April. reverterentur.

April, Aprilis m.: April, 2
Cassius, -ī m.: Cassius, 1
concēdō, -ere; go away, withdraw, yield, 2
cōnsul, -is m.: consul, 3
contendō, -ere, -ī, -ntus: strive; hasten, 4
dēliberō (1): consider, consult, weigh, 1
Genava, -ae f.: Geneva, 3
impetrō (1): to obtain, accomplish, 3
inimīcus, -a, -um: hostile, unfriendly, 4
iniūria, -ae f.: wrong, insult, injustice, 4
intercēdō, -ere, -cessī, -cessum: come or go
   between, intervene, 1
Idūs, -uum f.: Ides (day of the month), 1
iugum, -ī n.: yoke, (mountain) range, 2
L.: Lucius, 2
lēgātio, -ōnis f.: embassy, envoy, 2
maleficium, -iī n.; wrongdoing, crime, 2
mātūrō (1); hasten; anticipate, ripen, 1
memoria, -ae. f.: memory, 4
Nammeius, -iī m.: Nammeius, 1
nōbilis, -e: noble, renowned, 3

nuntiō (1): announce, report, 2
occīdō, -ere, occidī, occīsus: kill, cut down 4
omnīnō: altogether, wholely, entirely, 2
pellō, -ere, pepulī, pulsus: drive, push, 2
pons, pontis m.; a bridge, 2
princeps, -cipis m./f.: chief, leader, 4
proptereā: on this account, therefore, 4
putō (1): to think, imagine, 3
rescindō, -ere, scidī, scissum: cut back, 1
respondeō, -ēre, -dī, -ōnsum: to answer, 3
revertor, -ī, reversus sum: to turn back, return, 2
rogō (1): to ask; tell, 2
spatium, -iī n.: space, room, extent, 4
sūmō, -ere, sumpsī, sumptum: take, spend, 1
temperō (1): refrain from, keep from, 1
ubi: where, when, 4
ulterior, -ius: farther, 2
urbs, urbis, f.: city, 1
Verucloētius, iī m.: Verucloetius, 1
voluntās, -tātis f.: will, wish, choice, 2

Subordinate Clauses in Indirect Discourse

In indirect discourse, the verbs of subordinate clauses become subjunctive, while the main verbs
become infinitives. These subjunctives often do not require a special translation. Simply translate the
verb in the appropriate tense and identify the subjunctive as "subordinate clause in indirect discourse."

| quod imperium obtentūrus esset | *because he was about to obtain the command* | p. 6 |
| quod…aliud iter habērent nūllum | *because they had no other route* | p. 10 |

1 **Caesarī**: *to Caesar*; Caesar talks about himself in the 3rd person; dat. sg. of nūntiātum esset
nūntiātum esset: plpf. pass. subjunctive in a temporal clause with cum, "after" or "when"
id…eōs…cōnārī: *this…(namely) that they attempt*; acc. subject and deponent inf. (indirect disc.) in apposition to id

2 **quam…itineribus**: *in as rapid marches as possible*; "with the greatest marches as it is possible," quam + superlative is "as X as possible," potest is impersonal: "it is possible"

3 **Gallia ulteriōrem**: *further Gaul*; i.e. the Province (Transalpine Gaul) in southern France
contendit: *hastens*

4 **Prōvinciae tōtī…imperat**: *ordered from the entire Province…*; dat. indirect object; tōtī is dat. sg. of tōtus (gen. tōtīus)
quam…numerum: *as great a number of soldiers possible*; "a greatest number of soldiers as it is able;" see line 2

4 **imperat….(et) pontem…iubet**: supply the missing conjunction "et," asyndeton, which suggests that Caesar is quick and decisive

5 **ad Genavam**: *near Geneva*
rescindī: present passive infinitive

6 **eius**: *his*; i.e. Caesar's
certiōrēs factī sunt: *were informed*; "were made more certain", common idiom in Caesar, certiōrēs is a pred. nominative

7 **cuius legātiōnis**: *of which embassy*; rel. adj.

8 **quī dīcerent**: *who would say…*; relative clause of purpose, impf. subj. dīcō, which one may translate as a regular purpose clause: "to say…"
sibi esse in animō: *that he had in mind*; + inf., "there is to him in mind," dat. of possession

9 **proptereā quod**: *because*; lit. "on this account because," 4th and final instance of this phrase
habērent: *they had*; impf. subj., subordinate clauses within indirect discourse govern verbs in the subjunctive
rogāre ut…liceat: *they asked that it be allowed…*; historical inf. and ind. command
eius voluntāte: *with his permission*

10 **memoriā tenēbat**: *in memory*; abl. of means, a common idiom for "he recalled" or "he remembered"
L. Cassium…occīsum (esse), exercitumque …pulsum (esse)…missum (esse): two separate instances of indirect discourses (two acc. subjects) governed by tenēbat, supply esse to form pf. passive infinitives

11 **occīsum (esse)**: *had been killed*; pf. pass. inf.
pulsum (esse): pf. pass. inf. pellō
sub iugum missum (esse): *had been sent under the yoke*; i.e. had been enslaved

12 **cōncēdendum nōn (esse sibi)**: *that he must not yield*; "that it is not going to be yielded by him," a passive periphrastic (gerundive + form of sum) which expresses obligation or necessity, often with a dative of agent
hominēs…temperātūrōs (esse): *that people…would not refrain*; fut. inf. governed by existimābat
inimīcō animō: *of hostile intent*; abl. of description modifying hominēs
datā facultāte: ablative absolute

13 **itineris faciendī**: *of making a journey*; "of a journey going to be made" gerundive modifies gen. iter which is better translated through a gerundive-gerund flip
ab inūriā..maleficiō: *from…*; abl. separation with temperātūrōs (esse)

14 **ut spatium…posset**: *so that…*; purpose clause with impf. subj.; spatium is subject

15 **sē…sūmptūrum (esse)**: *that he…*; indirect discourse, supply esse for the future inf.
ad dēliberandum: *for deliberating*; ad + gerund expressing purpose, which can also be translated as an infinitive: "to deliberate"

16 **quid**; *anything*; aliquis, aliquid is a common indefinite pronoun (anyone, anything), but quis, quid is commonly used as an indefinite (who → anyone; what → anything) after sī, nisi, num, and nē. The mnemonic for this construction is the jingle "After sī, nisi, num, and nē, all the ali's go away" (in other words indefinite aliquid becomes just quid)
sī…vellent,…reverterentur: *if they should wish, they could return…*; in direct disc. a future less vivid condition (sī pres. subj., pres. subj.) which are placed in impf. subjunctive in indirect discourse in secondary sequence
ad Id(ūs) April(is): *near the Ides of April*; the 13th of April, the Ides denotes the time of the month when there is a full moon; Idūs is 4th decl. acc. pl. and Aprilis is gen. sg.

Numbers of Helvetians Killed During Caesar's Campaign

In I.29 Caesar claims that 368,000 Helvetians and allies left Helvetia (only 92,000 were able to bear arms) and 110,000 returned. Therefore, 258,000 either fled or perished at Caesar's hand.

24.1 At barbarī, cōnsiliō Rōmānōrum cognitō, praemissō equitātū et 1
ēssedariīs, quō plērumque genere in proeliīs ūtī consuērunt, reliquīs copiīs
subsecūtī nostrōs nāvibus ēgredī prohibēbant. 2. Erat ob hās causās summa
difficultās, quod navēs propter magnitūdinem nisi in altō cōnstituī nōn
poterant, mīlitibus autem, ignōtīs locīs, impedītīs manibus, magnō et gravī 5
onere armōrum oppressīs simul et dē nāvibus desiliendum et in fluctibus
consistendum et cum hostibus erat pugnandum, 3. cum illī aut ex āridō aut
paulum in aquam progressī omnibus membrīs expedītīs, nōtissimīs locīs,
audacter tēla coicerent et equōs insuēfactōs incitārent. 4. Quibus rēbus nostrī
perterritī atque huius omnīnō generis pugnae imperītī, nōn eādem alacritāte 10
ac studiō quō in pedestribus ūtī proeliīs consuerant utēbantur.

25.1 Quod ubi Caesar animadvertit, nāvēs longās, quārum et speciēs erat
barbarīs inūsitātior et motus ad usum expedītior, paulum removērī ab
onerāriīs nāvibus et rēmīs incitārī et ad latus apertum hostium constituī atque
inde fundīs, sagittīs, tormentīs hostēs propellī ac submovērī iussit; quae rēs 15
magnō usuī nostrīs fuit. 2. Nam et nāvium figūrā et rēmōrum mōtū et
inusitātō genere tormentōrum permōtī barbarī constitērunt ac paulum modo
pedem rettulērunt.

alacritās, -tātis f.: eagerness, ardor, 1
aperiō, -īre, -uī, -ertus: open, disclose, 3
aqua, -ae f.: water, 1
aridus, -a, -um: dry, 3
audacter: boldly, 1
consistō, -ere, -stitī: to stand (still), stop 2
dēsiliō, -īre, -luī: to jump down, dismount, 4
difficultās, -tātis f.: trouble, difficulty, 1
equus, -ī m.: horse, 4
ēssedārius, -ī m.: charioteer, driver, 1
expedītus, -a, -um: unimpeded, fast, 4
figūra, -ae f.: form, shape, figure, 1
fluctus, -ūs m.: wave, billow, 2
funda, ae f.: sling, 3
ignōtus, -a, -um: unknown; obscure 1
imperītus, a, um: unskilled, inexperienced, 2
impeditus, -a, -um: hindered, impeded, 3
inde: from there, then, afterward, 3
insuefactus, -a, -um: accustomed, inured, 1
inūsitātus, -a, -um: unusual, uncommon, 1
latus, -eris n.: side, flank, 3
membrum, -ī n.: limb, member, 1
modo: only, merely, simply; just now, 4
mōtus, -ūs m.: motion, 3

nōtus, -a, -um: known, familiar, famous, 2
omnīnō: altogether, wholely, entirely, 2
onerārius, -a, -um: freight (ship); 2
onus, oneris n.: burden, load, freight, 1
opprimō, -ere, -pressī, -pressum: burden,
  overwhelm, 3
pedester, -tris, -tre: on foot, infantry, 1
perterreō, -ēre, -terruī: terrify thoroughly, 1
praemittō, -ere: send forward, send ahead, 2
prōgredior, -gredī, -gressus: step forward,
  go forth, advance, 2
prōpellō, -ere, -pellī, -pulsum: drive forward
  or push away, 3
referō, ferre, tulī, lātum: report, bring back, 3
removeō, -ēre, -mōvī, -mōtus: remove, 2
remus, ī m.: oar, 2
sagitta, -ae f.: arrow, 1
simul: at the same time (as); together, 4
speciēs, -ēi f.: sight, appearance, aspect, 1
studium, -ī n.: zeal, enthusiasm, pursuit, 3
submoveō, -ēre, -mōvī: move up; remove, 1
tormentum, -ī n.: missile-launcher, 3
ubi: where, when, 4

1 **cōnsiliō…cognitō**: abl. absolute
praemissō…ēssedariīs: abl. absolute with two nouns; mobile troops were sent in advance

2 **quō…genere**: *which kind (of warfare)*; abl. obj. of ūtī, the deponent complementary inf. of ūtor

3 **cōnsu(ev)ērunt**: *were accustomed*; 3p pf.
reliquīs copiīs subsecūtī: *having followed behind with the rest of the troops*; dep. pf. pple modifies barbarī, the cavalry went in advance and the foot-soldiers followed

3 **navibus**: *from…*; abl. of place from which
ēgredī: *from disembarking*; "to step out," dep. inf. ēgredior

4 **nisi in altō**: *except in the deep*; the Roman ships did not have flattened keels to come closer to the shore
cōnstituī: *to be stopped*; pass. inf. with poterant

5 **mīlitibus…oppressīs**: *the soldiers having been overcome…*; dat. of agent of pass. periphrastic, the dat. of agent is better translated as a subject intervening words are ablative of cause/means
gravī: i-stem abl. sing. modifies onere

6 **et desiliendum (erat)…et consistendum (erat)…et pugnandum (erat)**: *(both) the soldiers had to…and had to…and had to…*; "it was going to be jumped down by soldiers…" passive periphrastic (gerundive + sum) with a dat. of agent expressing obligation or necessity; it is better translated in the active with the verb "must" or, as here, "had to" (see pg. 21)

7 **cum…coicerent…incitārent**: *when…*; temporal cum-clause with impf. subjunctive

8 **paulum**: *a little*; inner acc. or acc. of extent

prōgressī: *having advanced*; pf. pple deponent
omnibus…expedītīs: abl. absolute
nōtissimīs locīs: abl. absolute, supply "being"

9 **īnsuēfactōs**: *experienced*; 'accustomed'
quibus rēbus: *by these matters*; "by which things," abl. means or cause; Caesar often uses relative pronoun for transition where English employs a demonstrative
nostrī: *our (men)*; as often

10 **huius generis pugnae**: gen. governed by the adjective imperitī, "unskilled in"
eādem…studiō: abl. objects of ūtēbantur

11 **quō…consuerant**: *which…*; quō is an abl. object of the inf. ūtī
proeliīs: *in battles*

12 **quod**: *this*; "which," acc. obj. of animadvertit
nāvēs longās…cōnstituī: acc. subj. and pass. infinitives governed by iussit below

13 **barbarīs**: *to the barbarians*; dat. of reference
inūsitātior: nom. sg. comparative adj.

14 **paulum**: *a little*; inner acc. or acc. of extent
removērī: pres. pass. inf.
cōnstituī: *to be stopped*; pass. inf.

15 **propellī, submovērī**: pass. infinitives, hostēs is acc. subject

16 **magnō ūsuī nostrīs fuit**: *served a great use to our men*; "was for a great use for our men," double dative construction (ūsuī is dat. of purpose, nostrīs is dat. of interest)

17 **paulum modo**: *just a little*; modo is adverbial, paulum is acc. of extent

18 **pedem**: *their step(s)*; i.e. they retreated
rettulērunt: 3rd pl. pf. referō

Background to Caesar's First Invasion of Britain on August 26, 55 BC

In IV.20 Caesar says that, although the winters were early (*matūrae*) in the north, he decided to go to Britain because he realized that assistance had been supplied from there (*inde subministrāta auxilia*) for the Gauls in almost every battle. Since Caesar knew very little about the region—its size (*magnitūdō*), inhabitants (*quantae nātiōnēs*), its practices in war (*ūsum bellī*), or its suitable ports (*idōneī portūs*)—he sent Gaius Volusenus in IV.21 as a scout to gather this information.

In the meantime, several states (*civitātēs*) of the Britons learned about his plan, sought out Caesar, and offered hostages as a show of loyalty. Caesar sent Commius, a loyal Gaul whom Caesar had placed as leader of the Atrebates and who had clout (*auctoritās*) over Gauls, back with the Britons. On the fifth day, Volusenus returned and reported what he had seen. In IV.22 after accepting hostages from the Gauls, Caesar placed the legates Q. Titurius Sabinus and L. Aurunculeius Cotta in charge of Roman forces in Gaul. Then he departed with 2 legions and about 80 transport ships.

In IV.23 Caesar set sail after midnight (*tertiā ferē vigiliā*) and around 10 a.m. (*hōrā diēī quārtā*) arrived in Britain. The Romans found themselves facing the sheer cliffs of Dover, and on top of all of the hills armed troops (*copiās armātās*) openly stood. Caesar now informed his legates about what Volusenus reported and sailed 7 miles up the coast to an open beach (*apertō ac plānō lītore*).

25.3 Atque nostrīs mīlitibus cunctantibus, maximē propter altitūdinem 1
maris, quī X legiōnis aquilam ferēbat, contestātus deōs ut ea rēs legiōnī
feliciter ēvenīret, 'Dēsilite,' inquit, 'militēs, nisi vultis aquilam hostibus
prōdere; ego certē meum reī pūblicae atque imperātōrī officium praestiterō.'
4. Hoc cum vōce magnā dīxisset, sē ex nāvī prōiēcit atque in hostēs aquilam 5
ferre coepit. 5. Tum nostrī cohortātī inter sē, nē tantum dēdecus
admitterētur, universī ex nāvī dēsiluērunt. 6. Hōs item ex proximīs primī
nāvibus cum conspēxissent, subsecutī hostibus appropinquāverunt.

26.1 Pugnātum est ab utrīsque ācriter. Nostrī tamen, quod neque ordinēs
servāre neque firmiter insistere neque signa subsequī poterant atque alius 10
aliā ex nāvī quibuscumque signīs occurrerat sē aggregābat, magnopere
perturbābantur; 2. hostēs vērō, nōtīs omnibus vadīs, ubi ex lītore aliquōs
singulārēs ex nāvī ēgredientēs conspēxerant, incitātīs equīs impedītōs
adoriēbantur, 3. plūrēs paucōs circumsistēbant, aliī ab latere apertō in
universōs tēla coniciēbant. 15

4. Quod cum animadvertisset Caesar, scaphās longārum nāvium, item
speculātōria navigia mīlitibus complērī iussit et, quōs laborantēs conspēxerat,
hīs subsidia submittēbat. 5. Nostrī, simul in āridō constitērunt, suīs omnibus
consecūtīs, in hostēs impetum fecērunt atque eōs in fūgam dedērunt; neque
longius prosequī potuērunt, quod equitēs cursum tenēre atque insulam capere 20
non potuerant. Hoc ūnum ad pristīnam fortūnam Caesarī defuit.

acriter: sharply, fiercely, 2
admittō, -ere, mīsī, missum: admit, allow, 2
adorior, -īrī, -ortus sum: rise up, attack, 2
aggregō (1): to crowd together, collect, 1
altitūdō, -inis f.: height, depth, altitude, 2
aperiō, -īre, -uī, -ertus: open, disclose, 3
appropinquō (1): approach, draw near, 3
aquila, -ae f.: eagle, eagle standard, 4
aridus, -a, -um: dry, 3
circumsistō, -ere, -stetī: to surround, 2
cohortor, -ārī, cohortātum: urge on, incite 3
consequor, -ī, secūtus: follow after; pursue 1
conspiciō, -ere, spexī, spectus: see, behold 5
contestor, -ārī, -ātum: to call to witness, 1
cunctor, -ārī, -ātum: to delay, hesitate 1
cursus, -ūs m.: course, running, haste, 3
dēdecus, -oris n.: dishonor, disgrace, shame, 1
dēsiliō, -īre, -luī: to jump down, dismount, 4
deus, -ī m.: god, divinity, deity, 4
ego: I, 2
equus, -ī m.: horse, 4
ēveniō, -īre, -iī, -itum: come or turn out, 1
fēlīciter: happily, favorably, 1
firmiter: firmly, steadfastly, 1

fortūna, -ae f.: fortune, chance, luck, 4
fuga, -ae f.: flight, haste, exile, speed, 3
impeditus, -a, -um: hindered, impeded, 3
imperātor, -oris m.: commander, leader, 2
inquam: say, 4
insistō, -ere, -stitī: set on, set about; stop, 2
insula, -ae, f.: island, 2
item: also, likewise, in like manner, 3
labōrō (1): work, toil, labor, strive, 2
latus, -eris n.: side, flank, 2
litus, litoris n.: coast, shore, beach, 1
magnōpere: greatly, very much, 2
mare,, -is n.: sea, 1
meus, -a, -um: my, mine, 1
nāvigium, -ī n.: vessel, sail, 1
nōtus, -a, -um: known, familiar, famous, 2
occurrō, -ere: run to meet, attack, 2
officium, -iī, n.: duty, obligation, 3
paucī, -ae, -a: little, few, scanty, 4
plūs (plūris): more, 4
pristinus, -a, -um: former, previous, earlier 2
prōdō, ere, didī, ditum: bring forth; betray 2
proiciō, -icere, -iēcī, -iectum: throw
   forward, project, 2

prosequor, sequī, secūtum: follow, pursue 1
quīcumque, quae-, quod-: whosoever, 4
scapha, -ae f.: skiff, small boat, 1
servō (1): save, keep, preserve, 2
simul: at the same time (as); together, 4
singulāris, -e: single, 2
speculātōrius, -a, um: of a look-out/scout, 1

submittō, -ere, -mīsī: send up, 1
ubi: where, when, 4
ūniversus, -a, -um: all together, whole, 3
vadum, -ī n.: shallow, shoal, ford, 2
vērō: in truth, truly, in fact, to be sure, 3
vōx, vōcis, f.: voice; utterance, word, 4

---

1 **nostrīs...cunctantibus**: abl. abs., pres. pple
2 **quī...ferēbat**: *(the one) who…*; i.e. the standard bearer, subject of inquit
contestātus...ut: *having implored the gods... that…*; ut + impf. subjunctive in ind. command
3 **dēsilite**: plural imperative
mīlitēs: vocative direct address
vultis: 2nd pl. pres. volō
aquilam: *the eagle (standard)*; the golden eagle on the staff that represents the 10th legion. The behavior toward the military standard is similar to the loyalty shown to the American flag.
4 **meum...officium praestiterō**: *I will have performed my duty to*; + dat. compound, fut. pf.
5 **cum...dīxisset**: *when he had…*; cum is an adverbial conjunction not a preposition
vōce magnā: *with…*; abl. of manner is often without "cum" when the object is modified by an adjective, here magnā
sē: *himself*; standard-bearer is the subject
ex navī: ablative, i-stem 3rd declension
6 **ferre**: infinitive ferō
nostrī: *our (men)*; nom. subject
conhortātī: pf. dep. pple cohortor
inter sē: *one another*; "among themselves"
nē...admitterētur: *that… not*; negative ind. command, impf. subj. in secondary sequence
7 **Hōs..conspēxissent**: *when (the other soldiers) had caught sight of (them)*; plpf. subjunctive
8 **subsecutī**: *having followed behind*; pf dep pple
pugnātum est: *each (side) fought*; "it was fought," impersonal pf. pass.
9 **Nostrī**: *our (men)*
10 **ordinēs servāre**: *to maintain their ranks*
subsequī: *to follow behind*; deponent inf.
alius aliā ex nāvī: *one from one ship…*

another from another ship; common meaning with two uses of alius, -a, -um
11 **quibuscumque signīs**: dat. of compound verb
12 **vērō**: *but indeed, but to be sure*; vērō is in an adversative clause; placed second in the sentence but first in English, it draws out a contrast between the Romans and the Britons
nōtīs...vadīs: ablative abs.
13 **ēgredientēs**: pres. act. pple
14 **plūrēs paucōs**: *More (Britons)…few (Romans)*; juxtaposition, which heightens the contrast; plūrēs is nom. subj. of plūs
aliī: *(and) others…*; asyndeton
16 **quod**: *this*; "which," acc. obj. animadvertisset
nāvium: i-stem gen. plural nāvis
17 **complērī**: pass. infinitive
quōs laborantēs conspēxerat: *whom he had seen struggling*; "toiling," against the enemy
18 **hīs**: *to these*; dat. i.o. or dat. with compound
Nostrī: *Our (men)*
19 **suīs omnibus**: *all their (fellow soldiers)…*; an abl. absolute with consecūtīs
in: *against*; a common meaning in this context
in fūgam dedērunt: *put them into flight*; "in fūgam dō" is a common idiom in Caesar
20 **longius**: *farther*; comparative adverb, longē
prosequī: pres. deponent complementary inf.
21 **īnsulam capere**: *to land on the island*; "catch the island," the horses had not disembarked yet because the ships were not close enough to the shore
ad pristīnam fortūnam: *(compared) to his previous good fortune*; "in proportion to…" suggests a comparison
22 **Caesarī defuit**: *failed Caesar*; "was lacking to Caesar," dat. of interest

---

Supine

A supine is a verbal noun formed by adding **-ū** in ablative and **-um** in accusative to the 4th principle part stem. It is often translated as an ablative of respect (specification) and accusative expressing purpose:

factū: *in doing (to do)* (p. 6, 20)	**frūmentātum**: *to get grain* (p. 20)	**oppugnātum**: *to assault* (p. 39)
	rogātum: *to ask* (p. 52)	**nocitum**: *to be harmed* (p. 52)

27.1 Hostēs proeliō superātī, simul atque sē ex fūgā recēpērunt, statim ad   1
Caesarem lēgātōs dē pace mīsērunt; obsidēs datūrōs quaeque imperāsset sēsē
factūrōs pollicitī sunt. 2. Ūnā cum hīs legātīs Commius Atrēbās vēnit, quem
suprā demonstrāveram ā Caesare in Britanniam praemissum. 3. Hunc illī ē
nāvī ēgressum, cum ad eōs ōrātōris mōdō Caesaris mandāta dēferret,   5
comprehenderant atque in vincula coiēcerant; 4. tum proeliō factō
remīsērunt. In petendā pace eius rēī culpam in multitūdinem coiēcērunt
et propter imprudentiam ut ignōscerētur petivērunt.

5. Caesar questus quod, cum ultrō in continentem lēgātīs missīs pacem ab
sē petissent, bellum sine causā intulissent, ignōscere <sē> imprudentiae dixit   10
obsidēsque imperāvit; 6. quōrum illī partem statim dedērunt, partem ex
longinquiōribus locīs arcessitam paucīs diēbus sēsē datūrōs dīxērunt. 7. Intereā
suōs remigrāre in agrōs iussērunt, principēsque undique convenīre et sē
civitātēsque suās Caesarī commendāre coepērunt.

28.1 Hīs rēbus pāce confirmātā, post diem quartum quam est in Britānniam   15
ventum nāvēs XVIII, dē quibus suprā demonstrātum est, quae equitēs
sustulerant, ex superiōre portū lēnī ventō solvērunt. 2. Quae cum
appropinquārent Britānniae et ex castrīs vidērentur, tanta tempestās subitō
coörta est ut nūlla eārum cursum tenēre posset, sed aliae eōdem unde erant
profectae referrentur, aliae ad inferiōrem partem insulae, quae est prōpius   20
sōlis occāsum, magnō suī cum perīculō deicerentur; 3. quae tamen, ancorīs
iactīs, cum fluctibus complērentur, necessāriō adversā nocte in altum
provectae continentem petiērunt.

---

adversus, -a, -um: opposite, in front, 2
ancora, -ae f.: anchor, 3
appropinquō (1): approach, draw near (dat.), 3
arcessō, -ere, -īvī, itum: summon, send for, 1
Atrebas, Atrebātis, m.: Atrebates, 3
coepī, coepisse, coeptum: to begin, 9
commendō (1): to commit, entrust, 1
Commius, -ī m.: Commius, 2
compleō, -ēre, -ēvī, -ētum: fill up, fill, 6
comprehendō, -ere, -dī: seize, arrest; grasp 4
continēns, continentis f.: the continent, mainland, 3
coörior, -īrī, coörtus: arise, break out, 2
culpa, -ae f.: blame, fault; cause, 1
cursus, -ūs m.: course, running, haste, 3
dēiciō, -ere, -iēcī, -iectum: cast down 2
fluctus, -ūs m.: wave, billow, 1
fuga, -ae f.: flight, haste, exile, speed, 3
iaciō, iacere, iēcī, iactum: to throw, 4
ignoscō, -ere, nōvī, nōtum: pardon, forgive 2
imprudentia, -ae, f.: lack of foresight, 2
inferus, -a, -um: below, lower, 3

insula, -ae, f.: island, 2
intereā: meanwhile, meantime, 3
lenis, -e: smooth, slippery, 1
longinquus, -a, -um; far, distant, remote, 2
mandō (1): order, command, commit, 2
modus, ī n.: manner, form; measure, 4
necessārius, -a, -um: necessary, inevitable, 1
occāsus, -ūs m.: fall, destruction, 2
ōrātor, -oris, m.: speaker, pleader, 1
paucī, -ae, -a: little, few, scanty, 4
polliceor, -cērī, -citus: promise, offer, 2
portus, -ūs m.: harbor, port, haven, 1
praemittō, -ere: send forward, send ahead, 2
princeps, -cipis m./f.: chief, leader, 4
proprius: more closely, nearer, 3
prōvehō, -ere, -vexī, vectum: carry forth, 1
quartus, -a, -um: the fourth, 2
queror, querī, questum: complain, lament, 1
referō, ferre, tulī, lātum: report, bring back, 3
remigrō (1): to travel back, wander back, 1
remittō, -ere, -mīsī: send back, let go, relax, 4

simul: at the same time (as); together, 4
sōl, sōlis m.: sun, 3
solvō, -ere, solvī, solūtum: loosen, set sail; pay, 1
statim: immediately, at once, 4
sufferō, -ere, sustulī: carry or hold up, bear 3
suprā: above, over, on the top, 3

tempestās, tempestātis f.: storm, 3
ultrō: voluntarily; moreover, beyond, 3
unde: whence, from which source, 3
ventus, ventī m.: wind, 3
vinculum, -ī n.: bond, chain, 2

---

1 **proeliō**: *in battle*; abl of respect or place where
simul atque: *as soon as...*
sē...recēpērunt: *they recovered*; "retreated"

2 **dē**: *about*
obsidēs: acc. d.o. of datūrōs (esse)
sēsē: *that they would*; reflexive as acc. subject of fut. infinitives datūrōs (esse) and factūrōs (esse) in secondary sequence
quaeque imperāsset: *and (the things) which he had ordered*; imperā(vi)sset is a syncopated plpf. subj. in a relative clause of characteristic, the missing antecedent is obj. of factūrōs (esse)
pollicitī sunt: perfect deponent polliceor
ūnā: *altogether, together*; ablative as adverb

3 **quem**: *whom...*; acc. subject of pf. passive inf. praemissum (esse) in ind. discourse with by demonstrāveram

4 **suprā demonstrāveram**: *I had shown above*; i.e. earlier in the narrative
illī: *those (Britons)*; subject of comprehenderant

5 **orātōris mōdō**: *in the manner of a public speaker*; ablative of manner

6 **mandāta**: *the orders*; "things ordered" acc. d.o.
deferret: *Commius carried*; impf. subj. deferō
coiēcerant: plpf. co(n)iciō, -ere
proeliō factō: abl. absolute

7 **in petendā pace**: *in seeking peace*; "in peace going to be sought," gerund-gerundive flip in which *pace* becomes acc. obj. of the gerund
eius rēī: *for this matter*; gen. of charge
coiēcerunt: pf. co(n)iciō, -ere

8 **ut ignōscerētur**: impf. subj., ind. command

9 **questus quod**: *having complained that...had waged*; intulisset is plpf. subj. for alleged cause
cum: *after*
in continentem: *to the continent*; i.e. continent of Europe, governed by missīs
petissent: *they had sought*; plpf. subjunctive
ab sē: *from him*; i.e. from Caesar, reflexive

8 **intulissent**: plpf. subj. inferō, alleged cause

10 **ignōscere <sē>**: *that he pardons*; + dat. obj.

11 **quōrum...partem...partem**: *part of which...(another) part...*; partitive gen.

12 **arcessitam**: *summoned*; modifies partem

paucīs diēbus: *within...*; abl. time within
sēsē: *that they...*; emphatic reflexive, acc. subject of fut. inf. datūrōs (esse) in indirect discourse

13 **suōs**: *their own (men)*; object of iussērunt
in agrōs: *to their fields, to their farms*

15 **Hīs rēbus**: abl. of means of cause
Pāce confirmātā: abl. absolute
post diēm quartum quam...ventum *during the fourth day after they came to Britain*; "the fourth day later than it was come into Britain," postquam as one word can be translated "after;" ventum est is an impersonal pf. passive which we translate in the active
nāvēs XVIII: subject of solvērunt

16 **suprā demonstrātum est**: *it has been revealed above*; i.e. earlier in the narrative
quae..sustulerant: *which had brought...*; modifies fem. pl. nāvēs, plpf. sufferō

17 **ex superiōre portū**: *from the upper harbor*
lēnī: abl. sg. i-stem 3rd decl. adj. with ventō, the wind was not strong, so the ships holding the cavalry arrived later than the ships that had already come ashore
solvērunt: *set sail*; "loosened"
quae cum: *when these (ships)...*; "when which (ships)," we prefer a demonstrative here where Caesar uses a relative pronoun
Britānniae: *to Britain*; dat. of compound verb

19 **coörta est**: deponent perfect, coörior
ut...posset: *that...was able*; result clause
nūlla eārum: the antecedents of the adj. and pronoun are the nāvēs (feminine, plural)
aliae...aliae: *some (ships)...others*
eōdem: *to the same place*; adverb
erant profectae: plpf. deponent proficīscor

20 **proprius**: *nearer to* + acc.

21 **magnō suī perīculō**: *with great risk for them*
quae tamen: *these (ships) however*; "which"

22 **cum...complerētur**: *when...*; cum is adverbial not a preposition; flūctibus is abl. means
necessāriō: *necessarily*; abl. as adverb
adversā nocte: *in the face of the coming night*

24 **provectae**: PPP prōvehō

29.1 Eādem nocte accidit ut esset luna plēna, quī diēs maritimōs aestūs 1
maximōs in Ōceanō efficere consuēvit, nostrīsque id erat incognītum. 2. Ita
ūnō tempore et longās nāvēs, quibus Caesar exercitum transportandum
curāverat, quāsque in aridum subdūxerat, aestus complēverat, et onerāriās,
quae ad ancorās erant deligātae, tempestās afflictābat, neque ūlla nostrīs 5
facultās aut administrandī aut auxiliandī dabātur.

3. Complūribus nāvibus fractīs, reliquae cum essent fūnibus, ancorīs
reliquīsque armamentīs amissīs ad navigandum inūtilēs, magna, id quod
necesse erat accidere, tōtīus exercitūs perturbātio facta est. 4. Neque enim
nāvēs erant aliae quibus reportārī possent, et omnia dēerant quae ad 10
reficiendās nāvēs erant usuī, et, quod omnibus constābat hiemārī in Galliā
oportere, frumentum in hīs lōcīs in hiemem provīsum nōn erat.

30.1 Quibus rēbus cognitīs, principēs Britānniae, quī post proelium ad
Caesarem convēnerant, inter sē collocutī, cum equitēs et nāvēs et
frumentum Rōmānīs dēesse intellegerent et paucitātem mīlitum ex 15
castrōrum exiguitāte cognōscerent, quae hōc erant etiam angustiora quod sine
impedimentīs Caesar legiōnēs transportāverat.

---

afflictō (1): agitate, knock about, 1
administrō (1): to manage, direct; help, 3
aestus, -ūs f.: tide, swell; heat, 2
āmittō, -ere, -mīsī, -missum: lose, let go, 2
ancora, -ae f.: anchor, 3
angustus, -a, -um: narrow, confined, 4
aridus, -a, -um: dry, 3
armāmentum, -ī m.: equipment, tackle, 1
auxilior, -ārī: to help, assist, support, 1
clam: secretly, in secret, 1s
coepī, coepisse, coeptum: to begin, 9
colloquor, -quī, -locūtum: to converse, 4
compleō, -ēre, -ēvī, -ētum: fill up, fill, 6
confīdō, -ere, confīsus sum: trust, believe, rely upon, 4
coniūrātio, -ōnis f.: pact, union, conspiracy 3
constō, -āre, -stitī: stand fixed; is agreed, 2
cūrō (1): care for, attend to, manage, 1
dēdūcō, -ere: to lead or draw down or away, 3
dēligō (1): to tie down, fasten, 2
enim: for, indeed, in truth, 3
exiguitās, -tātis, f.: smallness, tininess, 1
frangō, -ere, frēgī, frāctus: break, 1
fūnis, -is m.: a rope, cord
hiemo (1): spend the winter, pass the winter, 3
hiems, hiemis f.: winter, storm, 4
incognitus, -a, -um: unknown, unexamined, 1
intellegō, -ere, -lēxī, -lēctum: to understand, 2
interclūdō, -ere, -clūsī, -clūsum: close off, 1

inūtilis, -e: useless, unprofitable, 1
lūna, -ae f.: moon, 1
maritimus, -a, -um: maritime, marine, 1
nāvigō (1): to sail, 2
necesse: necessary; (it is) necessary, 4
nēmō, nūllīus, nēminī, -em, nūllō: no one, 3
Oceānus, ī m.: Oceanus, 3
onerārius, -a, -um: transport ship; 2
oportet: it is proper, fitting, necessary, 2
optimus, -a, -um: best, noblest, finest, 1
paucitās, -tātis f. (1): fewness, scarcity, 3
paulātim: gradually, little by little, 3
perturbātio, -tiōnis f.: confusion, disorder, 1
plēnus, -a ,-um: full, full of, 1
posteā: thereafter, afterwards, 1
princeps, -cipis m./f.: chief, leader, 4
prōdūcō, -ere, -duxī, ductum: lead forward 2
prōvideō, -ēre, -vīdī, -visum: to foresee, take precautions, prepare for 3
rebellio, -lliōnis f.: revolt, renewal of war, 1
reditus, -ūs m.: a return, a coming back, 1
reficiō, -ere, -fēcī, -fectum: restore, repair, 2
reportō (1): to carry back, 1
rursus: again, backward, back, 4
subdūcō, -ere, -dūxī, -ductus: draw up,, 2
tempestās, tempestātis f.: storm, 3
transportō (1): carry over, take across, 3

1 **Eādem nocte** *on...*; abl. of time when
accidit ut: *it happened that...*; noun result
clause commonly follows impersonal accidit
esset: *there was*; impf. subj. sum
quī diēs: *which time...*; "which day," rel. adj.
aestūs maximōs: calculated to be August 30,
55 BC thus dating the entire expedition
2 **nostrīs**: *to our (men)*; dat. of interest
3 **ūnō tempore**: abl. of time when
et longās nāvēs....et onerāriās (nāvēs): *both
the long ships and the freight (ships)*
quibus: abl. of means, relative pronoun
transportandum (esse): *that...was to be
transported*; "was going to be transported"
passive periphrastic (gerundive + missing inf.
of sum) express obligation or necessity;
exercitum is acc. subject of this infinitive in
indirect discourse
4 **subdūxerat**: *drew up*; as a prefix sub- often
means "up from under" or just "up"
5 **nostrīs**: *to our (men)*; dat. of indirect object
6 **administrandī aut auxiliandī**: gen. sg.
gerunds (verbal nouns), translate in English
with –ing, modifying the subject facultās
7 **complūribus...fractīs**: abl. absolute
relīquae cum essent...inūtilēs: *since the*

remaining (ships) were...; causal; impf. subj.
8 **ad navigandum**: *for...*; ad + gerund expresses
purpose, here qualifying inūtilēs
7 **magna**: modifies fem. sg. perturbātio below
id quod: *that which...*; apposition to perturbātiō
9 **tōtīus exercitūs**: subjective gen. sg.
10 **possent**: *they might be able*; impf. subj. in a
relative clause of purpose
dēerant: impf. dēsum
ad reficiendās nāvēs: *for repairing...*; ad +
noun + gerundive expressing purpose; employ
a gerund-gerundive flip in the translation
11 **erant usuī**: *were of use*; dative of purpose
constābat: *it was agreed to all to...*; "stood
fixed" + oportere, Caesar had planned to
spend the winter in Gaul, so he brought
insufficient amount of grain to Britain
12 **in hiemem**: *(well) into the winter*
13 **quibus rēbus**: *these things...*; abl. abs.
inter sē: *to one another*; "among themselves"
Rōmānīs dēesse: *were falling short for the
Romans*; dat. of interest, inf. dēsum
16 **quae...erant angustiora**: *which was...*;
neut. pl. castra is the antecedent
hōc...quod: *because of this...(namely)
because*," abl. of cause

Popular Uses of Subjunctive in Caesar
Practical Note: identify and translate most subjunctives in the tense you find them.

	How to identify	special translation	example
1. Purpose, adverbial or relative	*ut/nē* (neg.)	may/might	*ut Caesar mitteret* *so that Caesar **might send***
2. Result, adverbial or noun clause	*ut/ut nōn* (neg.)	none	*ut Caesar mitteret* *that Caesar **sent***
3. Cum-Clauses	*Cum* + subjunctive	none	*Cum Caesar mitteret* *When Caesar **sent***
4. Indirect Question	interrogatives: e.g. *quis, cūr*	none	*nōvit quōs Caesar mitteret* *he learned whom Caesar **sent***
5. Indirect Command	commanding verb + *ut/nē* (neg.)	none	*persuāsit ut Caesar mitteret* *he persuaded that Caesar **send***
6. Relative Clause of Characteristic	*quī, quod* + subj.	none/would	*quōs Caesar mitteret* *the sort whom Caesar would **send***
7. Verb in Subordinate Clause in Ind. Disc.	any subordinate verb in an acc. + inf. construction	none	*eōs, sī id mitteret, lēgere* *that they read it, if he **sent** it*
8. Future-Less-Vivid	sī pres. subj., pres. subj.	should/would	*sī sit, mittat* *if he **should** be...he **would send***
9. Pres. Contrafactual	sī impf. subj., impf. subj.	were/would	*sī esset, mitteret* *if he **were**...he **would send***
10. Past Contrafactual	sī plpf. subj., plpf. subj.	had/would have	*sī fuisset, mīsisset* *if he **had** been...he **would have***

30.2. optimum factū esse dūxērunt rebelliōne factā frūmentō commeātūque   1
nostrōs prohibēre et rem in hiemem prodūcere, quod eīs superātīs aut redītū
interclūsīs nēminem posteā bellī īnferendī causā in Britanniam trānsitūrum
cōnfīdēbant. 3. Itaque rursus coniūrātiōne factā paulātim ex castrīs discēdere
et suōs clam ex agrīs dēdūcere coepērunt.   5

31.1 At Caesar, etsī nōndum eōrum cōnsilia cognōverat, tamen et ex
ēventū nāvium suārum et ex eō quod obsidēs dare intermīserant fore id quod
accidit suspicābātur. 2. Itaque ad omnēs casūs subsidia comparābat. Nam et
frūmentum ex agrīs cotīdiē in castra cōnferēbat et, quae gravissimē afflictae
erant nāvēs, eārum māteriā atque aere ad reliquās reficiendās ūtēbātur et quae   10
ad eās rēs erant ūsuī ex continentī comportārī iubēbat. 3. Itaque, cum summō
studiō ā mīlitibus administrārētur, XII nāvibus āmissīs, reliquīs ut nāvigārī
satis commodē posset effēcit.

32.1 Dum ea geruntur, legiōne ex cōnsuētūdine ūnā frūmentātum missā,
quae appellābātur VII., neque ūllā ad id tempus bellī suspiciōne interpositā,   15
cum pars hominum in agrīs remanēret, pars etiam in castra ventitāret, eī quī
prō portīs castrōrum in statiōne erant Caesarī nūntiāvērunt pulverem
maiōrem quam cōnsuētūdō ferret in eā parte vidērī quam in partem legiō iter
fēcisset.

adflictō (1): damage, agitate, knock about, 1
administrō (1): to manage, direct; help, 3
aes, aeris n.: bronze, copper, 2
āmittō, -ere, -mīsī, -missum: lose, let go, 2
clam: secretly, in secret, 1
coepī, coepisse, coeptum: to begin, 9
commeātus, -ūs m.: convoy, traffic, trip, 1
commodus, -a, -um: convenient, suitable, 2
comparō (1): prepare, get ready, provide, 4
comportō (1): carry together, collect, 3
cōnferō, -ferre, -tulī, -lātum: bring together, gather, 2
cōnfīdō, -ere, cōnfīsus sum: trust, believe, rely upon, 4
coniūrātiō, -ōnis f.: pact, union, conspiracy 3
conlocō (1): place, settle, arrange, 1
continēns, continentis f.: the continent, mainland, 3
cotīdiē: daily, every day, 1
dēdūcō, -ere: lead or draw down or away, 3
ēventus, -ūs m.: outcome, consequence, result, 2
factū: to do (supine), 2
frūmentor, -ārī: to forage, fetch corn, 1
hiems, hiemis f.: winter, storm, 4
interclūdō, -ere, -clūsī, clūsum: close off, 1
interpōnō, -ere, -posuī; include, introduce, 2
materia, -ae f.: timber, wood, material, 2

nāvigō (1): to sail, 2
nēmō, nūllīus, nēminī, -em, nūllō: no one, 3
nondum: not yet, 3
nuntiō (1): announce, report, 2
optimus, -a, -um: best, noblest, finest, 1
paucitās, -tātis f. (1): fewness, scarcity, 3
paulātim: gradually, little by little, 3
porta, -ae f.: gate, entrance, 1
posteā: thereafter, afterwards, 1
princeps, -cipis m./f.: chief, leader, 4
prōdūcō, -ere, -duxī, ductum: lead forth, 2
pulvis, pulveris m.: dust, dirt, 1
rebellio, -lliōnis f.: revolt, renewal of war, 1
reditus, -ūs m.: a return, a coming back, 1
reficiō, -ere, -fēcī, -fectum: restore, repair, 2
remaneō, ēre, mansī, mansum: remain, 1
rursus: again, backward, back, 4
satis: enough, sufficient, 2
statio, statiōnis f.: post, station, anchorage, 3
studium, -ī n.: zeal, enthusiasm, pursuit, 3
suspīcio, -ciōnis f.: mistrust, suspicion, 4
suspicor, -ārī, suspicātum: to suspect, 3
transportō (1): carry over, take across, 3
ventitō (1): to come often, resort to, 2

1 **optimum esse**: *that it was best*; ind. discourse, the subject is prohibēre and prodūcere
 factū: *in fact*; supine (verbal noun), abl. respect
 dūxērunt: *they considered*; "they calculated"
 rebelliōne factā: abl. absolute
 frumentō commeātūque: *from....*; abl. of separation governed prohibēre

2 **nostrōs** *our (men)*
 prodūcere *to prolong, to draw out*
 eīs...interclusīs: abl. absolute; eīs = hīs
 redītū: *from a return*; abl. separation

3 **nēminem**: *no one*; acc. subject from nēmō
 bellī inferendī causā: *for the sake of waging...*; causā behaves as a preposition with a preceding gen.; here a gerundive which we translate with the gerundive-gerund flip
 transitūrum (esse): fut. inf. transeō with acc. subject nēminem

5 **suōs**: *their (men)*; i.e. the Britons, obj. of dēdūcere

6 **et...et**: *both...and*

7 **ex eō quod**: *from the fact that*; "from this (fact) because," eō is a demonstrative
 dare intermīserant: *had ceased to give...*
 fore...accidit: *that it would be that which happened*; ind. discourse, fore is equivalent to futūrum esse, the fut. inf. of sum, governed by suspicābātur

8 **ad omnēs casūs**: *for...*; expressing purpose
 et...et: *both...and*;

9 **quae...nāvēs, eārum...aere**: *the timber and bronze of those (ships), which ships...*; the relative clause precedes the antecedent eārum, materia atque aere are abl. object of impf. ūtor

10 **ad...reficiendās:** *for...*; ad + gerundive again expressing purpose, readers should employ the gerundive-gerund flip, and translate the verb form as a gerund with an acc. object
 reliquās (nāvēs): *the rest (of the ships)*

11 **quae...usuī**: *the (things) which were of use...*; usuī is dative of purpose, cf. 29.4
 ad eās rēs: *for...*; ad + acc expressing purpose
 continentī: 3rd declension i-stem abl. sg.

12 **summō studiō**: abl. of manner with adjective does not require "cum;" this cum begins a causal cum-clause (since) with administrārētur
 administrārētur: *it was managed*; impf. subj.
 reliquīs ut...effēcit: *he brought it about that that the remaining ships were able to be sailed conveniently enough*; a noun result clause after effēcit, "brought it about"

14 **ex consuetūdine**: *according to custom*; abl. of source; the adj. ūnā modifies legiōne
 frumentātum: *to get grain*; supine, acc. usually expresses purpose

15 **VII**: *the 7th (legion)*; predicate nominative
 ūllā...suspiciōne interpositā: abl. absolute

16 **cum pars hominum...pars**: *while some of the men...(and) others...*; asyndeton
 ventitāret: *kept coming*; impf. subj. with cum, frequentative form of veniō
 eī quī...: *those who...*

17 **pulverem...vidērī**: *that...*; indirect discourse, pulverem is acc. subj.
 pulverem maiōrem quam: *more dust than...*; comparative

18 **consuetūdo ferret**: *custom bore out*; i.e. usual impf. subj., verbs in subordinate clauses in indirect discourse are subjunctive
 in eā parte: *in that direction*
 quam in partem: *into which direction*; in quam partem

19 **fēcisset**: plpf. subj., relative cl. of characeristic

Gerundives

A gerundive, a future passive participle (stem + nd + 1st & 2nd decl. endings) agrees with a noun in case, number, and gender. Though it can be translated many ways: "going/about/worthy to be freed" or "to be freed," we often employ a gerund-gerundive flip and translate it as a gerund:

Genitive	suī liberandī	*for freeing themselves*	
	bellī inferendī causā	*for the sake of waging war*	gen. + causā expresses purpose
Accusative	ad nāvēs reficiendās	*for repairing ships*	ad + gerundive expresses purpose
Ablative	in petendā pāce	*in seeking peace*	

Passive Periphrastic (gerundive + sum) expresses obligation or necessity and governs a dative of agent. Translate it with "must" or "has to" or "ought" in the present and "had to" in the past.

faciendum esset	*it had to be done*	in subjunctive
sibi iter faciendum esse	*that a journey must be made by him*	in ind. discourse

32.2 Caesar id, quod erat, suspicātus, aliquid nōvī ā barbarīs inītum cōnsiliī,   1
cohortēs quae in statiōne erant sēcum in eam partem proficīscī, ex reliquīs
duās in statiōnem succēdere, reliquās armārī et confestim sēsē subsequī iussit.

   3. Cum paulō longius ā castrīs processisset, suōs ab hostibus premī atque
aegrē sustinēre et, cōnfertā legiōne, ex omnibus partibus tēla coīcī   5
animadvertit. 4. Nam quod omnī ex reliquīs partibus demessō frūmentō pars
ūna erat reliqua, suspicātī hostēs hūc nostrōs esse ventūrōs noctū in silvīs
delituerant; 5. tum dispersōs dēpositīs armīs in metendō occupātōs subitō
adortī paucīs interfectīs reliquōs incertīs ordinibus perturbāverant, simul
equitātū atque ēssedīs circumdederant.   10

   33.1 Genus hoc est ex ēssedīs pugnae. Prīmō per omnēs partēs perequitant
et tēla coīciunt atque ipsō terrōre equōrum et strepitū rotārum ordinēs
plērumque perturbant et, cum sē inter equitum turmās insinuāverunt, ex
ēssedīs dēsiliunt et pedibus proeliantur. 2. Aurigae interim paulātim ex proeliō
excēdunt atque ita currūs conlocant ut, sī illī ā multitudine hostium   15
premantur, expedītum ad suōs receptum habeant. 3. Ita mobilitātem
equitum, stabilitātem peditum in proeliīs praestant, ac tantum ūsū
cotidiānō et exercitātiōne efficiunt utī in declivī ac praecipitī lōcō incitātōs
equōs sustinēre et brevī moderārī ac flectere et per temonem percurrere et in
iugō insistere et sē inde in currūs citissimē recipere consuerint.   20

adorior, -īrī, -ortus sum: rise up, attack, 2
aeger, -gra, -grum: sick, weary, 4
armō (1): to arm, 1
auriga, ae m.: charioteer, driver, 1
brevis, -e: short, 3
circumdō, -are, -dedī, -datus: surround, 1
citus, -a, -um: swift, quick, 1
confertus, a, um: crowded together, dense, 3
cōnfēstim: immediately, 4
conlocō (1): place, settle, arrange, 1
cotidiānus, -a, -um: daily, of every day, 3
currus, -ūs m.: chariot, cart, 2
dēclīvis, -e: sloping, inclined downwards, 1
dēlitescō, -ere, -tuī: conceal oneself, lie hid 1
dēmetō, -ere, messuī, messum: reap, mow 1
dēpōnō, -ere, -posuī, -positum: put down, 1
dēsiliō, -īre, -luī: to jump down, dismount, 4
dispergō, -ere, -spersī, spersum: scatter, 1
equus, -ī m.: horse, 4
ēssedum, -ī n.: war-chariot (Gallic word), 3
excēdō, -ere, cessī, -cessum: go out, 3
exercitātio, -iōnis f.: training, practice, 2
expedītus, -a, -um: unimpeded, fast, 4
flectō, -ere, flexī, flectum: turn, bend, 1
hūc: to this place, hither, here 2

incertus, -a, -um: unreliable, doubtful, 2
inde: from there, then, afterward, 3
ineō, -īre, iī, -itum: go into, enter, 1
insinuō (1): to insinuate, wind a way in, 1
insistō, -ere, -stitī: set on, set about; stop, 2
iugum, -ī n.: yoke, (mountain) range, 2
metō, -ere, messuī, messum: reap, harvest, 1
mobilitās, -tātis f.: mobility, 1
moderor, -ārī, -ātum: restrain, regulate, 1
noctū: by night; abl. as adv. nox, noctis, 4
noscō, -ere, nōvī, nōtum: to learn, 1
occupō (1): seize, occupy, 4
paucī, -ae, -a: little, few, scanty, 4
paulātim: little by little, gradually, 3
pedes, peditis m.: foot soldier, infantry; adj. on foot, 1
percurrō, -ere, -cucurrī: run through, 1
perequitō (1): to ride (a horse) through, 1
praeceps, praecipitis adj.: headlong; steep, 1
prōcēdō, -ere, -cessī, -cessum; proceed, 3
proelior, -ārī: to give battle, fight, 1
rota, -ae f.: wheel, 1
silva, -ae f.: wood, forest, woodland, 4
simul: at the same time (as); together, 4
stabilitas, -tātis f.: stability, firmness, 1
statio, statiōnis f.: post, station, anchorage, 3

strepitus, -ūs m.: creaking, rustling, rushing, 1
succēdō, -ere, -cessī, -cessus: go up, approach, 2
suspicor, -ārī, suspicātum: to suspect, 3

tēmō, -ōnis m.: pole, beam (of a wagon), 1
terror, terroris m.: terror, fear, 1
turma, -ae f.: troop of cavalry (30 men), 1

---

1 **id, quod erat**: *that which was (the case)*
aliquid nōvī...cōnsiliī: *(namely that) some new plan*; partitive gen., aliquid is acc. subj. of inītum (esse),
inītum (esse): *had been initiated*; pf. pass. ineō

2 **cohortēs...duās...reliquās...iussit**: *ordered the cohorts to...two (cohorts) to... the remaining (cohorts) to...*; acc. object of iussit
in eam partem: *into that direction*
ex reliquīs: *from the remaining (cohorts)*

3 **armārī**: *to arm themselves*; "to be armed"
subsequī: present deponent inf.

4 **paulō longius**: *a little farther*; abl. of degree of difference with comparative adverb
processisset: plpf. subjunctive
suōs: *that his (soldiers)*; acc. subj. of pass. inf. premī, sustinēre and pass. inf. coīcī in an ind. discourse governed by animadvertit

5 **partibus**: *directions*
coīcī: pass. inf. coīciō, -ere

6 **omnī...demessō frūmentō**: abl. abs., omnī is i-stem 3ʳᵈ decl. adj. modifying frūmentō

7 **ūna, reliqua**: pars is feminine in gender
suspicātī hostēs: *the enemy having suspected that..*; hostēs is nom. subj. of deliituerant
nostrōs: *that our (men)*; acc. subj.
esse ventūrōs: ventūrōs esse; fut. inf. veniō

8 **dispersōs...occupātōs**: *(our soldiers) dispersed...and occupied*; acc. d.o. of adortī
adortī: *(the enemy) having attacked...*
depōsitīs armīs: abl. absolute; the men put down their weapons to gather food

metendō: *harvesting*; gerund of meteō

9 **paucīs interfectīs**: abl. absolute
incertīs ōrdinibus: *in unfixed ranks*

11 **pugnae**: *of fighting*; modifies genus
prīmō: *at first*; abl. time when
partēs: *directions*

13 **cum...insinuāverunt**: *when...*; + indicative, cum is adverbial not a prep.; sē is acc. d.o.

14 **pedibus**: *on foot*; "by feet," abl. of manner
Aurigae: *drivers*; the drivers carried soldiers to battle, waited at a safe distance, and then returned to pick up soldiers when summoned

15 **ita...ut**: *in such a way...that*; introducing a result clause, pres. subj. in primary sequence

16 **expedītum...receptum**: *an easy recovery for their (people)*; "an unencumbered recovery"

17 **tantum**: *only*; adverb

18 **efficiunt utī...consuerint**: *they bring it about that they have become accustomed...*; noun result clause, utī is another form for ut (ūtī is inf. of ūtor) and consuerint is perfect subj.

19 **sustinere**: *to restrain*; "hold up"
brevī (tempore): *in a short (time)*; time when
per temōnem...in iugō: The Britons ran out from the chariot onto the wooden pole (*tēmō*) attached between the two horses to the chariot. Then they stood on the harness (*iugum*) binding the horses together

22 **sē...recipere**: *retreat*; a common idiom, "take themselves back"
citissimē: superlative adverb

Indirect Discourse: Accusative Subject + Infinitive

In secondary sequence, translate a present infinitive as imperfect, perfect as pluperfect, and "will" as "would."

Present	Caesarem mīlitēs **mittere**	mīlitēs ā Caesar **mittī**
	*(says) that Caesar **is sending** soldiers*	*(says) that the soldiers **are sent** by Caesar*
	*(said) that Caesar **was sending** soldiers*	*(says) that the soldiers **were sent** by Caesar*
Perfect	Caesarem mīlitēs **mīsisse**	mīlitēs ā Caesar **missōs esse**
	*(says) that Caesar **has sent*** soldiers*	*(says) that the soldiers **has been sent*** by C.*
	*(said) that Caesar **had sent** soldiers*	*(said) that the soldiers **had been sent** by C.*
Future	Caesarem mīlitēs **missūrum esse**	
	*(says) that Caesar **will send** soldiers*	
	*(said) that Caesar **would send** soldiers*	*alternatives: sent, were sent*

34.1 Quibus rēbus perturbātīs nostrīs novitate pugnae tempore 1
opportunissimō Caesar auxilium tulit: namque eius adventū hostēs
constitērunt, nostrī sē ex timore recepērunt. 2. Quō factō, ad lacessendum
hostem et committendum proelium aliēnum esse tempus arbitrātus suō sē
locō continuit et brevī tempore intermissō in castra legiōnēs redūxit. 3. Dum   5
haec geruntur, nostrīs omnibus occupātīs quī erant in agrīs reliquī
discessērunt. 4. Secutae sunt continuōs complūrēs diēs tempestātēs, quae et
nostrōs in castrīs continērent et hostem ā pugnā prohibērent.

    5. Interim barbarī nuntiōs in omnēs partēs dimīsērunt paucitātemque
nostrōrum mīlitum suīs praedicāvērunt et quanta praedae faciendae atque in   10
perpetuum suī liberandī facultās darētur, sī Rōmānōs castrīs expulissent,
demonstrāvērunt. Hīs rēbus celeriter magnā multitudine peditātūs
equitātūsque coactā ad castra vēnērunt.

    35.1 Caesar, etsī idem quod superiōribus diēbus acciderat fore vidēbat, ut, sī
essent hostēs pulsī, celeritāte perīculum effugerent, tamen nactus equitēs   15
circiter XXX, quōs Commius Atrēbās, dē quō ante dictum est, sēcum
transportāverat, legiōnēs in aciē prō castrīs constituit. 2. Commissō proeliō
diutius nostrōrum mīlitum impetum hostēs ferre non potuērunt ac terga
vertērunt. 3. Quōs tantō spatiō secutī quantum cursū et vīribus efficere
potuērunt, complūrēs ex eīs occidērunt, deinde omnibus longē lātēque   20
aedificiīs incensīs sē in castra recēpērunt.

    36.1 Eōdem diē lēgātī ab hostibus missī ad Caesarem dē pace vēnērunt.

ācer, ācris, ācre: sharp, fierce, eager, bitter 2	**namque**: to be sure, for, 1
aciēs, -ēī f.: sharp edge, battle line, army, 2	**nanciscor, nanciscī, nactus**: obtain, meet, 1
aedificium, -iī n.: building, edifice, 2	**novitās, -tātis f.**: newness, strangeness, 1
aliēnus, -a, -um: of another, foreign, 2	**occīdō, -ere, occidī, occīsus**: kill, cut down 4
ante: before, in front of (acc); *adv.* before, 4	**occupō (1)**: seize, occupy, 4
Atrebas, Atrebātis, m.: Atrebates, 3	**opportūnus, -a, -um**: fit, suitable, useful, 2
auxilium, -ī n.: help, aid, assistance, 3	**paucitās, -tātis f. (1)**: fewness, scarcity, 3
brevis, -e: short, 3	**peditātus, -ūs m.**: infantry, 3
committō, -ere: commence, commit, entrust 4	**pellō, -ere, pepulī, pulsus**: drive, push, 2
Commius, -ī m.: Commius, 2	**perpetuus, -a, -um**: constant, everlasting, 4
continuus, -a, -um: continuous, unceasing, 1	**praeda, -ae f.**: loot, spoils, cattle, 2
cursus, -ūs m.: course, running, haste, 3	**praedicō (1)**: proclaim, publish, declare, 2
deinde: then, next, from that place, 1	**redūcō, -ere, -dūxī, -ductus**: to bring back, 3
dīmittō, -ere, -mīsī, -missus: send (away), 3	**sequor, -ī, secūtus**: follow, pursue, 4
diū: a long time, long, 1	**spatium, -iī n.**: space, room, extent, 4
effugiō, -ere, -fūgī: flee out, escape, 1	**tempestās, tempestātis f.**: storm, 3
expellō, ere, pulī, pulsum: drive out, expel 2	**tergum, -ī n.**: back, hide, rear, 1
incendō, -ere, -ī, -ēnsus: kindle, burn, 2	**timor, -oris m.**: fear, dread, anxiety, 2
lacessō, -ere, -īvī: provoke, goad, irritate, 1	**transportō (1)**: carry over, take across, 3
latē: widely, far and wide, 2	**vertō, -ere, -sī, -rsus**: turn, change, 1
līberō (1): free, liberate, 3	**vīs, vīs, f.**, pl. **virēs**: force, power, violence, 4

1 **quibus rēbus**: *because of these things*; "which things," abl. of cause
perturbātīs nostrīs: *our (men) having been set into confusion*; abl. abs.
novitāte pugnae: abl. of means with perturbātīs
tempore opportunissimō: abl of time when

2 **tulit**: perfect, ferō
hostēs: nom. subject

3 **constitērunt**: *stopped*; "stood still"
sē...recēpērunt: *retreated*; idiom
quō factō: *this having been done*; " which having been done," abl. abs.
ad...aliēnum esse tempus: *that it was an unfavorable time...*; ind. discourse governed by perfect deponent pple arbitratus
ad lacessendum...commitendum: *for provoking...*; ad + gerundives: in a gerund-gerundive flip: the gerundives should be translated as gerunds (-ing) with acc. objs.

4 **suō sē locō continuit**: *he held his ground*; "held himself in his position"

6 **quī erant...reliquī**: *(those) who...*; the antecedent is subject of discessērunt

7 **secūtae sunt**: pf. deponent, subject tempestātēs
continuōs...diēs: *for...*; acc. of duration
quae...continenērent...prohibērent: *which (sort) contained..*; or "which would contain..." relative clause of characteristic with impf. subj.

10 **suīs**: *to their people*; dat. indirect object
quanta...facultās...darētur: *how great an opportunity would...*; indirect question governed by demonstrāvērunt
praedae faciendae: *of freeing...*; gerund-gerundive flip; translate the gerundive as a gerund; modifying facultās
in perpetuum: *forever*; "into perpetuity"

11 **suī liberandī**: *of freeing themselves*; gerund-gerundive flip; modifying facultās
castrīs: *from...*; abl. separation
expulissent: plpf. subj.

12 **hīs rēbus**: *because of these matters*; abl. cause
multitudine...coactā: ablative absolute

14 **idem fore**: *the same thing....would happen...*; "same thing...would be," ind. disc. governed by vidēbat, fore is equivalent to futūrum esse, fut. infinitive of sum, esse;
superiōribus diēbus: *in the days before yesterday*; abl. time when
ut...effugerent: *(namely) that...*; noun result clause in apposition to idem

15 **essent pulsī**: plpf. passive subjunctive, pellō
celeritāte: *with speed*; abl. of manner
nactus: pf. deponent pple, nanciscor
dē quō: *concerning whom*

16 **dictum est**: *it was mentioned (by me)*

17 **commissō proeliō**: *the battle having been begun*; common idiom, proelium committō

18 **diūtius**: *longer*; comparative adv. diū
nostrōrum mīlitum: subject gen. + impetum
hostēs: nom. subject of potuērunt, pf. possum
ferre: *to endure*

19 **quōs...secūtī**: *having pursued these (Britons)*; "having pursued whom"
tantō spatiō...quantum: *by as great an interval as*; abl of degree of difference

19 **cursū et vīribus**: *with speed and (troop) force*; vīribus denotes troop size; abl. manner

20 **potuērunt...occidērunt**: the Roman cavalry is the subject, complūrēs is the direct object
omnibus...incensīs: abl. absolute
longē lātēque: *far and wide*

21 **sē recēpērunt**: *retreated*, "took themselves back"

22 **Eōdem diē**: abl. time when

Gerunds

A gerund (present stem + nd + 2nd decl. neut. sg. endings) is a verbal noun. It can govern an acc. obj. and is easy to distinquish from a gerundive because a gerund has only -ī/-ō/-um endings and does not modify a nearby noun.

Gen.	navigandī	*of sailing*
Dat.	navigandō	*for sailing*
Acc.	navigandum	*sailing*
Abl.	navigandō	*by sailing*

Nominative	Navigāre est difficile.	*To sail is difficult.*	an infinitive not gerund as subject
Genitive	facultās navigandī	*opportunity for sailing*	
	navigandī causā	*for the sake of sailing*	gen. + causā/grātiā expresses purpose
Dative	ūtilis navigandō	*useful for sailing*	dative of purpose
Accusative	ad navigandum	*for sailing (to sail)*	ad + gerund expresses purpose
Ablative	navigandō	*by sailing*	ablative with or without a preposition
	in navigandō	*in sailing*	
	ulcīscendī Rōmānōs	*of avenging the Romans*	occasionally with an acc. object

13.1 In omnī Galliā eōrum hominum, quī aliquō sunt numerō atque honōre,   1
genera sunt duo. Nam plebēs paene servōrum habētur locō, quae nihil audet
per sē, nūllō adhibētur cōnsiliō. 2. Plērīque, cum aut aere aliēnō aut
magnitūdine tribūtōrum aut iniūriā potentiōrum premuntur, sēsē in
servitūtem dicant nōbilibus: in hōs eadem omnia sunt iūra, quae dominīs in   5
servōs. 3. Sed dē hīs duōbus generibus alterum est Druidum, alterum equitum.
4. Illī rēbus dīvīnīs intersunt, sacrificia publica ac prīvāta prōcūrant, religiōnēs
interpretantur: ad hōs magnus adulēscentium numerus disciplīnae causā
concurrit, magnōque hī sunt apud eōs honōre. 5. Nam ferē dē omnibus
controversiīs publicīs prīvātīsque constituunt et, sī quod est admissum   10
facinus, sī caedēs facta, sī dē hērēditāte, dē fīnibus contrōversia est, īdem
decernunt, praemia poenāsque constituunt; 6. sī quī aut prīvātus aut populus
eōrum dēcrētō nōn stetit, sacrificiīs interdicunt. Haec poena apud eōs est
gravissima. 7. Quibus ita est interdictum, hī numerō impiōrum ac
scelerātōrum habentur, hīs omnēs dēcēdunt, aditum sermonemque   15
dēfugiunt, nē quid ex contāgiōne incommodī accipiant, neque hīs petentibus
ius redditur neque honōs ūllus commūnicātur. 8. Hīs autem omnibus
Druidibus praeest ūnus, quī summam inter eōs habet auctoritātem.

---

aditus, -ūs m.: approach, access, entrance, 2
adhibeō, -ēre, -uī, -itum: hold toward, admit, apply, 1
admittō, -ere, mīsī, missum: admit, commit, allow, 2
adulescens, -ntis m./f.: youth, 1
aes, aeris n.: bronze, copper, 2
alienus, -a, -um: of another, foreign, 2
auctōritās, -tātis f.: influence, clout, 3
audeō, -ēre, ausus sum: dare, venture, 4
caedēs, caedis f.: murder, slaughter, killing 2
communicō (1): share, impart, 4
concurrō, -ere, -currī, -cursus: run eagerly, clash, 2
contāgio, -giōnis f.: contact; contagion, 1
dēcēdō, -ere, cessī, cessum: depart, withdraw, die, 4
dēcernō, ere, crēvī, crētum: decide, judge, 3
dēfugiō, -ere, -fūgī: to flee away, avoid, 1
dicō, -āre, -āvī, -ātum: dedicate, devote, 1
dīvinus, -a, -um: divine, 1
dominus, -ī m.: master, 1
facinus, facinoris n.: deed; bad deed, crime 2
hērēditas, -tātis f.: inheritance, 1
honor(s), -ōris m.: honor, glory; offering, 2
impius, -a, -um: unholy, impious, 1
incommodus, -a, -um: unfortunate, disastrous, 3
iniūria, -ae f.: wrong, insult, injustice, 4

interdīcō, -ere, -dīxī, -dictum: to forbid, prohibit, outlaw, 2
interpretor, -ārī, : to translate, interpret, 1
intersum, -esse, -fuī: take part in, engage in, 1
iūs, iūris n.: justice, law, right, 2
nōbilis, -e: noble, renowned, 3
paene: almost, nearly, 2
plebs, plēbis, f.: common people, masses, 2
plērusque, -raque, -rumque: very many, 2
poena, poenae, f.: punishment, penalty, 3
potēns, -entis: powerful, ruling (*gen.*), 2
praesum, -esse, -fuī: be over, preside over, 2
prōcūrō (1): take care of, look after, 1
reddō, -ere, -didī, -ditus: give back, return, 2
religiō, religiōnis f.: susperstitious rites, ritual, divine manifestation, 3
sacrificium, ī n.: sacrifice, 4
scelerātus, -a, -um: wicked, profane, guilty 1
sermo, -mōnis m.: conversation, discourse, 3
servitūs, servitūtis, f.: servitude, 2
servus, -ī, m.: slave, 1
stō, -āre, stetī, stātum: stand still, stop, 3
tribūtum, -ī n.: tribute, tax, contribution, 2

1 **eōrum hominum quī**: *of all these peoples who*; partitive genitive
   aliquō numerō…honōre: *are of some account and honor*; abl. of description, here predicate of sunt
2 **plēbēs**: *the masses*; though plural, it governs a 3rd sg. verb
   habētur: *are considered (to be)*; "are held"
   locō: *in the position…*; i.e. status in life
3 **per sē**: *by themselves*; lit. 'through themselves"
   adhibētur: *are admitted*; + dat. of compound
   cōnsiliō: *council*; "assembly," dat. compound
4 **cum…premuntur**: *when they are overwhelmed*; cum is an adverbial conjunction
   aere aliēnō: *by debt*; lit. "another's money"
   portentiōrum: *of those more powerful*; gen. pl.
   sēsē: *themselves*; emphatic form of sē
   dicant: *they dedicate*; 1st conj. pres., not dīcō
5 **sunt**: *(they) have*; "are (to them)," supply dat. of possession eīs, parallel to dominīs
   in hōs: *over them*; "towards them," i.e. plebēs
   quae dominīs: *which masters (have)*; "which (there are) to masters," dat. of possession with missing linking verb sunt
   in servōs: *over slaves*; "towards slaves"
6 **alterum (genus)…alterum (genus)**: *one…the other*; neuter in agreement with missing genus
7 **illī**: i.e. Druids, nom. pl.
   rēbus dīvīnīs: dat. obj. of compound intersunt
   intersunt…(et) prōcūrant…(et) interpretantur: asyndeton, add conjunctions
9 **disciplīnae causā**: *for the sake of training*
   magnō…honōre: *of great honor*; abl. of description in the predicative position after sunt
   apud eōs: *among them*; i.e. among the Gauls
10 **sī quod…facinus**: *if any crime…*; aliquis, aliquod is a common indefinite adjective

(any, some), but quī, quod is commonly used as an indefinite (which → any, some) after sī, nisi, num, and nē. The mnemonic for this construction is the jingle "After sī, nisi, num, and nē, all the ali's go away" (in other words indefinite aliquod becomes just quod)
11 **facta (est)**: *has been committed*; pf. pass.
   dē hērēditāte (aut) dē fīnibus: asyndeton, supply "aut"
12 **īdem**: *likewise*
   sī quī: *if anyone…*; quī indefinite before sī, see line 10 above
13 **dēcrētō nōn stetit**: *did not abide by the decision*; "did not stand by the (thing) having been decided; abl. place where; pf. stō, stāre
   sacrificiīs: *from the sacrifices*; abl. separation
14 **apud eōs**: *among them*; i.e. among the Gauls
   quibus…est interdictum, hī: *these for whom it has been prohibited*; "for whom it has been prohibited, these…" hī is the antecedent of the relative clause beginnning with quibus
   numerō: *in the number, group*; place where
15 **habentur**: *are considered (to be)*; "are held (to be)," see line 2 above
   hīs: *from these*; i.e. from those placed in the group of the wicked; abl. of separation
   dēcēdunt (et)…dēfugiunt: asyndeton, supply a conjunction
   aditum: *an encounter*
16 **nē quid incommodī**: *lest anything unsuitable*; quid is indefinite following sī, nisī, num, or nē; incommodī is a partitive gen.
   neque…neque: *neither…nor*
   hīs petentibus: *to these seeking*; pres. pple petō is condition in force; dat. indirect object
17 **praeest**: *is over (+ dat)*; compound verbs often govern a dative object

---

Common Uses of the Dative

construction	example	translation
Dative of Indirect Object	**eī** fīliam dat	*gives his daughter **to him***
Dative of Compound Verbs	**Druidibus** praeest	*is over **the Druids***
Dative of Agent + Pass. Periphrastic	**sibi** iter faciendum esse	*a journey must be made **by him***
Dative of Purpose	**hibernīs** mūnītum	*fortified **for winter-quarters***
Dative of Possession + sum	quae **dominīs** sunt	*which are **to masters** (= masters have)*
Dative of Interest (Advantage)	**nostrīs** gravissimus	*most grievous **for our men***
Dative of Reference*	**mihi** vidētur	*it seems **to me** (i.e. from my viewpoint)*
Dative of Special Adjectives	**fūgae** similem	*similar **to flight***
Double Dative (purpose + <u>interest</u>)	**magnō ūsuī** <u>nostrīs</u> fuit	*was **for a great use to our men** → served a great use to our men*

*for some, interest and reference are the same construction

13.9 Hōc mortuō aut sī quī ex reliquīs excellit dignitāte succēdit, aut, sī sunt   1
plūrēs parēs, suffrāgiō Druidum, nōnnumquam etiam armīs dē principātū
contendunt. 10. Hī certō annī tempore in fīnibus Carnūtum, quae regiō
tōtīus Galliae media habētur, consīdunt in locō cōnsecrātō. Hūc omnēs
undique, quī contrōversiās habent, conveniunt eōrumque decrētīs iudiciīsque   5
parent. 11. Disciplīna in Britanniā reperta atque inde in Galliam trānslāta esse
exīstimātur, 12. et nunc, quī dīligentius eam rem cognōscere volunt,
plērumque illō discendī causā proficīscuntur.

14.1 Druidēs ā bellō abesse cōnsuērunt neque tribūta ūnā cum reliquīs
pendunt; mīlitiae vacātiōnem omniumque rērum habent immunitātem. 2.   10
Tantīs excitātī praemiīs et suā sponte multī in disciplīnam conveniunt et ā
parentibus propinquīsque mittuntur. 3. Magnum ibi numerum versuum
ēdiscere dicuntur. Itaque annōs nōnnullī vīcēnōs in disciplīnā permanent. 4.
Neque fās esse exīstimant ea litterīs mandāre, cum in reliquīs ferē rēbus,
publicīs privātīsque ratiōnibus, Graecīs litterīs ūtantur. Id mihi duābus dē   15
causīs īnstituisse videntur, quod neque in vulgum disciplīnam efferrī velint
neque eōs, quī discunt, litterīs cōnfīsōs minus memoriae studēre: quod ferē
plērīsque accidit, ut praesidiō litterārum dīligentiam in perdiscendō ac
memoriam remittant. 5. In prīmīs hoc volunt persuādēre, nōn interīre
animās, sed ab aliīs post mortem transīre ad aliōs, atque hōc maximē ad   20
virtūtem excitārī putant metū mortis neglēctō. Multa praetereā dē sīderibus
atque eōrum mōtū, dē mundī ac terrārum magnitūdine, dē rērum nātūrā, dē
deōrum immortālium vī ac potestāte disputant et iuventūtī trādunt.

---

anima, -ae f.: breath, spirit, soul, 1
Carnūtēs, -um: Carnutes, 4
confīdō, -ere, confīsus sum: trust, believe, rely upon, 4
consecrō (1): dedicate to a god, make holy 2
consīdeō, -ēre, -sēdī: to sit down, settle, 2
contendō, -ere, -ī, -ntus: strive; hasten, 4
dēcernō, ere, crēvī, crētum: decide, judge, 3
deus, -ī m.: god, divinity, deity, 4
dignitās, -tātis f.: worth, merit, worthiness, 1
dīligēns, -entis: careful, diligent, accurate, 2
diligentia, -ae f.: diligence, attentiveness, 1
discō, -ere, -didicī: learn, get to know, 2
disputō (1): reckon, debate, argue, 1
ēdiscō, -ere, -didicī: to learn thoroughly, 1
efferō, -ferre, -tulī, ēlātus: raise, lift up 4
ego: I, 2
excellō, -ere, : be distinguished, excel, 1
excitō (1): excite, rouse up, raise, inspire, 3
fās n.: right, divine law, duty, 1
Graecus, -a, -um: Greek, 2
hūc: to this place, hither, here 2

immortālis, -e: immortal, 3
immūnitās, -tātis f.: exception, immunity, 1
inde: from there, then, afterward, 3
instituō, -ere, -uī, -ūtum: set, establish, 3
intereō, -īre, -īvī, -ītum: to die, perish, 3
iudicium, -ī n.: decision, judgment; trial 3
iuventūs, -tūtis f.: youth, 1
mandō (1): order, command, commit, 2
medius -a –um: in the middle of, 3
memoria, -ae. f.: memory, 4
metus, -ūs f.: dread, fear, 2
mīlitia, -ae f.: military service; military, 2
morior, morī, mortuus sum: die, 2
mōtus, -ūs m.: motion, 3
mundus, -ī m.: the world, 1
nātūra, -ae. f.: nature, 3
neglegō, ere, -lēxī, neglēctum: to neglect, 3
nōnnullus, -a, -um: some, not none, 2
nōnnumquam: sometimes, not never, 1
nunc: now, at present, 2
pār, paris: equal, similar, even, 2

parens, -rentis m.: parent, ancestor, 1
pāreō, -ēre, -uī, pāritum: obey, yield (dat) 1
pendō, -ere, pependī, pensum: pay, weigh 2
perdiscō, -ere, -didicī: learn thoroughly, 1
permaneō, -ere, -mansī: to remain, stay, 1
plērusque, -raque, -rumque: very many, 2
plūs (plūris): more, 4
potestās, -tātis f.: power, ability, capacity, 3
praesidium, -iī n.: guard, protection; assistance, 2
praetereā: besides, hereafter, 2
principātus, -ūs m.: leadership, rule, 2
propinquus, -a, -um: near, close; *subst.* kinsman, 2
putō (1): to think, imagine, 3
regiō, regiōnis f.: region, area, 1
remittō, -ere, -mīsī: send back, let go, relax, 4

reperiō, -īre, repperī, repertum: to discover, find, 1
sīdus, sīderis n.: star; group of stars, constellation, 1
sponte: willingly, voluntarily, 2
studeō, -ēre, uī: be eager, strive after, 1
succēdō, -ere, -cessī, -cessus: go up, approach, 2
suffrāgium, -iī n.: a vote, 1
terra, -ae. f.: earth, ground, land, 2
trādō, -dere, -didī, -ditum: to give over, hand down, 3
transferō, ferre, tulī, lātum: carry across, 1
tribūtum, -ī n.: tribute, tax, contribution, 2
vacātiō, -tiōnis f.: exemption, immunity 1
vertō, -ere, -sī, -rsus: turn, change, 1
vīcenī, -a, -um: twenty each, 1
vīs, vīs, f., pl. **virēs**: force, power, violence, 4
vulgus, -ī n.: mass, mob, multitude, 2

---

1 **Hōc mortuō**: *this (one) having died*; i.e. "if this one has died," abl. abs. is conditional in force, mortuus is pf. dep. pple morior, "having died,' or can be translated as a simple adj., 'dead'
sī quī ex reliquīs: *if (anyone) who out of the rest…*; missing antecedent is subj. of succēdit
dignitāte: *in dignity*; abl. of respect, governed by excellit not by succēdit

2 **plūrēs**: *more*; nom. subj., parēs is nom. pred.
nōnnumquam etiam: *(and) sometimes even*; suffrāgiō and armīs are parallel, abl. of means

3 **certō…tempore**: abl. of time when
fīnibus: *territory*

4 **media**: *center*; nom. predicate, the gen. tōtīus Galliae modifies media
habētur: *is considered*; "is held," quae regiō is subject, quae is a relative adjective

6 **reperta (esse)**: *to have been invented*; pf. pass. inf. governed by exīstimātur
trānslāta esse: pf. pass. inf. trānsferō
dīligentius: comparative adverb
plērumque: *frequently*
illō: *to that place*; adverb
discendī causā: *for the sake of learning*; causā governs a preceding gen.; gerund gen. sg.

9 **cōnsu(ēv)ērunt**: *are accustomed*; present sense
ūnā: *together*; adverb

10 **pendunt**: *pay*; "weigh out"

11 **suā sponte**: *by their own will*

12 **versuum**: *of verses*; gen. pl.

13 **annōs…vīcēnōs**: *for twenty years*; duration
nōnnūllī: *several*; "not none"

14 **fās esse**: *that it is right*; impersonal verb in ind. discourse, mandāre is subject of esse
ea: *these (things)*; neut. pl., i.e. these teachings
litterīs: *to letters (of the alphabet)*; i.e. writing
cum…ūtantur: *although…*; this cum + pres.

subjunctive is concessive

15 **id…īnstituisse**: *to have established this*; i.e. not entrusting training to letters; pf. inf.
duābus dē causīs…quod: *for two reasons…(namely) because)*; as often, the adjective precedes the preposition; dat. and abl. pl. of duō is duābus/duōbus not duīs
mihi videntur: *they seem to me*; "seem" is a common translation for the passive of video

16 **in vulgum**: *to the masses*
efferrī: pass. inf., disciplīnam is acc. subj.
velint: *they wish*; pres. subj. of vōlō; quod + subjunctive denotes an alleged, not real, cause

17 **cōnfīsōs**: *having trusted in* + dat; pf. dep. pple
minus…studēre: *pay less attention to memory* "have less enthusiasm for memory" eōs is acc. subj., minus is a comparative adverb

18 **plērīsque**: *to very many*; dat. of interest; -que does not decline, but plērus- does
quod…accidit ut: *because it happens…that*; accidit governs a noun result clause
praesidiō litterārum: *with the assistance of (written) letters*; "with the protection of…"
in perdiscendō: gerund abl. sg.

19 **remittant**: *they weaken*; "they let go"
in prīmīs: *in particular*; "among the first"
hoc…nōn interīre animās: *this…(namely) that…*; neuter sg. acc. object of persuādēre, animās is acc. subject in indirect discourse
ab aliīs…ad aliōs: *from some…into others*

20 **transīre**: animās is still acc. subject
hōc: *because of this*; i.e. the reincarnation of souls, abl. of cause

21 **excitārī**: *that (people) are roused*; add hominēs as acc. subject
metū…neglectō: abl. abs.
Multa: *many (things);* neut. pl. acc. d.o.

15.1 Alterum genus est equitum. Hī, cum est ūsus atque aliquod bellum   1
incidit (quod ferē ante Caesaris adventum quotannīs accidere solēbat, utī aut
ipsī iniūriās inferrent aut illātās prōpulsārent), omnēs in bellō versantur, 2.
atque eōrum ut quisque est genere copiīsque amplissimus, ita plūrimōs circum
sē ambactōs clientēsque habet. Hanc ūnam grātiam potentiamque nōvērunt.   5

16.1 Nātiō est omnis Gallōrum admodum dēdita religiōnibus, 2. atque ob
eam causam, quī sunt adfectī graviōribus morbīs quīque in proeliīs
periculīsque versantur, aut prō victimīs hominēs immolant aut sē
immolātūrōs vovent administrīsque ad ea sacrificia Druidibus ūtuntur, quod,
prō vītā hominis nisi hominis vīta reddātur, 3. nōn posse deōrum   10
immortālium nūmen placārī arbitrantur, pūblicēque eiusdem generis habent
īnstitūta sacrificia. Aliī immānī magnitūdine simulācra habent, 4. quōrum
contexta vīminibus membra vīvīs hominibus complent; quibus succensīs,
circumventī flammā exanimantur hominēs. 5. Supplicia eōrum quī in furtō
aut in latrōciniō aut aliquā noxiā sint comprehēnsī grātiōra dīs immortālibus   15
esse arbitrantur; sed, cum eius generis cōpia dēfēcit, etiam ad innocentium
supplicia dēscendunt.

17.1 Deum maximē Mercurium colunt. Huius sunt plūrima simulācra:
hunc omnium inventōrem artium ferunt, hunc viārum atque itinerum
ducem, hunc ad quaestūs pecūniae mercatūrāsque habēre vim maximam   20
arbitrantur. Post hunc Apollinem et Mārtem et Iovem et Minervam.

adficiō, -ere, -fēcī, -fectum: afflict, affect, 3
administer, -strī m.: performer, 1
admodum: completely, quite; just about, 2
ambactus, -ī m.: vassal, 1
amplus, -a, -um: ample, full, spacious, 2
ante: before, in front of (acc); *adv.* before, 4
Apollo, Apollinis m.: Apollo, 2
ars, artis f.: art, 1
circum: around, round about, 2
cliens, -entis m.: client, dependent, 4
colō, -ere, coluī, cultum: till, farm; worship, 1
comprehendō, -ere, -dī: seize, arrest; grasp 4
contegō, -ere, -texī, -tectum: to cover over, 1
dēscendō, -ere, ī, ēnsus: descend; sink to; stoop to, 1
dēditus, -a, -um: given to, devoted to, 1
dēficiō, -ere, -fēcī, -fectum: fail, give out, 3
deus, -ī m.: god, divinity, deity, 4
dux, ducis m../f.: leader, guide, chief, 4
exanimō (1): deprive of breath; kill, stun, 2
flamma, ae f.: flame, 3
furtum, -ī n.: theft, robbery, deceit, 1
grātia, -ae f.: gratitude; favor, thanks, 2
grātus, -a, -um: pleasing; grateful, 1

immānis, -e: immense, enormous, 1
immolō (1): to sacrifice, immolate, 3
immortālis, -e: immortal, 3
incidō, -ere, -cidī, -cisum: happen, fall in with, 1
iniūria, -ae f.: wrong, insult, injustice, 4
innocens, innocentis: harmless, blameless, 1
instituō, -ere, -uī, -ūtum: set, establish, 2
inventor, -ōris m.: inventor, 1
Iuppiter, Iovis m.: Jupiter, 2
latrōcinium, -ī n.: banditry, robbery, 1
Mars, Martis m.: Mars, god of victory, 2
membrum, -ī n.: limb, member, 1
mercātūra, -ae f.: trade, traffic, 1
Mercurius, -ī m.: Mercury, 1
Minerva, -ae f.: Minerva, 2
morbus, -ī m.: disease, sickness, illness, 2
nātiō, nātiōnis f.: nation, people, tribe, 1
noscō, -ere, nōvī, nōtum: to learn, 1
noxia, -ae f.: fault, offence, crime, 1
nūmen, -minis n.: divine spirit or consent 1
pecūnia, -ae f.: money, 3
placō (1): soothe, calm, appease, placate, 1
plūrimus, -a, -um: most, very many, 4

potentia, -ae f.: power, might, strength, 1
prōpellō, -ere, -pellī, -pulsum: drive forward
    or push away, 3
quaestus, -ūs m.: gain, profit, advantage, 1
quotannis: every year, year by year, 1
reddō, -ere, -didī, -ditus: give back, return, 2
religiō, religiōnis f.: susperstitious rites, ritual,
    divine manifestation, 3
sacrificium, ī n.: sacrifice, 4
simulācrum, -ī n.: likeness, image, 2

soleō, -ēre, -itus sum: be accustomed, 1
succendō, -ere, -dī, censum: kindle under, 2
supplicium, -iī n.: punishment, 3
versor (1): be engaged in, move about, deal with, 3
via, -ae, f.: road, way, path, 2
victima, -ae f.: animal for sacrifice, victim, 1
vīmen, vīminis n.: twig, wicker, withe, 1
vīs, vīs, f., pl. **virēs**: force, power, violence, 4
vīvus, -a, -um: living, alive, 2
vovō, -ere, vōvī, vōtum: to vow; pray 1

---

1 **alterum genus**: *the other kind*; In 13.3 Caesar
    distinguished two groups, Druids and Knights.
    Here Caesar addresses the latter group.
    equitum: *of knights*
    Hī: *these*; i.e. the knights
    cum est ūsus: *when there is a need*; "is a use"
2 **incidit**: *occurs, happens*
    quod: *which*
    utī...inferrent...prōpulsārent: *(namely) that..*;
    ūti is an alternative to ut; noun result clause in
    apposition to quod with impf. subjunctives
    (secondary sequence) governed by accīdere
3 **ipsī**: *they themselves*; i.e. the knights
    illātās: *carried on*; PPP inferō, supply *inūriās*
4 **eōrum ut quisque...ita**: *in the proportion as
    each one of them is...so..*; in other words "the
    more...the more," ut and ita are correlatives
    genere copiīsque: *in birth and...*; abl. respect
    amplissimus: *very distinguished*
5 **hanc...grātiam**: *this lone (form) of influence*
    nōvērunt: *they have come to learn*; or "they
    know," pf. noscō
6 **dēdita**: *devoted to*; governs a dative plural
    ob eam causam: *for this reason*
7 **quī**: *(those) who...*
    sunt adfectī: pf. passive adficiō, + abl. means
    quīque: *and (those) who...*; second parallel
    clause parallel to the first
8 **prō victimīs**: *instead of sacrifical animals*
    immolātūrōs (esse): *will sacrifice (them)*; fut.
    inf., sē is acc. subj.; governed by vovent
9 **administrīs...Druidibus**: *Druids as
    performers*; abl. obj. of ūtuntur
    ad...: *for...*; expressing purpose

   quod: *because*
10 **prō vītā hominis**: *for the life of a man*;
    governed by the nisi...reddātur
    posse...placārī: numen is acc. subject
    prō vītā hominis: *for the life of a man*;
11 **eiusdem generis**: *of the same sort*; gen. of
    quality
12 **immānī magnitūdine**: *of immense size*; abl. of
    quality, immānis is an i-stem 3rd decl. adj.
    simulācra: *likeness*; Caesar describes image
    in the likeness of a man made of wicker
13 **membra**: acc. direct object of complent
    vīvīs hominibus: abl. of means
    quibus succensīs: *with these (images)...*; gen.
    abs. Caesar prefers to use a relative pronoun
    where English prefers the demonstrative
14 **quī...sint comprehensī**: *who...have been
    caught*; pf. pass. subj. in a relative clause of
    characteristic
15 **grātiōra**: *more pleasing*; acc. pred. with esse
    dīs immortālibus: *to the immortal gods*; an
    alternative form for dat. pl. deīs
16 **eius generis cōpia**: *supply of this sort*; i.e. of
    criminals
18 **Huius**: *of this one*; i.e. Mercury, gen. sg.
19 **ferunt**: *they call this one the inventor...*;
    governs a double accusative, inventōrem is
    in the predicative position
    hunc...ducem: *they call this one the guide...*;
20 **hunc...habēre**: *that this one...*; ind. discourse
    governed by arbitrantur
    vim maximam: *the greatest influence*
21 **Apollinem...Minervam**: supply colunt

---

volō, velle, voluī: to wish: Regular 3rd Conj. except the infinitive, present indicative and present subjunctive

pres.	vult	*she wishes*	present indicative		present subjunctive		imperfect subjunctive	
impf.	volēbat	*she was wishing*	volō	volumus	velim	velimus	vellem	vellēmus
fut.	volet	*she will wish*	vīs	**vultis**[1]	velīs	velītis	vellēs	vellētis
perf.	voluit	*she wished*	vult	**volunt**[2]	**velit**[3]	**velint**[4]	vellet	**vellent**[5]
plupf.	volerat	*she had wished*						
fut. pf	volerit	*she will have wished*	[1]p. 14, 46	[2]p. 28	[3]p.52	[4]p. 28, 42, 58, 60	[5]p. 10, 40, 52, 58, 62	

17.2. Dē hīs eandem ferē, quam reliquae gentēs, habent opiniōnem:　1
Apollinem morbōs dēpellere, Minervam operum atque artificiōrum initia
trādere, Iovem imperium caelestium tenēre, Martem bella regere. 3. Huic,
cum proeliō dīmicāre constituērunt, ea quae bellō cēperint plērumque
dēvovent: cum superāvērunt, animalia capta immolant reliquāsque rēs in　5
ūnum locum cōnferunt. 4. Multīs in civitātibus hārum rērum exstrūctōs
tumulōs locīs consecrātīs conspicārī licet; 5. neque saepe accidit ut neglēctā
quispiam religiōne aut capta apud sē occultāre aut posita tollere audēret,
gravissimumque eī reī supplicium cum cruciātū constitūtum est.

18.1 Gallī sē omnēs ab Dīte patre prōgnātōs praedicant idque ab Druidibus　10
prōditum dīcunt. 2. Ob eam causam spatia omnis temporis nōn numerō
diērum sed noctium fīniunt; diēs nātālēs et mēnsum et annōrum initia sic
observant ut noctem diēs subsequātur. 3. In reliquīs vītae īnstitūtīs hōc ferē ab
reliquīs differunt, quod suōs līberōs, nisi cum adolēvērunt, ut mūnus mīlitiae
sustinēre possint, palam ad sē adīre non patiuntur filiumque puerīlī aetāte in　15
pūblicō in cōnspectū patris adsistere turpe dūcunt.

adeō, -īre, i(v)ī, itus: approach, encounter, 2
adolescō, -ere, adolevī: to grow up, 1
adsistō, -ere, adstitī: stand by, set near, 1
aetās, aetātis f.: age, time, lifetime, 1
animal, animalis n.: animal, 2
Apollo, Apollinis m.: Apollo, 2
artificium, -ī m.: work, craft, work of art, 1
audeō, -ēre, ausus sum: dare, venture, 4
caelestis, -e: celestial, heavenly; *subs.* gods, 1
cōnferō, -ferre, -tulī, -lātum: bring together, gather, 2
conficiō, -ere: to exhaust, finish, 4
consecrō (1): dedicate to a god, make holy 2
conspectus, -ūs, m.: look, sight, view, 2
conspicor, -ārī: catch sight of, perceive, 1
cruciātus, -ūs m.: torture, torment, 2
dēpellō, -ere, -pulī, -pulsum: drive out, 1
dēvoveō, -ere, vōvī, vōtum: vow, sacrifice, 1
differō, -ferre, distulī: differ, be different, 2
dīmicō (1): brandish weapons; contend, 1
Dis, Ditis, -ī m.: Dis, Pluto, 1
exstruō, -ere, -struxī, -structum: build up, 1
finiō, -īre: to end, limit, bound, 1
gens, gentis, f.: people, tribe, nation, 1
immolō (1): to sacrifice, immolate, 3
institum, ī n.: institution, practice, custom, 2
Iuppiter, Iovis m.: Jupiter, 2
līberī, -ōrum m.: children 2
Mars, Martis m.: Mars, god of victory, 2
mensis, -is m.: month, 2
mīlitia, -ae f.: military service; military, 2

Minerva, -ae f.: Minerva, 2
morbus, -ī m.: disease, sickness, illness, 2
mūnus, -eris n.: service, duty; tax, gift, 1
nātālis, -e: natal, of birth, 1
neglegō, ere, -lēxī, neglēctum: to neglect, 3
observō (1): watch, observe, attend to, 2
occultō (1): hide, conceal, 3
opus, -eris n.: work, deed, toil, 2
opīniō, -niōnis f.: opinion, thought, belief, 2
palam: openly, publicly, 2
pater, patris, m.: father, 4
patior, -ī, passus: suffer, endure; allow, 2
praedicō (1): proclaim, publish, declare, 2
prōdō, ere, didī, ditum: bring forth; betray 2
prognātus, -a, -um: born, sprung from, 1
puerīlis, -e: youthful, childish; silly, 1
quispiam, quae-, quod-: anyone, anything (adj. any), 2
regō, -ere, rēxī, rectum: rule, lead, direct, 1
religiō, religiōnis f.: susperstitious rites, ritual,
　divine manifestation, 3
saepe: often, 3
sīc: thus, in this way, 3
spatium, -iī n.: space, room, extent, 4
supplicium, -iī n.: punishment, 3
tollō, ere, sustulī, sublātum: raise, destroy, 2
trādō, -dere, -didī, -ditum: to give over,
　hand down, pass down, 3
tumulus, -ī m.: pile, heap, mound, hill, 1
turpis, turpe: ugly, shameful, 2

1 **Dē hīs**: *concerning these*; i.e. Apollo, Minerva, Juno, Jupiter
eandem...quam reliquae gentēs: *the same... as the rest of the people (have)*; "the same... which the rest of the people (have)," eandem modifies opiniōnem

2 **Apollinem...Minervam...Iovem...Martem**: *that Apollo...(and) that Minerva...(and) that Jupiter...(and) that Mars...*; acc. subjects of ind. discourse in apposition to opiniōnem; asyndeton, supply conjunctions

3 **huic**: *to this one*; i.e. Mars

4 **cum proeliō**: *when...in battle*; cum is adverbial
ea quae...cēperint: *those things which...*; ea is neuter pl. object of dēvovent; cēperint is pf. subjunctive in a relative clause of characteristic

5 **cum superāvērunt**: *when they have overcome (an enemy)*

6 **multīs**: modifies cīvitātibus; placing the adj. before the preposition emphasizes the role of the adjective
hārum rērum: *with these things*; modifies tumulōs

7 **locīs consecrātīs**: *in...*; abl. place where
ut quispiam...audēret: *that anyone...dare to*; noun result clause, impf. subjunctive audeō which governs complementary infinitives
neglēctā...religiōne: *with religious observance...*; ablative absolute

8 **capta**: *things seized*; PPP capiō in neuter pl., i.e. the rēs in line 5
apud sē: *in their home*

posita tollere: *to destroy things having be put aside*; PPP pōnō, -ere in neuter pl.

9 **eī reī**: *for this matter*; dat. sg.

10 **sē...prōgnātōs (esse)**: *that they were born*; prōgnātōs is either an acc. predicate with missing inf. esse or part of a pf. passive inf.
id...prōditum (esse): *that this was brought forth...*; pf. pass. inf. prōdō in ind. discourse

11 **ob eam causam**: *for this reason*
spatia omnis temporis: *intervals of every (period of) time*

12 **noctium**: i-stem gen. plural nox, noctis
et mēnsum (initia) et annōrum initia: *and the beginnings of months and of years*; acc. object of observant
sīc...ut: *in this way...so that*; result clause

13 **hōc...quod**: *in this...(namely) because*; abl. of respect governed by differunt
suōs līberōs...adīre: *that their children...*; acc. subj. of ind. discourse following patiuntur

14 **mūnus mīlitiae**: *military service;* "service of the military"

15 **nōn patiuntur**: *do not allow*; 3rd pl. pres. patior

16 **fīliumque...adsistere (esse) turpe dūcunt**: *and they consider it is shameful that a son... stand...*; supply (esse); the infinitive adsistere is subject of the missing esse and turpe is acc. predicate; all indirect discourse governed by dūcunt, fīlium is acc. subject of adsistere
puerīlī aetāte: *of a boy's age*; abl. of quality

Common Uses of the Ablative

construction	example	translation
Ablative Absolute	urbe captā	*the city having been captured*
Ablative of Means	stilō scrībēns	*writing with a stylus*
Ablative of Agent	ā matre vocātur	*he is called by his mother*
Ablative of Separation (includes From Which)	timore līberātur	*she is free from fear*
Ablative of Manner	cum dīligentiā	*with diligence*
Ablative of Accompaniment	cum amīcīs	*with friends*
Ablative of Place Where	in urbibus	*in the cities*
Ablative of Place From Which	ab marī	*from the sea*
Ablative of Time When	eō tempore	*at that time*
Ablative of Respect (Specification)	linguā differunt	*differ in respect to language*
Ablative of Quality (Description)	est animō bonō	*is of good will*
Ablative of Cause	gaudiō commōtus	*moved by joy*
Ablative of Comparison	clārior luce	*brighter than light*
Ablative of Degree of Difference	multō clārior	*much brighter*
w/ verbs: *potior, utor, fungor, fruor, vescor*	utī gladiō	*to employ a sword*
w/ adjectives: *dignus, indignus*	glōriā indignus	*unworthy of glory*

19.1 Virī, quantās pecūniās ab uxōribus dōtis nōmine accēpērunt, tantās ex   1
suīs bonīs aestimātiōne factā, cum dōtibus commūnicant. 2. Huius omnis
pecūniae coniūnctim ratiō habētur frūctūsque servāntur: uter eōrum vītā
superāvit, ad eum pars utrīusque cum frūctibus superiōrum temporum
pervenit. 3. Virī in uxōrēs, sīcutī in līberōs, vītae necisque habent potestātem;   5
et cum paterfamiliae illūstriōre locō nātus dēcessit, eius propinquī conveniunt
et, dē morte sī rēs in suspiciōnem venit, dē uxōribus in servīlem modum
quaestiōnem habent et, sī compertum est, ignī atque omnibus tormentīs
excruciātās interficiunt. 4. Fūnera sunt prō cultū Gallōrum magnifica et
sūmptuōsa; omniaque quae vīvīs cordī fuisse arbitrantur in ignem īnferunt,   10
etiam animālia, ac paulō suprā hanc memoriam servī et clientēs, quōs ab eīs
dīlēctōs esse cōnstābat, iustīs fūneribus cōnfectīs ūnā cremābantur.

20.1 Quae cīvitātēs commodius suam rem pūblicam administrāre
exīstimantur, habent lēgibus sānctum, sī quis quid dē rē pūblicā ā fīnitimīs
rūmōre aut fāmā accēperit, utī ad magistrātum dēferat nēve cum quō aliō   15
commūnicet, 2. quod saepe hominēs temerāriōs atque imperītōs falsīs
rūmōribus terrērī et ad facinus impellī et dē summīs rēbus cōnsilium capere
cognitum est. 3. Magistrātūs quae vīsa sunt occultant quaeque esse ex ūsū
iūdicāvērunt multitūdinī prōdunt. Dē rē pūblicā nisi per cōncilium loquī nōn
concēditur.   20

administrō (1): to manage, direct; help, 3
aestimātio, -tionis f.: valuation, assessment 1
animal, animalis n.: animal, 2
bonus, -a, -um: good, kind(ly), useful 2
cliens, -entis m.: client, dependent, 4
commodus, -a, -um: convenient, suitable, 2
communicō (1): share, impart, 4
comperiō, -īre, -perī, -pertum: find out, discover, 1
concēdō, -ere; go away, withdraw, yield, 2
conficiō, -ere: to exhaust, finish, 4
coniūnctim: jointly, in common, 1
cōnstō, -āre, -stitī: stand together, 2
cor, cordis n.: the heart, 1
cremō (1): burn, consumer by fire, 2
cultus, -ūs m.: culture, refinement, 2
dēcēdō, -ere, -cessī, -cessum: depart, die, 4
dīligō, -ere, -lexī, -lectum: to love, esteem, 1
dōs, dotis f.: dowry, gift, 2
excruciō (1): torture, torment, 1
facinus, facinoris n.: deed; bad deed, crime 2
falsus, -a, -um: wrong, mistaken, misled, 1
fāma, -ae f.: rumor, story, hearsay, 2
fructus, -ūs m.: profit, advantage, benefit, fruit, 2
fūnus, fūneris n.: funeral, burial; death, 2
ignis, ignis, m.: fire, 4

illustris, -e: bright, distinguished, 1
impellō, -ere, -pulī, -pulsus: drive, rouse 2
imperītus, a, um: unskilled, inexperienced, 2
iūdicō (1): judge, decide, assess, 2
iustus, -a, -um: just, fair, 1
lēx, lēgis f.: law, regulation, decree, 3
līberī, -ōrum m.: children, 2
loquor, -ī, locūtum: speak, say, 2
magistratus, -ūs m.: magistrate, officer, 3
magnificus, -a, -um: magnificent, splendid 1
memoria, -ae. f.: memory, 4
modus, ī n.: manner, form; measure, 4
nascor, nascī, nātus sum: be born, grow, 3
nēve: or not, and not, nor, 2
nex, necis f.: death, violent death, murder, 1
nōmen, nōminis n.: name, 2
occultō (1): hide, conceal, 3
paterfamiliās, -ae m.: paterfamilias, 1
pecūnia, -ae f.: money, 3
potestās, -tātis f.: power, ability, capacity, 3
prōdō, ere, didī, ditum: bring forth; betray 2
propinquus, -a, -um: near, close; *subst.* kinsman, 2
quaesītio, -tiōnis f.: investigation, inquiry, 1
rūmor, rūmoris f., -ae f.: rumor, hearsay, 2
saepe: often, 3

sanctus, -a, -um: consecrated, hallowed, 1
servīlis, -e: slavish, servile, of a slave, 1
servō (1): save, keep, preserve, 2
servus, -ī, m.: slave, 1
sicut: just as, so as, as if, 2
sumptuōsus, -a, -um: sumptuous, expensive, 1
suprā: above, over, on the top, 3
suspīcio, -ciōnis f.: mistrust, suspicion, 4

temerārius, -a, -um: rash, inconsiderate, 1
terreō, -ēre, terruī, territum: to terrify, 2
tormentum, -ī n.: missile-launcher, torture, 3
uter, utra, utrum: each or one (of two), 2
uxor, ūxōris f.: wife, spouse, 3
vir, virī m.: man, 4
vīvus, -a, -um: living, alive, 2

---

1 **Virī**: *husbands*; an appropriate translation in light of the discussion of wives, uxōrēs
quantās...tantās: *as much money...so much*; correlatives; relative and demonstrative respectively
dōtis nōmine: *in the name of a dowry*
ex suīs...factā: ablative absolute
commūnicant: *contribute (an equal share)*; i.e. the husband makes a contribution matching the value of the dowry

2 **huius omnis pecūniae**: *of...*; objective gen. governed by ratiō

3 **ratiō habētur**: *an account is made*; "is held"
fructūs: *the profits*; nom., the word "usufruct" denotes a husband's ability to enjoy the use and profits of a wife's dowry as long as he does not diminish the original value of the dowry
uter eōrum vītā superāvit, ad eum: *which one of them has survived (the other) in life, to this one...*; abl. of respect; eum, though masculine, can apply to the surviving husband or wife

4 **pars utrīusque**: *the portion of each one*; i.e. the dowry and the husband's contribution
superiōrum: *previous*; gen. pl. comparative

5 **in uxōrēs...in līberōs**: *toward...toward*
sīcutī: alternative to sīcut

6 **paterfamiliae**: *the paterfamilias*; nom. subject
illūstriōre locō: *in a more illustrious position*
nātus: pf. passive pple. nascor
dēcessit: *has died*; "departed," a euphemism

7 **dē morte**: *concerning death*; modifies rēs
in servīlem modum: *in the manner of slaves*; i.e. just as they investigate slaves after the death of a master, so a wife after the death of her husband

8 **compertum est**: *it is discovered*; incriminating evidence
ignī: i-stem abl. singular

9 **prō cultū**: *according to the culture*

10 **vīvīs cordī fuisse**: *to have been dear to the living*; cordī is a predicative dative commonly found with inf. of sum; vīvīs is dat. of interest

11 **paulō**: *a little*; abl. of degree of difference
suprā hanc memoriam: *before our time*; "before this (living) memory"

12 **constābat**: *it was agreed*; "it stood fixed"
ab eīs: *by them*; i.e. by the dead
dīlēctōs esse: pf. pass. inf.
iustīs fūneribus cōnfectīs: *the due funerals completed*; abl. absolute
ūnā: *together*; living burned with the dead

13 **quae cīvitātēs..exīstimantur**: *the cities which they consider to...*
commodius: *more advantageously*; comparative adverb
habent lēgibus sānctum...utī...: *have it ordained by laws....that*; utī (ut) introduces an indirect command with pres. subjunctive

14 **sī quis quid...accēperit**: *if anyone has received anything...*; aliquis, aliquid is a common indefinite pronoun (anyone, anything), but quis, quid is commonly used as an indefinite (who → anyone, what → anything) after sī, nisi, num, and nē. The mnemonic for this construction is the jingle "After sī, nisi, num, and nē, all the ali's go away" (in other words indefinite aliquid becomes just quid); accēperit is pf. subj.
ā fīnitimīs: *from neighbors, from those near*

15 **cum quō aliō**: *with anyone else*; see note l. 15
quod: *because*

16 **hominēs...terrērī...impellī...capere**: *that people...*; infs. are subject of cognitum est

17 **dē summīs rēbus**: *concerning the most important matters*
quae vīsa sunt: *(those things) which seemed best (to hide)*
quaeque...iūdicāvērunt: *and (those things) which...*; missing antecedent is obj. of prōdunt
esse ex ūsū: *is of use*; i.e. advantagous

19 **multitūdinī**: dat. indirect object
prōdunt: *bring forth*; in contrast to occultant
loquī: pres. deponent infinitive

20 **concēditur**: *it is allowed*; "it is yielded"

24.1 Subductīs nāvibus conciliōque Gallōrum Samarobrīvae perāctō, quod eō   1
annō frūmentum in Galliā propter siccitātēs angustius prōvēnerat, coāctus
est aliter ac superiōribus annīs exercitum in hībernīs collocāre legiōnēsque in
plūrēs civitātēs distribuere; 2. ex quibus ūnam in Morinōs ducendam Gaiō
Fabiō lēgātō dedit, alteram in Nerviōs Quintō Cicerōnī, tertiam in Esubiōs   5
Lucio Rōsciō; quartam in Rēmīs cum Titō Labiēnō in confīniō Trēverōrum
hiemāre iussit. Trēs in Belgīs collocāvit: 3. eīs Marcum Crassum quaestorem
et Lucium Munātium Plancum et Gaium Trebōnium lēgātōs praefēcit. 4. Ūnam
legiōnem, quam proximē trāns Padum cōnscrīpserat, et cohortēs V in
Eburōnēs, quōrum pars maxima est inter Mosam ac Rhēnum, quī sub   10
imperiō Ambiorīgis et Catuvolcī erant, mīsit. 5. Eīs mīlitibus Quintum
Titūrium Sabīnum et Lucium Aurunculēium Cottam lēgātōs praeesse iussit.
6. Ad hunc modum distribūtīs legiōnibus, facillimē inopiae frūmentāriae sēsē
medērī posse exīstimāvit. 7. Atque hārum tamen omnium legiōnum hīberna
praeter eam, quam Luciō Rōsciō in pācātissimam et quiētissimam partem   15
dūcendam dederat, mīlibus passuum centum continēbantur. 8. Ipse intereā,
quoad legiōnēs collocātās mūnītaque hīberna cōgnōvisset, in Galliā morārī
cōnstituit.

aliter: otherwise, 2
angustus, -a, -um: narrow, confined, 4
Aurunculeius, -ī m.: Aurunculeius, 2
Catūvolcus –ī m.: Catuvolcus, 2
centum: one hundred, 1
collocō (1): place together, arrange, set up, 4
confīnium, -iī n.: a confine, limit, border, 1
conscrībō, -ere, -scrīpsī: enlist, enroll, 2
distribuō, -ere, -buī, -būtum: divide up, 2
Ēsubiī, -ōrum m.: the Esubii, 1
Fabius, -ī m.: Fabius, 3
frūmentārius, -a, -um: full of grain, 2
Gaius, -ī m.: Gaius, 4
hiemō (1): spend the winter, 3
inopia, -ae f.: poverty, want (of), need, 1
intereā: meanwhile, meantime, 3
Marcus, -ī m.: Marcus, 1
medeor, -ērī: heal, cure; assist, alleviate (dat) 1
modus, ī n.: manner, form; measure, 4
Morinī, -ōrum m.: Morini, 1
moror, -ārī, -ātus: delay, linger; detain, 3
Mosa, -ae f.: Mosa (Meuse) river, 1
Munātius, -ī m.: Munatius, 1
muniō, -īre, -īvī, -ītum: to fortify, build, 3

pācātus, -a, -um: peaceful, quiet, 1
Padus, -ī m.: Padus (Po) river, 1
peragō, -ere, ēgī, actum: pass, go through, 1
Plancus, -ī m.: Plancus, 2
plūs (plūris): more, 4
praeficiō, -ere, -fēcī, -fectum: set (acc) over (dat), put (acc) in charge over (dat), 2
praesum, -esse, -fuī: be over, preside over (dat), 2
praeter: beyond, past (+ acc.), 2
prōveniō, -īre, -vēnī: come forward, grow 1
quaestor, -oris m.: quaestor, 3
quartus, -a, -um: the fourth, 2
quiētus, -a, -um: resting, calm, undisturbed 1
quoad: until, as far as, as long as, 1
Rēmī, -ōrum m.: Rheims (town), 1
Roscius, ī m.: Roscius, 2
Samarobrīva, -ae f.: Samarobriva (a town) 2
siccitās, -tātis f.: dryness, 1
subdūcō, -ere, -dūxī, -ductus: draw up,, 2
Titus, -ī m.: Titus, 4
trans; over, across (+ acc.), 3
Trebōnius , -ī m.: Trebonius, 1
Trēveri , -ōrum m.: Treveri (Germanic), 4

Background: Upon return from the second expedition to Britain, Caesar discovers that on account of drought the grain supply will be low for the winter. Since no one region can supply the grain for the army, Caesar distributes his forces into a number of smaller camps which, one assumes, can live off the grain in their particular region.

1 **Subductīs nāvibus**: *the ships drawn up (on shore)*; sub- as a prefix often means "up from under," the ships were driven onto the beach
cōnciliō...perāctō: abl. absolute
Samarobrīvae: *at Samarobriva*; locative case
quod: *because*
2 **eō annō**: *on that...*; eō is demonstrative; abl. place where
angustius: *more limited, scarcer*; "narrower," i.e. less grain, comparative adj. neut. sg. with frūmentum the subject of prōvēnerat
coāctus est: *he was compelled*; pf. pass. cōgō
3 **aliter ac**: *otherwise than*; common translation of aliter with ac or atque
superiōribus: *in previous.*; "higher" time when
hībernīs: *winter-quarters*
4 **plūrēs**: acc. pl. plūs, comparative of multus
ex quibus: *from these*; "from which," in a transition Caesar prefers a relative pronoun where English prefers a demonstrative
ūnam: *one (legion)*
in Morinōs: *among the Morini*
ducendam: *to be led*; "going to be led," gerundive expressing purpose modifying ūnam and governing "in Morinōs"
Gaiō Fabiō...Rōsciō: dative indirect object
5 **dedit**: pf. dō, dare
alteram...tertiam: *another (legion)...a third (legion)...*; parallel to "ūnam...dedit," supply to each clause "ducendam" and "dedit" which are missing through ellipsis (omission)
6 **quartam**: *the fourth (legion)*
7 **Trēs**: *three (legions)*

eīs: *over them*; dat. with compound praefēcit
8 **praefēcit**: *put (acc) in charge of (dat)*
9 **proximē**: *very recently*; "nearest (in time) superlative adverb
10 **quōrum**: *of which*; partitive genitive
11 **Eīs**: *over them*; dat. with compound praeesse
12 **Quintum...lēgātōs**: acc. subject of praeesse
13 **Ad hunc modum**: *in this manner*; "according to this manner" part of the ablative absolute distribūtīs legiōnibus
inopiae...medērī: *to alleviate the need*; dat. object of dep. medeor
sēsē: *that he...*; reflexive acc. subject of posse
15 **praeter eam, quam**: *except that (legion) which...*;
Luciō Rōsciō: dat. i.o. of dederat, plpf. dō
In...partem: *into...part (of Gallia)*
pācātissimam, quiētissimam: superlatives
16 **ducendum**: *to be led*; "going to be led," gerundive expressing purpose modifying quam (legiōnem) and governing "in...partem"
mīlibus...centum: *by 100 miles*; "by 100 thousand of paces"
continēbantur: hīberna is the neut. pl. subject
17 **quoad...cōgnōvisset**: *until he had learned*; plpf. subjunctive; i.e. he delayed in Gaul until he had learned all had been arranged
legiōnēs collocātās (esse): *that the legions...*; ind. discourse, supply esse for pf. pass. inf.
hīberna mūnīta (esse): *that winter-quarters*; ind. discourse, supply esse for pf. pass. inf.
morārī: present deponent inf. moror

Command in the Winter-Quarters

The highest officer in the Roman Army was the **dux**, general. When a Roman dux won an important victory, he might be given the title **imperātor**, commander, by his own men. The officers who ranked immediately below the dux and were selected by him to lead a single legion were called **legātī**, a word that means "the commissioned" but is often translated as lieutenant-generals or more commonly legates. This word "legātus" is also used to describe envoys commissioned to convey information on behalf of the dux or senate, so readers should be careful to distinguish a legātus who leads a legion from a legātus who carries news, for example, from Caesar to his allies.

In the passage above, Caesar assigns a legion to each of a number of legātī who will play a role in the events that follow in Book V: **Gaius Fabius**, **Quintus Cicero**, brother of the famous orator, **Lucius Roscius**, **Titus Labienus**, **Lucius Munatius Plancus**, **Gaius Trebonius**, **Quintus Titūrius Sabinus** and **Lucius Aurunculeius Cotta**. In order to possess *imperium*, the power to command, these legates had to have been elected by the Centuriate Assembly in Rome at some point in the past to the office of praetor or consul. All the legates, therefore, were members of the senatorial class.

In addition to the legates, Caesar appointed a legion in winter-quarters to the **quaestor** Marcus Crassus, son of the wealthy M. Licinius Crassus. Elected by Rome's Tribal Assembly, quaestors were financial officers. On a military campaign, a quaestor would be chosen by the dux from among the elected quaestors and was responsible for distributing soldiers' pay and procuring supplies.

25.1 Erat in Carnūtibus summō locō nātus Tasgetius, cuius māiōrēs in suā   1
civitāte regnum obtinuerant. 2. Huic Caesar prō eius virtūte atque in sē
benevolentiā, quod in omnibus bellīs singulārī eius operā fuerat ūsus,
maiōrum locum restituerat. 3. Tertium iam hunc annum regnantem inimicī,
multīs palam ex civitāte eius auctōribus, eum interfēcērunt. 4. Defertur ea rēs   5
ad Caesarem. Ille veritus, quod ad plūrēs pertinēbat, nē cīvitās eōrum impulsū
dēficeret, Lucium Plancum cum legiōne ex Belgiō celeriter in Carnūtēs
proficiscī iubet ibique hiemāre quōrumque operā cognōverat Tasgetium
interfectum, hōs comprehēnsōs ad sē mittere. 5. Interim ab omnibus lēgātīs
quaestōreque, quibus legiōnēs trādiderat, certior factus est in hīberna   10
perventum locumque hībernīs esse mūnītum.

26.1 Diēbus circiter XV, quibus in hīberna ventum est, initium repentīnī
tumultūs ac dēfectiōnis ortum est ab Ambiorīge et Catuvolcō; 2. quī, cum ad
fīnēs regnī suī Sabīnō Cottaeque praestō fuissent frūmentumque in hīberna
comportāvissent, Indūtiomārī Trēverī nūntiīs impulsī, suōs concitāvērunt   15
subitōque oppressīs lignātōribus magnā manū ad castra oppugnātum
vēnērunt. 3. Cum celeriter nostrī arma cepissent vallumque adscendissent
atque ūnā ex parte Hispānīs equitibus ēmissīs equestrī proeliō superiōrēs
fuissent, dēspērātā rē hostēs suōs ab oppugnātiōne redūxērunt.

ascendō, -ere, -ī, -ēnsus: ascend, mount 2
auctor, auctoris m.: agent, doer, cause, 4
Belgium –ī n.: Belgium (part of Belgae), 2
benevolentia, -ae, f.: goodwill, kindness, 1
Carnūtēs, -um: Carnutes, 4
Catūvolcus –ī m.: Catuvolcus, 2
comportō (1): carry together, collect, 3
comprehendō, -ere, -dī: seize, arrest; grasp 4
concitō (1): stir up, incite, impel, 2
dēfectio, -tiōnis f.: rebellion, defection, 1
dēficiō, -ere, -fēcī, -fectum: fail, give out, 3
dēspērō (1): to have no hope, give up, 2
ēmittō, -ere, -mīsī, -missum: send away 1
equester, -stris, -stre: equestrian, 1
hiemō (1): spend the winter, 3
Hispānī, -ōrum m.: Spaniard, 1
iam: now, already, soon, 4
impellō, -ere, -pulī, -pulsus: drive, rouse 2
impulsus, -ūs m.: incitement, pressure, 1
Indūtiomārus, -ī m.: (chief of Treveri), 1
inimīcus, -a, -um: hostile, unfriendly, 4
lignātor, -ōris m.: wood-cutter, 1

muniō, -īre, -īvī, -ītum: to fortify, build, 3
nascor, nascī, nātus sum: be born, grow, 3
opera, operae f.: service, hard work, effort, 3
opprimō, -ere, -pressī, -pressum: crush,
  burden, overwhelm, 3
orior, -īrī, ortus: arise, rise, spring, 3
palam: openly, publicly, 2
Plancus, -ī m.: Plancus, 2
plūs (plūris): more, 4
praestō: at hand, present, at the service of (dat) 1
quaestor, -oris m.: quaestor, 3
redūcō, -ere, -dūxī, -ductus: to bring back, 3
regnō (1): to reign, rule as a king, 1
repentīnus, -a, -um: sudden, unexpected, 4
restituō, -ere, -stituī, -ductus: to restore, replace, 1
singulāris, -e: single, individual, alone, 2
Tasgetius, -ī m.: Tasgetius, 3
trādō, -dere, -didī, -ditum: to give over,
  hand down, pass down, 3
Trēveri , -ōrum m.: Treveri (Germanic), 4
tumultus, -ūs m.: uproar, tumult, confusion, 1
vereor, -ērī, -itus: be afraid, fear; revere, 4

1 **erat...nātus**: plpf. nascor
in Carnūtibus: *among the Carnutes*
summō locō: *in the highest position*; i.e. status,
abl. of quality
cuius: gen. sg. quī, quae, quod
māiōrēs: *ancestors*; "greater (in birth),"
comparative adj. of magnus, nom. subject
suā: *their*; possessive reflexive adjective

2 **Huic**: *to this one*; dat. i.o. of restituerat
prō virtūte...benevolentiā: *(in return) for...*
eius: *his*; i.e. Tasgetius'
in sē: *toward him*; i.e. toward Caesar

3 **singulārī eius operā fuerat ūsus**: *there had
been a need for his singular service*; ūsus est
(here plpf.) just as opus est is idiomatic for
"there is a need for" and governs an ablative,
singulārī is i-stem 3rd decl. abl. with operā,
which is 1st decl. and not from opus, operis

4 **māiōrum**: *of his ancestors*; see line 1
Tertium...annum: *for...*; acc. of duration
inimicī: nom. pl. subject

5 **multīs palam...auctōribus**: *many openly
(being) promoters...*; abl. absolute, subject and
pred., supply the missing pple "being"
ea: *this*; demonstrative adj. with fem. sg. rēs

6 **veritus**: *having begun to fear*; inceptive pf. dep.
pple vereor
quod...pertinēbat: *because...*; i.e. the murder
was not limited to one murderer but many
nē...dēficeret: *that...*; nē is translated
positively in this clause of fearing; impf.
subj. in secondary seq. governed by veritus

7 **impulsū**: *because of their incitement*; "by the
incitement" abl of cause
Lucium Plancum: acc. subject of proficīsī,
hiemāre, and mittere, all governed by iubet

8 **quōrumque operā...hōs**: *and these by whose
effort...*; the antecedent of the relative clause
quōrum...interfectum comes after the clause;
operā, as in line 3, is 1st decl. abl. sg.

9 **interfectum (esse)**: pf. pass. inf. in indirect
disc. with Tasgetium as acc. subject
comprehēnsōs: *arrested*

10 **certior factus est**: *he was informed*; "he was
made more certain," a common idiom, certior
is a comparative adjective, predicate nom.;
this construction governs indirect discourse

10 **perventum (esse)**: *that they had arrived*; this
pf. passive infinitive in ind. disc is impersonal:
"it has been arrived (by them)..." with the
legates and quaestor as assumed agents; in
translation, translate the pf. pass. as pf. active

11 **locum...mūnītum esse**: *that their positions
were fortified*; plural, though each legate may
have informed Caesar about his single
position, there were collectvely many different
winter-camps set up
hībernīs: *for winter-quarters*; dat. of purpose

12 **Diēbus...XV**: *within...*; abl. of time within
quibus: *in which (days)*; abl. of time within
ventum est: *they came*; "it has been come,"
impersonal passive
repentīnī...dēfectiōnis: subjective gen. of
initium, which is nom. subj.

13 **ortum est**: pf. deponent orior
ab: *from...*; abl. of origin, not abl. of agent

14 **regnī suī**: *of their kingdom*; gen. sg.
praestō fuissent: *had been at hand for*; + dat.
praestō is an adv. commonly found with a
form of sum, here plpf. subj. in a cum-clause

15 **Indūtiomārī Trēverī**: *of Indutiomarus, one of
the Treveri*; "of the Treverian Induiomarus,"
both are gen. sg. modifying abl. pl. nuntiīs
impulsī: *having been incited*; nom. pl.
modifies quī and governs preceding 3 words
suōs: *their own (men)*

16 **subitō...lignātōribus**: abl. abs.
magnā manū: *with a large body (of men)*; abl.
of means
oppugnātum: *to assault*; "to capture by
assault," supine in acc. sg. expresses purpose
and may be translated as an infinitive

17 **nostrī**: *our (men)*
cēpissent: plpf. subj. capiō

18 **ūnā ex parte**: *on one side*; "from one side"
Hispānīs...ēmissīs: abl. absolute
equestrī proeliō: *in an equestrian battle*;
i-stem 3rd decl. adjective in abl. sg.
superiōrēs: nom. pred. of plpf. subj. of sum

19 **dēspērātā rē**: abl. absolute
hostēs: nom. subj.
suōs: *their (men)*
ab: *from...*; abl. of separation

Quintus Titūrius Sabīnus and Lucius Aurunculeius Cotta.

Caesar commonly calls the first legate by the cognomen **Sabīnus** (line 14) or nomen **Titūrius**. Keep in mind that these names identify one and the same person. In V.27.1, the same legatus is called Quintus Titūrius. Caesar identifies the second legate, Lucius Aurunculeius Cotta, almost always by the cognomen **Cotta**.

26.4 Tum suō mōre conclāmāvērunt utī aliquī ex nostrīs ad colloquium   1
prōdiret: habēre sēsē, quae dē rē commūnī dicere vellent, quibus rēbus
contrōversiās minuī posse spērārent.

27.1 Mittitur ad eōs colloquendī causā Gaius Arpīnēius, eques Rōmānus,
familiāris Quintī Titūrī, et Quintus Iūnius ex Hispāniā quīdam, quī iam ante   5
missū Caesaris ad Ambiorīgem ventitāre cōnsuērat; apud quōs Ambiorīx ad
hunc modum locūtus est: 2. sēsē prō Caesaris in sē beneficiīs plūrimum eī
cōnfitērī dēbēre, quod eius operā stīpendiō līberātus esset, quod Aduatucīs,
fīnitimīs suīs, pendere cōnsuēsset, quodque eī et fīlius et fratris fīlius ab
Caesare remissī essent, quōs Aduatucī obsidum numerō missōs apud sē in   10
servitūte et catēnīs tenuissent; 3. neque id, quod fēcerit de oppugnātiōne
castrōrum, aut iūdiciō aut voluntāte suā fēcisse, sed coāctū civitātis, suaque
esse eiusmodī imperia, ut nōn minus habēret iūris in sē multitūdō quam ipse
in multitūdinem. 4. Cīvitātī porrō hanc fuisse bellī causam, quod repentīnae
Gallōrum coniūrātiōnī resistere nōn potuerit. Id sē facile ex humilitāte suā   15
probāre posse, quod nōn adeō sit imperītus rērum ut suīs copiīs populum
Rōmānum superārī posse cōnfīdat. 5. Sed esse Galliae commūne cōnsilium:
omnibus hibernīs Caesaris oppugnandis hunc esse dictum diem, nē qua legiō
alterae legiōnī subsidiō venīre posset; 6. nōn facile Gallōs Gallīs negāre
potuisse, praesertim cum dē recuperandā commūnī libertāte cōnsilium   20
initum vidērētur.

---

adeō: to such a degree, such an extent, so, 1
ante: before, in front of (acc); *adv.* before, 4
Arpineius, -ī m.: Arpineius, 2
beneficium, -ī n.: favor, benefit, kindness, 2
catena, -ae f.: chain, fetter, shackle, 1
coactus, -ūs m.: compulsion, coercion, 1
colloquium, -iī n.: conversation, talk, 1
colloquor, -quī, -locūtum: to converse, 4
conclamō (1): cry out together, shout, 2
confīdō, -ere, confīsus sum: trust, believe, rely upon, 4
confiteor, -ērī, -fessum: admit, reveal, 1
coniūrātio, -ōnis f.: pact, union, conspiracy 3
dēbeō, -ēre, dēbuī, dēbitum: ought, owe 1
eiusmodī: of this kind, such; so, 3
familiāris, -e: of the family; close friend, 1
frāter, -tris m.: brother, 2
Gaius, -ī m.: Gaius, 4
Hispania, -ae f.: Spain, 2
humilitās, -tātis f.: weakness, lowliness, 1
iam: now, already, soon, 4
imperītus, a, um: unskilled, inexperienced (gen), 2
iudicium, -ī n.: decision, judgment; trial, 3
Iūnius, -ī m.: Junius, 2

iūs, iūris n.: justice, law, right, 2
līberō (1): free, liberate, 3
lībertās, -tātis f.: freedom, liberation, 2
loquor, -ī, locūtum: speak, say, 2
minuō, -ere, minuī: diminish, ebb, 2
missus, -ūs m.: a sending, launching, 1
modus, ī n.: manner, form; measure, 4
mōs, mōris m.: custom, manner, law, 4
negō (1): to deny, say that…not, 2
opera, operae f.: service, hard work, effort, 3
pendō, -ere, pependī, pensum: pay, weigh 2
plūrimus, -a, -um: most, very many, 4
porrō: furthermore, further; long ago, far back, 1
praesertim: especially, particularly, 2
prōdeō, -īre, -iī, -itum: advance, go forth, 1
quīdam, quaedam, quiddam: a certain, 4
recuperō (1): gain again, regain, recover, 1
remittō, -ere, -mīsī, -missum: send back, 4
repentīnus, -a, -um: sudden, unexpected, 4
servitūs, servitūtis, f.: servitude, 2
stipendium, -iī n.: payment, tribute; military service, 1
ventitō (1): to come often, resort to, 2
voluntās, -tātis f.: will, wish, choice, 2

1 **suō mōre**: *according to their custom*; cf. I.4.1
utī aliquī...prōdiret: *that someone go forth*; ut + impf. subj. prōdeō in an ind. command; aliquī is a nom. sg. indefinite adj., alternate to aliquis
nostrīs: *our (men)*
ad: *for...*; expressing purpose

2 **habēre sēsē**: *(and) that they had...*; either ind. discourse governed by conclāmāvērunt just as the ind. command or governed by a missing verb of speech: "(stating) that they had"
quae...vellent: *(things) which they wanted*; impf. subj. volō in a subordinate clause in ind. disc.; the missing antecedent is obj. of habēre
dē rē commūnī: *about their common interests*; "about common affairs"
quibus rēbus: *by which things*; abl. of means

3 **contrōversiās**: acc. subject of inf. posse
minuī: pres. passive inf.
spērārent: impf. subj., same as vellent above

4 **colloquendī**: *of discussing*; gerund, gen. obj. of causā
eques: in apposition to Arpineius; Arpineius was an equestrian in rank, the term "eques" refers to his rank in society rather than his occupation as a horseman

5 **familiāris**: *a close friend*; nom. appositive
iam ante: *already before*

6 **missū**: *at Caesar's sending*; "by the sending of Caesar," Caesar is a subjective gen.; abl. cause
ventitāre: *to come often*; frequentative of veniō
apud quōs: *among these*; i.e. to these men; English prefers a demonstrative to the relative
ad hunc modum: *in this manner*; "according to this manner"

7 **locūtus est**: pf. deponent, loquor
sēsē...cōnfitērī debēre: *that he confessed to owe*; not "ought to confess," cōnfitērī is a dep. inf. in ind. discourse that extends at length through quod-clauses to tenuissent; in ind. disc. subordinate verbs not already subjunctive are made subjunctive
prō...beneficiīs: *(in return) for...*; prō + abl.
plūrimum eī: acc. object and dat. i.o. of debēre

8 **quod...liberātus esset**: *because...*; plpf. subj. Ambiorix lists the reasons he is indebted to Caesar; the verbs are subj. because subordinate verbs in ind. disc. are commonly subjunctive
stīpendiō: *from...*; abl. of separation
quod...cōnsuē(vi)sset: *which he had been accustomed*; plpf. subj., subordinate verb in ind. disc.; the antecedent is neuter stīpendiō

9 **quodque...remissī essent**: *and because...*; plpf. pass. subj., remittō, subordinate verbs in

ind. discourse become subjunctive
eī: *to him*; i.e. to Ambiorix, dat. indirect object

10 **quōs...tenuissent**: *whom...;* relative clause of characteristic, here with plpf. subj. teneō
obsidum numerō: *in a group of hostages*; abl. place where or accompaniment
apud sē: *among them*; i.e. among the Aduatuci

11 **neque id...fēcisse**: *and that (he) had not done it*; ind. discourse parallel to cōnfitērī in l. 8, reflexive sēsē in l. 7 is acc. subject; "id" is acc. d.o. and refers to Ambiorix's assault
quod fēcerit: *which...*; relative clause of characteristic with perfect subj. faciō

12 **iūdiciō (suō), voluntāte suā**: abl. cause
coāctū cīvitātis: *by the compulsion of the state*; abl. of cause
suaque...imperia, ut: *and that his powers were of such a kind that...*; a result clause with impf. subj. in secondary sequence follows

13 **nōn minus...iūris...quam ipse**: *no less (of) authority...than he himself (had)*; minus is comparative adj. neut. acc. d.o., iūris is a partitive gen.; supply habēret after ipse
in: *over*

14 **cīvitātī...hanc fuisse...**: *that to the state this...*; ind. discourse, hanc is acc. subj. with pf. inf. of sum; cīvitātī is a dat. of reference, i.e. from the viewpoint of the state
quod...potuerit: *(namely) because...*; pf. subj. of possum, subjunctive because it is a subordinate verb in ind. discourse; the verb in direct disc. is subjunctive for alleged cause, the subject of potuerit is a missing cīvitās

15 **coniūrātiōnī**: dat. obj. of resistere
Id sē...posse *that he is able...*; ind. disc., id is acc. d.o. of probāre, sē is acc. subject
facile: adverb of 3rd decl. facilis, facile

16 **quod...rērum**: *because...*
sit: *he is*; Ambiorix is nom. subject
ut...cōnfidat: *that...*; result clause, pres. subj.
suīs copiīs: abl. means; Ambiorix's troops
populum Rōmānum: acc. subject of posse

17 **sed esse**: *but that it is...*;

18 **omnibus...oppugnandīs**: *for assaulting...*; dat. purpose, employ a gerund-gerundive flip
dictum diem: *the appointed day*; PPP dīcō
nē...posset: *lest any legion...*; purpose clause

19 **alterae legiōnī subsidiō**: double dative (dat. of interest and dat. of purpose respectively)
Gallōs...potuisse: *Gauls could not deny Gauls*

20 **cum...vidērētur**: *since...seemed*
dē recuperandā...: gerund-gerundive flip

21 **initum (esse)**: *to have been entered*; pf. inf.

27.7 Quibus quoniam prō pietāte satisfēcerit, habēre nunc sē ratiōnem officī 1
prō beneficiīs Caesaris: monēre, ōrāre Titūrium prō hospitiō, ut suae ac
mīlitum salūtī cōnsulat. 8. Magnam manum Germānōrum conductam
Rhēnum trānsīsse; hanc adfore bīduō. 9. Ipsōrum esse cōnsilium velintne
priusquam fīnitimī sentiant ēductōs ex hībernīs mīlitēs aut ad Cicerōnem aut 5
ad Labiēnum dēdūcere, quōrum alter mīlia passuum circiter quinquaginta,
alter paulō amplius ab eīs absit. 10. Illud sē pollicērī et iūreiūrandō cōnfirmāre
tūtum iter per fīnēs datūrum; 11. quod cum faciat, et cīvitātī sēsē cōnsulere,
quod hībernīs levētur, et Caesarī prō eius meritīs grātiam referre. Hāc
ōrātiōne habitā discēdit Ambiorīx. 10

28.1 Arpinēius et Iūnius, quae audīerunt, ad lēgātōs dēferunt. Illī repentīnā
rē perturbātī, etsi ab hoste ea dīcēbantur, tamen nōn neglegenda
exīstimābant maximēque hāc rē permovēbantur, quod cīvitātem īgnōbilem
atque humilem Eburōnum suā sponte populō Rōmānō bellum facere ausam
vix erat crēdendum. 2. Itaque ad cōnsilium rem dēferunt magnaque inter eōs 15
exsistit contrōversia. 3. Lucius Aurunculēius complūrēsque tribūnī mīlitum et
prīmōrum ōrdinum centuriōnēs nihil temerē agendum neque ex hībernīs
iniūssū Caesaris discēdendum exīstimābant: quantāsvīs magnās etiam cōpiās
Germānōrum sustinērī posse mūnītīs hībernīs docēbant: rem esse testimōniō,
quod prīmum hostium impetum multīs ultrō vulneribus illātis fortissimē 20
sustinuerint: rē frumentāriā non premī; intereā et ex proximīs hībernīs et ā
Caesare conventūra subsidia: postrēmō quid esse levius aut turpius quam,
auctōre hoste, dē summīs rēbus capere cōnsilium?

adsum, -esse, -fuī: be present, assist, (dat.), 3
agō, agere, ēgī, āctum: drive, lead, do, 4
amplus, -a, -um: ample, full, spacious, 2
Arpineius, -ī m.: Arpineius, 2
auctor, auctoris m.: agent, doer, cause, 4
audeō, -ēre, ausus sum: dare, venture, 4
audiō, -īre, -īvī, audītum: to hear, listen to, 1
Aurunculeius, -ī m.: Aurunculeius, 2
beneficium, -ī n.: favor, benefit, kindness, 2
biduum, -ī n.: a period of two days, 2
centurio, -iōnis m.: centurion, 4
condūcō, -ere: bring together, gather, 2
cōnsulō, -ere, -suluī, sultum: consult, consider, 3
credō, -ere, -didī, creditum: believe, trust 1
dēdūcō, -ere: lead or draw down or away, 3
discō, -ere, -didicī: learn, get to know, 2
doceō, -ēre, -uī, -ctus: teach, tell, 4
ēdūcō, -ere, -dūxī, -ductus: lead out, 3
exsistō, -ere, -stitī, -stitum: arise, appear, 1
frūmentārius, -a, -um: full of grain, 2
grātia, -ae f.: gratitude; favor, thanks, 2

hospitium, -ī n.: hospitality; guest-host tie, 1
humilis, -e: on the ground, low; humble, 1
ignōbilis, -e: ignoble, obscure, unknown, 1
impetus, -ūs m.: attack, onset, assault, 7
iniussū: without orders, 1
intereā: meanwhile, meantime, 3
Iūnius, -ī m.: Junius, 2
ius-iūrandum, iūrisiūrandī n.: sworn oath, 2
levīs, -e: light, not heavy; unimportant, 1
levō (1): lift up, relieve; make smooth, 1
meritum, -ī n.: service, merit, favor, 1
moneō, -ēre, -uī, -itum: to warn, advise, 2
muniō, -īre, -īvī, -ītum: to fortify, build, 3
-ne: whether (opens yes/no question), 1
neglegō, ere, -lēxī, neglēctum: to neglect, 3
nunc: now, at present, 2
officium, -iī, n.: duty, obligation, 3
ōrō (1): plead, pray (for), entreat, 2
pietās, -tātis f.: piety, devotion, 1
polliceor, -cērī, -citus: promise, offer, 2
postrēmō,: *at last, finally*; abl. as adv. 2

priusquam: before, earlier than, 1
quantusvīs, -avis, -umvis: however much, 1
quinquaginta: fifty, 1
quoniam: since, inasmuch as, seeing that, 1
referō, ferre, tulī, lātum: report, bring back, 3
repentīnus, -a, -um: sudden, unexpected, 4
satisfaciō, -ere, fēcī, factum: to do enough 1
sentiō, -īre, -sī, sēnsum: to realize, feel, 3

sponte: willingly, voluntarily, 2
temere: heedlessly, blindly, without cause, 1
testimonium, -iī n.; witness, testimony, 1
tribūnus, -ī m.: tribune, officer, 2
turpis, turpe: ugly, shameful, 2
ultrō: voluntarily; moreover, beyond, 3
vix: with difficulty, with effort, scarcely, 2
vulnus, -eris n.: wound, blow, 3

---

1 **quibus...satisfēcerit**: *Since he accomplished enough for these*; pf. subjunctive satisfaciō, use a demonstrative instead of relative pronoun
prō pietāte: *out of devotion*; i.e. patriotism
habēre...sē: *he had*
ratiōnem officī: *a regard for his duty*; "a calculation for," objective genitive

2 **prō**: *(in return) for...*; + ablative
manēre, orāre...hospitiō: *(he said) that he advised (and) that he pleaded with Titūrius on behalf of hospitality*; asyndeton, Ambiorix said
ut...cōnsulat: *that...*; ind. command with pres. subj. governed by monēre and ōrāre

3 **salūtī**: *for his own and the soldiers' safety*; dat. of purpose, suae is a possessive adj. agreeing with salūtī while mīlitum is a gen. plural
manum: *body*; i.e. group, acc. subject

4 **trānsīsse**: pf. inf. trānseō in ind. discourse
hanc: *this (body)*; supply manum, acc. subject
adfore: *would be present*; alternative to the fut. inf. of adsum: adfutūrum esse
bīduō: *in...*; abl. of time within
Ipsōrum...cōnsilium, velintne: *that it is the consideration (of the Romans) themselves whether they are willing...*; ind. question with the pres. subjunctive of volō

5 **priusquam...sentiant**: i.e. before the Gauls find out
ēductōs...mīlitēs: acc. d.o. of dēdūcere

6 **dēdūcere**: complementary inf. of velint
quōrum alter..alter: *of whom one...the other*; i.e. Cicero and Labiēnus; partitive genitive
mīlia passuum: *for...miles*; "thousands of paces," acc. of extent; add "ab eīs absit"

7 **paulō**: *a little*; "by a little," abl. of degree of difference with comparative adv. of amplus
ab eīs: *from them*; i.e. from Titūrius' troops
absit: *is away*; pres. subj. subordinate verb in indirect discourse
Illud...tūtum iter...datūrum (esse): *that... (namely) that (he)*; illud is acc. d.o. of pollicērī and cōnfirmāre, "tūtum...datūrum (esse)" is in apposition to illud; datūrum esse is fut. inf. dō

sē pollicērī: *that he promised...*; deponent inf.
iūre-iūrandō: often as two words; abl. means

8 **quod**: *this*; i.e. removing Titūrius' troops and advising Titūrius on flight; translate the relative as a demonstrative, acc. object of faciat
et...et: *both...and*

9 **et cīvitātī sēsē cōnsulere**: *both that he was consulting the state*; cīvitātī is dat. obj.
quod hībernīs levētur: *because (the state) is relieved from the winter-quarters*; i.e. from supplying the Romans with grain for winter
et...referre: *and he returned...*; Ambiorix is able to be loyal to the Gauls and to Caesar

10 **Hāc...habitā**: abl. absolute
quae: *the things (which)*; or "what," the missing antecedent is obj. of dēferunt
audī(v)erunt: syncopated pf. 3rd pl.

11 **etsī**: *even if, although*; the clause is concessive
ea: *they*; "those things," neuter plural

12 **(ea) nōn neglegenda (esse)**: *that they must not be neglected*; passive periphrastic (gerundive + sum); supply esse to form the infinitive

13 **suā sponte**: *by its own will*

14 **populō Rōmānō**: *(against) the Roman people*
ausam (esse): *had dared*; pf. deponent inf. of semi-deponent audeō, audēre, ausus sum; the acc. subj. is fem. cīvitātem

15 **erat crēdendum**: *was to be believed*; the subj. is "cīvitātem...ausam (esse);" passive periphratic (gerundive + sum) as in line 12
cōnsilium: *council*; i.e. discussion in assembly

17 **nihil...agendum (esse)**: passive periphastic, see note for line 15 above
discedendum (esse): *that (they) must not depart*; "it must not be departed," see line 12

19 **rem esse testimōniō**: *that the matter served as evidence*; "was for evidence" dat. of purpose

20 **quod**: *namely because...*; in apposition to rem

21 **rē frūmentāriā**: *by the grain supply*; means

22 **conventūra (esse)**: *would convene*; fut. inf.

23 **turpius**: *more shameful than...*; comparison
auctōre hoste: *enemy being author*; absolute
capere cōnsilium: *to adopt a plan*; idiom

29.1 Contrā ea Titūrius sērō factūrōs clāmitābat, cum māiōrēs manūs   1
hostium adiūnctīs Germānīs convēnissent, aut cum aliquid calamitātis in
proximīs hībernīs esset acceptum. Brevem cōnsulendī esse occāsiōnem.
Caesarem arbitrārī profectum in Ītaliam; 2. neque aliter Carnūtēs interficiendī
Tasgetī cōnsilium fuisse captūrōs, neque Eburōnēs, sī ille adesset, tantā   5
contemptiōne nostrī ad castra ventūrōs esse. 3. Nōn hostem auctōrem, sed
rem spectāre: subesse Rhēnum; magnō esse Germānīs dolōrī Ariovistī
mortem et superiōrēs nostrās victōriās; 4. ārdēre Galliam, tot contumēliīs
acceptīs sub populī Rōmānī imperium redāctam, superiōre glōriā reī mīlitāris
exstīnctā. 5. Postrēmō quis hoc sibi persuādēret, sine certā rē Ambiorīgem ad   10
eiusmodī cōnsilium dēscendisse? 6. Suam sententiam in utramque partem
esse tūtam: sī nihil esset dūrius, nūllō cum perīculō ad proximam legiōnem
perventūrōs; sī Gallia omnis cum Germānīs cōnsentīret, ūnam esse in
celeritāte positam salūtem. 7. Cottae quidem atque eōrum, quī dissentīrent,
cōnsilium quem habēre exitum, in quō sī praesēns perīculum nōn, at certē   15
longinquā obsidiōne famēs esset timenda?

adiungō, -ere, iunxī, iunctum: join, attach, 1
adsum, -esse, -fuī: be present, assist, (dat.), 3
aliter: otherwise, 2
ardeō, -ēre, arsī, arsum: burn, be eager, 1
Ariovistus, -ī m.: (leader of the Germans) 1
auctor, auctoris m.: agent, doer, cause, 4
brevis, -e: short, 3
Carnūtēs, -um: Carnutes, 4
clāmitō (1): to cry violently or repeatedly, 1
consentiō, -īre, sensī: to agree, assent, 1
cōnsulō, -ere, -suluī, sultum: consult, 3
contemptio, -tiōnis f.: scorn, disdain, 1
contrā: opposite, facing (acc.), 2
contumēlia, -ae f: outrage, insult; violence, 1
dēscendō, -ere, -ī, -ēnsus: descend, 1
dissentiō, -īre, sensī: to disagree, oppose, 1
dolor, -ōris m.: pain, grief, anger, passion, 2
dūrus, -a, -um: hard(y), harsh, stern, 1
eiusmodī: of this kind; such; so, 3
exitus, -ūs m.: going out, exit, result, issue, 1

exstinguō, -ere, -stinxī, -stinctum: put out,
    snuff out, extinguish, 1
famēs, -is f.: hunger, 2
glōria, -ae, f.: glory, fame, 2
Ītalia, -ae f.: Italy, 1
longinquus, -a, -um; far, distant, remote, 2
militāris, -e: military, of a soldier, 1
obsidio, -iōnis f.: seige, blockade, 2
occāsio, -iōnis f.: opportunity, occasion, 2
postremō,: *at last, finally*; abl. as adv. 2
praesēns, -ntis: present, instant, 1
redigō, -ere, -ēgī, -actum: to bring back, 1
sententia, -ae f.: opinion, purpose, 2
sērō: late, too late, 1
spectō (1): watch, observe, behold, inspect, 3
subsum, -esse, -fuī: to be near, close at hand, 1
Tasgetius, -ī m.: Tasgetius, 3
timeō, -ēre, timuī: to be afraid, be scared, 1
tot: so many, 2

1 **contrā ea**: *in reply to these things*; "against
clāmitābat: *kept shouting*; frequentative impf.
sērō factūrōs (esse): *that (the Romans)
would...*; ind. disc. with fut. inf., add acc. subj.
cum...convēnissent: *after...*; plpf. subjunctive
māiōrēs: comp. adj. of magnus with manūs
manūs: *bodies*; i.e. groups of troops, nom. pl.
2 **adiūnctīs Germānīs**: abl. absolute
cum...esset acceptum: *after...*; plpf. pass.
aliquid calamitātis: *some calamity*; neut. nom.
subject;"something of calamity"
3 **Brevem...occāsiōnem**: *that...*; occāsiōnem is
acc. subj. but the predicate brevem is placed
first in the clause for emphasis
cōnsulendī: gerund (-ing), with occāsiōnem
4 **arbitrārī**: *that (he) thought*; add sē (Titūrius) as
acc. subject; pres. dep. inf. of arbitror
Caesarem...profectum (esse): *that Caesar*;
pf. dep. inf. proficīscor, governed by arbitrārī
5 **interficiendī Tasgetī**: *of killing Tasgetius*; gen.
sg. gerundive modifying gen. Tasgetius, which
through a gerund-gerundive flip is translated as
a gerund and acc. object
cōnsilium...captūrōs: cōnsilium capere is
an idiom: "to adopt an argument"
fuisse captūrōs: *would have adopted*; pf. inf.
sum + fut. pple capiō; in direct discourse this
would be cēpissent, an apodosis in a mixed
contrary-to-fact condition; parallel with
ventūrōs esse, it complementing the protasis
sī...adesset below; see page 61
neque Eburōnēs: acc. subj. with ventūrōs esse
6 **sī...adesset**: *if that one were present*; i.e.
Caesar, impf. subjunctive adsum, in direct disc.
a protasis in a mixed contrary-to-fact condition
with fuisse captūrōs and ventūrōs esse; cf. p. 61
nostrī: *for us*; nostrī is gen. sg. of the personal
pronoun nōs; this gen. is an objective gen.
modifying contemptiōne
ventūrōs esse: *would come*; fut. inf. (fut. pple +
inf. of sum); in direct discourse it would be
venīrent, an apodosis in a pres. contrary-to-fact
condition with sī...adesset above; parallel to
the 1st apodosis fuisse captūrōs, see note, p. 61
Nōn hostem...spectāre: *that (he) saw not the
enemy but the situation (as) the authority*; add
sē as acc. subj.; spectāre governs a double acc.
where auctōrem is an an acc. predicate
7 **subesse Rhēnum**: Rhēnum is acc. subj.
magnō....dolōrī: *served as great grief for the
Germans*; "was for great grief for the
Germans," double dative construction: "magnō
dolōrī" is dat. of purpose and "Germānīs" is

dat. of interest
8 **Ariovistī mortem...victōriās**: subject of esse
9 **ārdēre**: *that Gaul is on fire*; "is eager (to act),"
fire is a common metaphor for passion, in this
case, feelings of anger and indignation
tot...acceptīs: abl. absolute
sub...imperium: *underneath...*; sub governs an
abl. place where or as here acc. place to which
redactam: PPP redigō, modifying Galliam
superiōre...exstīnctā: abl. absolute
reī mīlitāris: *of military affairs*; with glōria
10 **quis...persuādēret** *who would persuade
himself this*; in dir. discourse a deliberative
pres. subjunctive, but in ind. discourse
secondary sequence it is impf. subj.
sine certā...dēscendisse: *(namely) that...*; ind.
disc. in apposition to neuter acc. sg. *hoc* above
sine certā rē: *without a reliable reason*
11 **dēscendisse**: *had lowered himself*; pf. inf.
Ambiorix is acting unbecoming of his status
Suam sententiam...: *that his opinion...*;
i.e. Ambiorix's opinion; Sabinus is still
employing Ambiorix as subject
in utramque partem: *on each side*
12 **sī...esset...perventūrōs (esse)**: *If...was...,
would arrive*; in dir. discourse a fut. more
vivid (sī erit, pervenient); in ind. disc. in
secondary seq. the protasis is impf. subj. and
the apodosis a fut. inf., see grammar box, p. 59
dūrius: neut. sg. comparative adj., nom. pred.
13 **sī...cōnsentīret, esse positam**: *if...agreed,
had been placed...*; in dir. disc., mixed simple
condition (sī cōnsentit, posita est); in ind. disc.
in secondary sequence the subordinate verb
becomes impf. subj. and the main verb pf.
pass. inf. (which we translate as plpf. in
secondary sequence); see the box, p. 59
14 **ūnam...salūtem**: *a single (means of) safety*
Cottae atque eōrum: gen. modifying
cōnsilium, the acc. subject of habēre
15 **quī dissentīrent**: i.e. those who disagreed
with Titūrius; verbs in subordinate clauses in
ind. disc. are commonly subjunctive
quem...exitium: *what outcome does the
plan...?*; interrog. adj. and noun introducing a
question; acc. d.o. of habēre in ind. disc.
in quō: *in which...*; the cōnsilium of Cotta and
others opposing Titūrius is the antecedent
16 **perīculum**: *(there was)...danger*; add esse
longinquā obsidiōne: *with...*; abl. of cause
esset timenda: *had to be feared*; "was going
to be feared" passive periphrastic (gerundive +
impf. subj. of sum) expressing necessity

30.1 Hāc in utramque partem disputātiōne habitā, cum ā Cottā prīmīsque   1
ōrdinibus ācriter resisterētur, 'Vincite,' inquit, 'sī ita vultis,' Sabinus, et id
clāriōre vōce, ut magna pars mīlitum exaudīret; 2. 'neque is sum,' inquit, 'quī
gravissimē ex vōbīs mortis perīculō terrear: hī sapient; sī gravius quid
acciderit, abs tē ratiōnem reposcent; 3. quī, sī per tē liceat, perendinō diē cum   5
proximīs hībernīs coniūnctī commūnem cum reliquīs bellī cāsum sustineant,
nōn, reiectī et relēgātī longē ab cēterīs, aut ferrō aut fame intereant.'

31.1 Cōnsurgitur ex cōnsiliō; comprehendunt utrumque et ōrant nē suā
dissēnsiōne et pertināciā rem in summum perīculum dēdūcant: 2. facilem esse
rem, seu maneant, seu proficīscantur, sī modo ūnum omnēs sentiant ac   10
probent; contrā in dissēnsiōne nūllam sē salūtem perspicere. Rēs disputātiōne
ad mediam noctem perducitur. 3. Tandem dat Cotta permōtus manūs:
superat sententia Sabīnī. Prōnūntiātur prīmā lūce itūrōs. 4. Cōnsūmitur
vigiliīs reliqua pars noctis, cum sua quisque mīles circumspiceret, quid sēcum
portāre posset, quid ex īnstrūmentō hībernōrum relinquere cōgerētur. 5.   15
Omnia excogitantur, quārē nec sine perīculō maneātur et languōre mīlitum
et vigiliīs perīculum augeātur. 6. Prīmā lūce sīc ex castrīs proficīscuntur, ut
quibus esset persuāsum nōn ab hoste, sed ab homine amīcissimo Ambiorige
cōnsilium datum, longissimō agmine maximīsque impedīmentīs.

ācriter: sharply, fiercely, 2
agmen, agminis n.: column, battle line, formation, 3
amīcus, -a, -um: friendly, 1
augeō, ēre, auxī, auctum: increase, enlarge 1
cēterī, -ae, -a: the remaining, rest, others, 1
circumspiciō, -ere: look around, consider, 1
clārus, a, um: clear; famous, distinguished 1
comprehendō, -ere, -dī: seize, arrest; grasp 4
coniungō, -ere, -jūnxī, -junctus: join, 1
consumō, -ere, -sumpsī: to use up, spend, 2
consurgō, -ere, -surrexī: rise up (together), 1
contrā: opposite, facing (acc.), 2
dēdūcō, -ere: lead or draw down or away, 3
disputātio, -tiōnis f.: disagreement, debate 2
dissensio, -siōnis f.: conflict, dissension, 2
eō, īre, īvī: to go, come, 4
exaudiō, -īre, -īvī, -ītum: hear out, listen to 1
excogitō (1): think out, devise, contrive, 1
famēs, -is f.: hunger, 2
ferrum, -ī n.: iron; sword; tool, 1
inquam: say, 4
instrumentum, -ī n.: tool, implement; stock, 1
intereō, -īre, -īvī, -ītum: to die, perish, 3
languor, -ōris m.: fatigue, weariness, sluggishness, 1
lūx, lūcis, f.: light, 3
maneō, -ēre, -sī, mānsus: remain, await 2

medius -a –um: in the middle of, 3
modo: only, merely, simply; just now, 4
nec: and not, nor (nec,nec = neither,nor) 2
ōrō (1): plead, pray (for), entreat, 2
perdūcō, -ere, dūxī, ductum: to draw out, 1
perendinus, a, um: of day after tomorrow, 1
perspiciō, -ere, -spexī, -spectum: perceive, 1
pertinācia, -ae f.: stubbornness, obstinacy, 1
portō (1): carry, bear, bring, 2
prōnuntiō (1): to proclaim, speak forth, 4
quārē: wherefore, therefore, why, 1
reiciō, -ere, -iēcī, -iectum: cast off or back, 1
relēgō (1): to send away, remove, 1
reposcō, -ere: to ask back again, demand, 1
sapiō, -ere, sapīvī: to taste; discern, think, 1
sententia, -ae f.: opinion, purpose, 2
sentiō, -īre, -sī, sēnsum: to feel, realize, 3
sīc: thus, in this way, 3
sīve, seu: whether, or (if), 2
tandem: finally, at last, at length, 2
terreō, -ēre, terruī, territum: to terrify, 2
vigilia, -ae f.: watch (1/4 period of night), 3
vincō, -ere, vīcī, victum: conquer, defeat, 1
vōs: you (all), 1
vōx, vōcis, f.: voice; utterance, word, 4

1 **hāc...habitā**: ablative absolute
  in utramque partem: *on each side*
  prīmīsque ōrdinibus: *and the first ranks*; i.e.
  centurions
2 **resisterētur**: *(Sabinus) was resisted*; impf.
  pass. subjunctive; cum is likely causal in sense
  Vincite: *Prevail*; i.e. win the dispute
  vultis: 2nd pl. present volō
  id clāriōre vōce: *and (he said) it with a rather
  loud voice*; supply inquit, ablative of manner
  loses "cum" when there is an adjective, here a
  comparative adjective
3 **ut...exaudīrent**: *so that...*; purpose clause with
  impf. subj., secondary sequence
  is...quī...terrear: *one who would be terrified*;
  i.e. "the sort of man who would...*; *is* is a
  predicate; relative clause of characteristic with
  a pres. subj.
  gravissimē: superlative adverb
4 **ex vōbīs**: *by you*; i.e. "danger (heard) from
  you," abl. source
  hī: *these (soldiers)*; i.e. at the meeting
  sapient: *will know*; future tense
  gravius quid: *anything more serious*; quid is
  indefinite after sī
5 **sī...acciderit, poscent**: *happens...will demand*;
  future more vivid (sī fut. pf., fut.), see, p. 59
  quī: *(and these) who*
  sī...liceat, sustineat...nōn...intereant: *should
  be allowed... would endure...would not perish*;
  future less vivid (sī + pres. subj., pres. subj.),
  licet, sustineō, and intereō; see box, p. 61
  per tē: *by you*; "through you"
  perendinō diē: *on...*; abl. time when
6 **hībernīs**: *winter-quarters*; throughout this
  episode hīberna denotes a winter camp
  commūnem...bellī cāsum: bellī is a genitive
  of description modifying cāsum
7 **nōn...intereant**: *would not die*; nōn modifies
  the finite verb, pres. subj. intereō
8 **cōnsurgitur**: *they rise from council*; "it is
  arisen (by them) from the council," impersonal
  passive governs a dat. of agent, here missing)
  and is often translated in the active, see p. 57
  comprehendunt utrumque: *they detain both*;
  i.e. the centurions stop Sabinus and Cotta
  ōrant nē: *plead that...not*; negative ind.
  command governs pres. subj. in primary seq.
9 **facilem esse rem**: *(and) that the matter*; ind.
  disc. governed by ōrant, asyndeton, add "et"
10 **seu...seu**: *whether...or*; sīve...sīve, introduces
   and indirect question with present subjunctives

sī modo: *provided that...*; "if only," a proviso
clause governs a present subjunctive
contrā: *on the other hand*
11 **nūllam sē salūtem perspicere**: *that they...*; sē
   is acc. subj., nūllam salūtem is acc. d.o. in
   indirect discourse governed by ōrant and
   parallel to "facilem esse rem" above
   Rēs: *the matter*; i.e. the discussions
12 **dat manūs**: *gives his hands*; i.e. surrenders
13 **sententia**: *the opinion*
   prīmā lūce: abl. of time when
   (eōs) itūrōs (esse): *that they...*; fut. inf. eō, īre
14 **vigiliīs**: *with night-watches*
   sua...circumspiceret: *looks over his own
   things*; i.e. inspects equipment, gear, property
   quisque: *each...*; an adjective modifying mīles
   quid..posset: *what he was able...*; impf. subj.
   possum in indirect question; with sua, this
   construction is an example of *prolepsis*
   (anticipation): "his things what he was able..."
   is equivalent to "what things he was able"
15 **quid...cōgerētur**: *(and) what he was forced*;
   ind. question parallel to the one above
   ex īnstrūmentō: *from the store, from the
   stock*; i.e. from the inventory
16 **quārē...maneātur...augeātur**: *for what
   reason they would remain not without
   danger and danger would be increased both
   by the fatigue and night-watches of the
   soldiers*; ind. question in apposition to omnia,
   the pres. subjunctive is potential subjunctive
17 **Prīma lūce**: *at...*; abl. time when
   castrīs: *the camp*; castra is plural in form but
   singular in translation
   ut...cōnsilium datum (esse): *as (if men) who
   had been persuaded that the plan had been
   given (to them) not by an enemy but by a man
   most friendly, Ambiorix*; ut here is equivalent
   to "ut sī," which introduces a conditional
   sentence of comparison with the subjunctive
   (apodosis is missing); plpf. pass. subj. of
   persuādeō is used impersonally (common in
   verbs governing a dative), the dat. obj. quibus
   may be translated as subject; dātum (esse) is a
   pf. pass. inf. in an acc. + inf. construction that
   is subject of persuāsum esset. An alternative
   translation is "as if (men) who had been
   persuaded by Ambiorix not as an enemy but as
   a man most friendly (to them)"
19 **longissimō agmine maximīs impedīmentīs.**:
   ablative absolutes; add pple "being" for each

32.1 At hostēs, posteāquam ex nocturnō fremitū vigiliīsque dē profectiōne   1
eōrum sēnsērunt, collocātīs īnsidiīs bipertītō in silvīs, opportūnō atque
occultō locō, ā mīlibus passuum circiter duōbus Rōmānōrum adventum
exspectābant 2. et, cum sē maior pars agminis in magnam convallem
dēmīsisset, ex utrāque parte eius vallis subitō sē ostendērunt novissimōsque   5
premere et prīmōs prohibēre ascensū atque inīquissimō nostrīs locō proelium
committere coepērunt.

33.1 Tum dēmum Titūrius, quī nihil ante prōvīdisset, trepidāre et
concursāre cohortēsque dispōnere, haec tamen ipsa timidē atque ut eum
omnia dēficere vidērentur; quod plērumque eīs accidere cōnsuēvit, quī in ipsō   10
negōtiō cōnsilium capere cōguntur. 2. At Cotta, quī cōgitāsset haec posse in
itinere accidere atque ob eam causam profectiōnis auctor non fuisset, nūllā in
rē commūnī salūtī dēerat, et in appellandīs cohortandīsque mīlitibus
imperātōris et in pugnā mīlitis officia praestābat. 3. Cum propter
longitūdinem agminis minus facile omnia per sē obīre et, quid quōque locō   15
faciendum esset, prōvidēre possent, iussērunt prōnūntiāre, ut impedīmenta
relinquerent atque in orbem cōnsisterent. 4. Quod cōnsilium etsī in eiusmodī
cāsū reprehendendum nōn est, tamen incommodē accidit:

agmen, agminis n.: column, battle line, formation, 3
ante: before, in front of (acc); *adv.* before, 4
ascensus, -ūs m.: ascent, climb, 1
auctor, auctoris m.: agent, doer, cause, 4
bipertītō: in two parts, 1
coepī, coepisse, coeptum: to begin, 9
cogitō (1): to think, ponder, turn over, 1
cohortor, -ārī, cohortātum: urge on, incite 3
collocō (1): place together, gather, arrange, 4
committō, -ere: commence, commit, entrust 4
concursō (1): to run about, rush about, 1
consistō, -ere, -stitī: to stand (still), stop 2
convallis, -is m: valley, deep lowland, 1
dēficiō, -ere, -fēcī, -fectum: fail, give out on, 3
dēmittō, -ere, -mīsī, -missum: drop, sink, 1
dēmum: at length, finally, 1
dispōnō, -ere: to arrange distribute, 1
eiusmodī: of this kind; such; so, 3
exspectō (1): look out for, wait for, await, 3
fremitus, -ūs m.: roaring, murmuring, 1
imperātor, -oris m.: commander, leader, 2
incommodus, -a, -um: unfortunate, disastrous, 3

inīquus, -a, -um: uneven, unequal, not fair, 1
insidiae, -ārum, f.: ambush, plot, trap, 2
longitūdo, -inis f.: length, width, 2
negōtium, iī n.: business, task, 2
nocturnus, -a, -um: nocturnal, nightly, 3
novus, -a, -um: new, fresh, young, recent, 2
obeō, -īre, -īvī, -ītum: go to meet, attend to, 1
occultō (1): hide, conceal, 3
officium, -iī, n.: duty, obligation, 3
opportūnus, -a, -um: fit, suitable, useful, 2
orbis, -is m.: sphere, circle (+ terrae: world), 2
ostendō, -ere, -ī, ntus: show, promise, 2
posteāquam: after (+ indicative), 1
prōnuntiō (1): speak forth or in advance, 4
prōvideō, -ēre, -vīdī, -visum: to foresee, take precautions, prepare for 3
reprehendō, -ere, -dī: blame; hold back, 1
sentiō, -īre, -sī, sēnsum: to feel, realize, 3
silva, -ae f.: wood, forest, woodland, 4
timidus, -a, -um: fearful, shy, 1
trepidō (1): be agitated, be in confusion, 1
vigilia, -ae f.: watch (1/4 period of night), 3

1 **ex nocturnō fremitū vigiliīsque**: *from the roar at night and the night-watches*; i.e .the Roman soldiers had not settled down but instead stayed awake and made much noise
sensērunt: *they realized*

2 **collocātīs īnsidiīs**: abl. absolute
bipertītō: *in two parts*; adverb
opportūnō...locō: *in...*; abl. place where in apposition to in silvīs

3 **ā mīlibus passuum circiter duōbus**: *about two miles away*; "from about two thousand of paces," partitive genitive;

4 **maior pars agminis**: i.e. the Romans
cum...dēmīsisset: *when...had dropped*; plpf. subjunctive

5 **ex utrāque parte**: *on both sides*; "from each side"
eius vallis: *of this valley*; eius is demonstrative
nōvissimōs: *the rear (soldiers)*; the "most recent" soldiers are the "last" or "rear" soldiers in a column of soldiers, the enemy is attacking the rear and front of the battle column

6 **premere, prohibēre, committere**: all of the infinitives are governed by coepērunt
prīmōs: *first (soldiers)*; the front of the column
ascensū: *from...*; abl. of separation
inīquissimō nostrīs locō: *(in) a place most unfair to our (men)*; place where, superlative
proelium committere: *commence battle*; idiom

8 **tum dēmum**: *then at last*
Titūrius: *Sabinus*; Quintus Titūrius Sabinus
quī...prōvīdisset: *since he had foreseen nothing beforehand*; "who had foreseen nothing beforehand," quī + plpf subjunctive is a relative clause causal in sense, equivalent to a cum-clause (quī = cum is) causal in sense; cf. l. 11
trepidāre, concursāre, dispōnere: historical infinitives with nom. Titūrius as subject, translate all three in the 3ʳᵈ sg. imperfect; at times used to give a rapid sequence of events

9 **haec ipsa**: *(he did) these very things*; neuter pl. acc., supply a verb
ut...omnia...vidērentur: *so that all (his wits) seemed*; a result clause, omnia is subject; videor is frequently translated as "seem;" the

word "omnia" pertains to his internal turmoil
eum: *him*; i.e. Titūrius, object of dēficere

10 **quod...cōnsuēvit**: *which was accustomed*
eīs: *to those*; dat. of interest with accidere

11 **cōnsilium capere**: *to adopt a plan*; idiom
quī cōgitāsset...fuisset: *since he had realized ...and had been*; "who had realized..." just as above quī + plpf. subjunctives in a relative clause causal in sense, equivalent to a cum-clause (quī = cum is) causal in sense
haec posse: *that these things...*; neut .pl. acc. subject of inf. of possum

12 **ob eam causam**: *for this reason*; "on account of this reason"
fuisset: pluperfect subjunctive of sum
nūllā in rē: in nūllā rē; order emphasizes adj.

13 **commūnī salūtī**: dat. object of impf. dēsum
in appellandīs cohortandīsque mīlitibus: both are gerundives modifying mīlitibus, use a gerund-gerundive flip

14 **(officia) imperātōris**: add "officia;" there is a contrast between the officia imperātōris and officia mīlitis
praestābat: *performed*

15 **minus**: *less*; comparative adv. modifies facile
facile: *easily*; irregular adv. of facilis, facile
omnia...obīre: *to attend to everything*
quōque: *in each...*; abl. place where, quisque

16 **faciendum esset**: *had to be done*; "was going to be done," gerundive + sum (here, impf. subj.) is a pass. periphrastic expressing necessity; subjunctive in an ind. question
possent: *they were able*; Cotta and Titūrius
prōnūntiāre: *that (the centurions) command...*; + indirect command
ut...cōnsisterent: ind. command, impf. subj.

17 **in orbem**: *in a circle*; so that all soldiers have their backs to one another and fight forward
Quod: *this...*; "which" translate the relative adj. as a demonstrative adj. with cōnsilium

18 **reprehendendum nōn est**: *must not be blamed*; gerundive + sum is a pass. periphrastic expressing necessity or obligation
incommodē: *unadvantageously, disastrously*

Cum-Clauses			
Cum haec verba audīvit	1. temporal	*When he heard these words*
Cum haec verba audīvisset	2. circumstantial	*When/After he had heard these words*
	3. causal	*Since/Because he had heard these words*
	4. concessive	*Although he had heard these words*

33.5 nam et nostrīs mīlitibus spem minuit et hostēs ad pugnam alacriōrēs   1
effēcit, quod nōn sine summō timōre et dēspērātiōne id factum vidēbātur.
Praetereā accidit, quod fierī necesse erat, ut vulgō mīlitēs ab signīs
discēderent, quae quisque eōrum cārissima habēret, ab impedīmentīs petere
atque arripere properāret, clāmōre et flētū omnia complērentur.   5

34.1 At barbarīs cōnsilium nōn dēfuit. Nam ducēs eōrum tōtā aciē
prōnūntiāre iussērunt, nē quis ab locō discēderet: illōrum esse praedam atque
illīs reservārī quaecumque Rōmānī reliquissent: proinde omnia in victōriā
posita existīmārent. 2. Erant et virtūte et studiō pugnandī parēs; nostrī,
tametsī ab duce et ā Fortūnā dēserēbantur, tamen omnem spem salūtis in   10
virtūte pōnēbant, et quotiēns quaeque cohors prōcurrerat, ab eā parte magnus
numerus hostium cadēbat. 3. Quā rē animadversā, Ambiorix prōnūntiārī
iubet, ut procul tēla coniciant neu propius accēdant et, quam in partem
Rōmānī impetum fēcerint, cēdant (levitāte armōrum et cōtidiānā
exercitātiōne nihil eīs nocērī posse), 4. rūrsus sē ad signa recipientēs   15
īnsequantur.

35.1 Quō praeceptō ab eīs dīligentissimē observātō, cum quaepiam cohors
ex orbe excesserat atque impetum fēcerat, hostēs vēlōcissimē refugiēbant.
2. Interim eam partem nūdārī necesse erat et ab latere apertō tēla recipī.

---

aciēs, -ēī f.: sharp edge, battle line, army, 2
alacer, alacris, alacre: eager, spirited, 1
aperiō, -īre, -uī, -ertus: open, disclose, 3
arripiō, -ere, -ripuī: to grab, snatch, lay hold of, 1
cadō, cadere, cecidī, cāsūrum: to fall, 1
cārus, -a, -um: dear, precious, costly, 1
cēdō, -ere, cessī, cessus: withdraw, move, 2
clāmor, clāmoris m.: shout, cry, 2
compleō, -ēre, -ēvī, -ētum: fill up, fill, 6
cotidiānus, -a, -um: daily, of every day, 3
dēserō, -ere, -ruī: desert, forsake, abandon, 1
dēspērātio, -tiōnis f.: hopelessness, despair 1
dīligēns, -entis: careful, diligent, accurate, 2
dux, ducis m../f.: leader, guide, chief, 4
excēdō, -ere, cessī, -cessum: go out, 3
exercitātio, -iōnis f.: training, practice, 2
fiō, fierī, factus: become, be made, 3
flētus, -ūs m.: weeping, wailing, 1
fortūna, -ae f.: fortune, chance, luck, 4
impetus, -ūs m.: attack, onset, assault, 7
insequor, -sequī, -secūtus: follow, ensue, 1
latus, -eris n.: side, flank, 2
levitās, -tātis f.: lightness; inconstancy, 1
minuō, -ere, minuī: to diminish, ebb, 2
necesse: necessary; (it is) necessary, 4
nēve, neu: or not, and not, nor, 2

noceō, -ēre, -uī, -itum: harm, injure, hurt, 2
nudō (1): to make naked or bare, uncover, 1
observō (1): watch, observe, attend to, 2
orbis, -is m.: sphere, (+ terrae: world), 2
pār, paris: equal, similar, even, 2
praecipiō, -ere, -cēpī, -ceptum: receive in
    advance, instruct, admonish, 2
praeda, -ae f.: loot, spoils, cattle, 2
praetereā: besides, hereafter, 2
procul: far, from a distance, from afar, 3
prōcurrō, ere, currī, cursum: run forward, 2
proinde: then, therefore, consequently, 1
prōnuntiō (1): speak forth or in advance, 4
properō (1): to hasten, complete quickly, 1
proprius: more closely, nearer, 3
quīcumque, quae-, quod-: whosoever, 4
quispiam, quae-, quod-: anyone, anything (adj. any), 2
quotiens: as often as, how often?, 1
refugiō, -ere, -fūgī: to flee back, run back, 1
reservō (1): lay up, save up, reserve, 1
rursus: again, backward, back, 4
studium, -ī n.: zeal, enthusiasm, pursuit, 3
tametsi: even if, although, though, 1
timor, -oris m.: fear, dread, anxiety, 2
vēlox, vēlōcis adj.: swift, rapid, quick, 1
vulgus, -ī n.: mass, mob, multitude, 2

1 **nostrīs mīlitibus**: *for our soldiers*; dat. interest
alacriōrēs: comparative adjective

2 **effēcit**: *made (x) (y)*; double acc., alacriōrēs is in the predicative position
quod: *because*
factum (esse): pf. pass. inf. following vidēbātur
vidēbātur: *seemed*; impf. pass.

3 **accidit**: *it happened*; governs the noun result clause ut…complērentur
quod fierī…erat: *(which it was necessary to happen)*; parenthetical, inf. fiō
vulgō: *commonly, generally*; abl. as adverb
signīs: *the standards*; i.e. military standards

4 **habēret**: *considered*; "held," impf. subj. in a relative clause of characteristic, governs a double accusative

6 **barbarīs…dēfuit**: *fail the barbarians*; dat. of interest
tōtā aciē: *on the entire battle line*; place where

7 **prōnūntiāre**: *commanded*; dūcēs is acc. subj., the inf. governs the ind. command (nē)
nē quis: *that not anyone…*; aliquis, aliquid is a common indefinite pronoun (anyone, anything), but quis, quid is commonly used as an indefinite (who → anyone, what → anything) after sī, nisi, num, and nē. The mnemonic for this construction is the jingle "After sī, nisi, num, and nē, all the ali's go away" (in other words indefinite aliquid becomes just quid)

7 **illōrum esse praedam**: *(and) that the loot was theirs*; i.e. the Gauls', the indirect discourse is parallel to the ind. command and likewise governed by prōnūntiāre
illīs: *for them*; dat. of interest

8 **quaecumque…reliquissent**: *whatsoever…*; relative clause of characteristic (plpf. subj.); the misssing antecedent is acc. subject of reservārī
proinde…existīmārent: *therefore let them*

think that; a jussive (volitive) subjunctive in indirect discourse remains a subjunctive; in secondary sequence the pres. subj. is impf.

9 **posita (esse)**: *have been put aside*; i.e. the loot from the Romans is waiting for the Gauls to take it; ind. discourse, omnia is acc. subject
et virtūte et studiō: *both in…*; abl. of respect qualifying parēs
pugnandī: gen. sg. gerund
nostrī: *our (soldiers)*; nom. subject

10 **Fortūnā**: fortūnā is personfied as a goddess

11 **ab eā parte**: *from that side*

12 **Quā rē animadversā**: *with this matter…*; abl. abs.; translate the relative as demonstrative
prōnūntiārī…ut: *it to be commanded that…*; pass. inf. governs indirect command

13 **neu**: *and not*; nēve
quam in partem: *in whatever direction…*; relative clause of characteristic with pf. subjunctive of faciō

14 **cēdant**: *they withdraw (from this direction)*

15 **nihil**: *not at all*; adverbial accusative
eīs…posse: *that it is possible for them*; ind. discourse with an impersonal inf. possum
sē…recipientēs: *(the Romans) while retreating to their standards*; i.e. attack the Romans as they try to relign themselves with the fixed military standards for each unit acc. d.o. of īnsequantur

16 **īnsequantur**: pres. subjunctive, part of the indirect command introduced by ut in line 13

17 **Quō praeceptō…**: *this instruction…*; abl. abs.
ab eīs: i.e. by the Gauls
dīligentissimē: superlative adverb
quaepiam cohors: *any cohort*

18 **vēlōcissimē**: superlative adverb, *vēlōx, vēlōcis*

19 **necesse erat**: *it was necessary*
recipī: pres. pass. inf., tēla is neuter acc. subj.

Ablative Absolute in Translation

Absolutes are circumstantial, causal, or concessive in sense, even if the translation does not reveal it. Cum-Clauses are just as versatile and can have a similar variety of uses within a Latin sentence.

verbīs audītīs	1. raw translation	*(with) the words having been heard…*
	2. Circumstantial	***When/After*** *the words had been heard…*
	3. Causal	***Since/Because*** *the words had been heard…*
	4. Concessive	***Although*** *the words had been heard…*
Caesar audiente	1. raw translation	*(with) Caesar listening*
	2. Circumstantial	***When/While*** *Caesar is/was listening…*
	3. Causal	***Since/Because*** *Caesar is/was listening…*
	4. Concessive	***Although*** *Caesar is/was listening…*

35.3 Rūrsus cum in eum locum unde erant ēgressī revertī coeperant, et ab   1
eīs quī cesserant et ab eīs quī proximī steterant circumveniēbantur; 4. sīn
autem locum tenēre vellent, nec virtūtī locus relinquēbatur neque ab tantā
multitūdine coniecta tēla confertī vitāre poterant. 5. Tamen tot incommodīs
cōnflictātī, multīs vulneribus acceptīs, resistēbant; et magnā parte diēī   5
cōnsūmptā, cum ā prīmā lūce ad hōram octāvam pugnārētur, nihil quod
ipsīs esset indignum committēbant. 6. Tum Titō Balventiō, quī superiōre
annō prīmum pīlum dūxerat, virō fortī et magnae auctōritātis, utrumque
femur trāgulā trāicitur; 7. Quintus Lucānius, eiusdem ōrdinis, fortissimē
pugnāns, dum circumventō fīliō subvenit, interficitur; 8. Lucius Cotta lēgātus   10
omnēs cohortēs ordinēsque adhortāns in adversum ōs fundā vulnerātur.

36.1 Hīs rēbus permōtus Quintus Titūrius, cum procul Ambiorīgem suōs
cohortantem cōnspexisset, interpretem suum Gnaeum Pompeium ad eum
mittit rogātum ut sibi mīlitibusque parcat. 2. Ille appellātus respondit: si velit
sēcum colloquī, licēre; spērāre ā multitūdine impetrārī posse, quod ad   15
mīlitum salūtem pertineat; ipsī vērō nihil nocitum īrī, inque eam rem sē
suam fīdem interpōnere. Ille cum Cottā sauciō commūnicat, 3. sī videātur,
pugnā ut excēdant et cum Ambiorīge ūnā colloquantur: spērāre ab eō de suā
ac mīlitum salūte impetrārī posse. Cotta sē ad armātum hostem itūrum negat
atque in eō persevērat.   20

adhortor, -ārī, -ātum: encourage, urge on, 1
adversus, -a, -um: opposite, in front, 2
armātus, -a, -um: armed, armor-clad, 2
auctōritās, -tātis f.: influence, clout, 3
Balventius, -ī m.: Balventius, 1
cēdō, -ere, cessī, cessus: withdraw, move, 2
coepī, coepisse, coeptum: to begin, 9
cohortor, -ārī, cohortātum: urge on, incite 3
colloquor, -quī, -locūtum: to converse, 4
committō, -ere: commence, commit, entrust 4
communicō (1): share, impart, 4
confertus, a, um: crowded together, dense, 3
conflictō (1): contend with, harm, 1
conspiciō, -ere, spexī, spectus: see, behold 5
consumō, -ere, -sumpsī: to use up, spend, 2
eō, īre, īvī, itum: to go, come, 4
excēdō, -ere, cessī, -cessum: go out, 3
femur, femorī n.: thigh, 1
fīdēs, eī f.: faith, honor, 4
funda, ae f.: sling, 3
Gnaeus, -ī m.: Gnaeus, 1
hora, -ae f.: hour, 4
impetrō (1): to obtain, accomplish, 3
incommodus, -a, -um: unfortunate, disastrous, 3
indignus, -a, -um: unworthy, undeserving, 1

interpōnō, -ere, -posuī; include, introduce, 2
interpres, interpretis m/f.: messenger, 1
Lucānius, -ī m.: Lucanius, 1
lūx, lūcis, f.: light, 3
nec: and not, nor (nec,nec = neither,nor) 2
negō (1): to deny, say that…not, 2
noceō, -ēre, -uī, -itum: harm, injure, hurt, 2
octāvus, -a, -um: eighth, 1
ōs, ōris n.: face, mouth 1
parcō, -ere, pepercī: to spare, refrain (dat), 2
persevērō (1): to persist, persevere, 1
pīlum, -ī n.: pilum, javelin, 3
Pompeius, -iī m.: Pompey, 1
procul: far, from a distance, from afar, 3
respondeō, -ēre, -dī, -ōnsum: to answer, 3
revertor, -ī, reversus sum: to turn back, return, 2
rogō (1): to ask; tell, 2
rursus: again, backward, back, 4
saucius, -a, -us: wounded, injured, hurt, 1
sīn: but if, if however, 1
stō, -āre, stetī, stātum: stand still, stop, 3
subveniō, -īre, -vēnī, -ventum: come up to, aid, relieve, 2
Titus, -ī m.: Titus, 4
tot: so many, 2

trāgula, -ae f.: tragula (a Gallic javelin) 3
trāiciō, -icere, -iēcī, -iectum: pierce, cast across, 2
unde: whence, from which source, 3
vērō: in truth, truly, in fact, to be sure, 3

vir, virī m.: man, 4
vītō (1): avoid, evade, shun, 1
vulnerō (1): wound, injure, 3
vulnus, -eris n.: wound, blow, 3

---

1 **unde erant ēgressī**: plpf. dep. ēgredior
   revertī: present deponent inf.
2 **cesserant**: *had withdrawn*; As some of the
   Romans made attacks from the circle (orbis),
   the opposing enemy withdrew temporarily and
   the flanks (quī proximī steterant) attacked.
   When the Romans returned to the circle, the
   opposing enemy would advance once again
3 **locum tenēre**: *to hold ground*; i.e. if the
   Romans did not advance in groups but instead
   remained together in the circle
   vellent: *they should wish*; an impf. subjunctive,
   the protasis of a mixed condition in secondary
   sequence;
   nec...neque: *neither...nor*; linking the apodosis
   locus: *opportunity*...
   virtūtī: *for valor*; dat. of purpose
4 **confertī**: modifies the nom. subject
   incommodīs cōnflictātī: *harmed by so many
   disadvantages*
5 **multīs...accēptīs**: ablative absolute
   resistēbant: *they kept on fighting*; iterative
   impf.
   magnā...cōnsūmptā: abl. absolute
6 **cum...pugnārētur**: *although they fought*; cum
   is concessive in force; impersonal passive p. 57
   quod ipsīs...indignum: *which was unworthy of
   the Romans themselves*; indignus, "unworthy
   of," governs an abl., here the intensive ipsīs
7 **Titō Balventiō**: *to Titus Balventius*; dat. of
   interest
   superiōre annō: *in...*; abl. of time when
8 **prīmum pīlum**: *the first pilum*; the officer
   known as Primus Pilus was the highly ranked
   centurion who threw the first pīlum in battle;
   Titus held this rank during the previous year
   virō fortī: dat. in apposition to Titō Balventiō
   magnae auctōritātis: *of great clout*; gen. of
   quality parallel with dative fortī
   utrumque femur: *each thigh*; neuter subject
9 **eiusdem ōrdinis**: *of the same rank*; gen. quality
   fortissimē: superlative adverb
   pugnāns: nom. sg. pres. pple, pugnō
10 **subvenit**: *he is approaching to help*
11 **in adversum ōs**: *full on the mouth*; "onto the
   opposing mouth," acc. place to which; another
   meaning for ōs, ōris is "face"

12 **hīs rēbus**: *because of these things*; abl. cause
   suōs: *his own (men)*; i.e. Ambiorix's men, the
   reflexive should grammatically refer to the
   subject Cotta's men but it does not
13 **eum**: *him*; i.e. Ambiorix
14 **rogātum**: *to ask*; supine (PPP + um) in the
   accusative expresses purpose, which in
   English is often expressed with an infinitive
   ut...parcat: ind. command following rogātum
   sibi mīlitibusque: *him and (his) soldiers*; i.e.
   Cotta and his soldiers
   sī velit: *if he wishes*; subordinate clauses in
   ind. discourse often fall into the subjunctive;
   here a pres. subjunctive of volō, velle in what
   was originally a present simple condition
15 **sēcum**: cum sē
   licēre: *it is allowed (for him)*; i.e. for Titurius,
   ind. discourse with an impersonal verb
   spērāre: *that (he) hoped*; i.e. Ambiorix hoped
   ā multitūdine: i.e. from the Gauls
   quod..pertineat: *(that) which...*; the missing
   antecedent is acc. subject of posse impetrārī;
   this is a relative clause of characeristic with
   the present subjunctive
16 **ipsī**: *that for (Titurius) himself*; dative interest
   or possible a dat. of agent *with nocitum īrī*
   nihil: *not at all*; "in no way," acc. of respect
   nocitum īrī: *it would not be harmed*; "it is
   going to be harmed:" a future passive inf.
   (supine + pres. pass. inf. of eō, īre), here
   impersonal
   ipsī...nocitum īrī: *that indeed he himself
   would not at all be harmed*; "indeed for him
   himself not at all it was going to be harmed,"
   a rare future passive inf. (supine + pres. pass.
   inf. of eō, īre), here impersonal
   sē...interpōnere: *he gave his pledge*
17 **Ille**: *that one*; i.e. Titurius speaks with Cotta
   videātur: *it seems good*; i.e. if he agrees
   with Ambiorix's terms; subordinate clauses in
   ind. discourse govern a subjunctive
   pugnā: *from battle*; abl. separation
   ut...colloquantur: *(namely) that...*; noun
   result clause governed by impersonal videātur
18 **spērāre**: *that (Cotta) hoped*; see also line 15
   ab eō: *from him*; i.e. from Ambiorix
19 **sē itūrum esse**: fut. inf. eō, īre

37.1 Sabīnus quōs in praesentiā tribūnōs mīlitum circum sē habēbat et　1
prīmōrum ōrdinum centuriōnēs sē sequī iubet et, cum propius Ambiorīgem
accessisset, iussus arma abicere, imperātum facit suīsque ut idem faciant
imperat. 2. Interim, dum dē condiciōnibus inter sē agunt longiorque cōnsultō
ab Ambiorīge īnstituitur sermō, paulātim circumventus interficitur. 3. Tum　5
vērō suō mōre 'Victōriam' conclāmant atque ululātum tollunt impetūque in
nostrōs factō ōrdinēs perturbant. 4. Ibi Lucius Cotta pugnāns interficitur cum
maximā parte mīlitum. Reliquī sē in castra recipiunt unde erant ēgressī; 5. ex
quibus Lucius Petrosidius aquilifer, cum magnā multitūdine hostium
premerētur, aquilam intrā vallum proiēcit; ipse prō castrīs fortissimē pugnāns　10
occīditur. Illī aegrē ad noctem oppugnātiōnem sustinent; 6. noctū ad unum
omnēs, dēspērātā salūte, sē ipsī interficiunt. 7. Paucī ex proeliō lapsī incertīs
itineribus per silvās ad Titum Labiēnum legātum in hīberna perveniunt atque
eum dē rēbus gestīs certiōrem faciunt.

38.1 Hāc victōriā sublātus Ambiorīx statim cum equitātū in Aduatucōs, quī　15
erant eius regnō fīnītimī, proficīscitur; neque noctem neque diem intermittit
peditātumque sēsē subsequī iubet. 2. Rē dēmonstrātā Aduatucīsque concitātīs
posterō diē in Nerviōs pervenit hortāturque, nē suī in perpetuum liberandī
atque ulcīscendī Rōmānōs prō eīs, quās acceperint, iniūriīs occāsiōnem
dīmittant: 3. interfectōs esse lēgātōs duōs magnamque partem exercitūs　20
interīsse dēmōnstrat; 4. nihil esse negōtī, subitō oppressam legiōnem quae
cum Cicerōne hiemet interficī; sē ad eam rem profitētur adiūtōrem. Facile
hāc ōrātiōne Nerviīs persuādet.

abiciō, -ere, -iēcī, -iectum: throw aside or away, 2
adiūtor, -ōris m.: helper, assistant, 2
aeger, -gra, -grum: sick, weary; *adv.* scarcely, 4
agō, agere, ēgī, āctum: drive, lead, do, 4
aquila, -ae f.: eagle, eagle standard, 4
aquilifer, -ferī m.: eagle-bearer, 1
centurio, -iōnis m.: centurion, 4
circum: around, round about, 2
concitō (1): stir up, incite, impel, 2
conclāmō (1): cry out together, shout, 2
condiciō, -ciōnis f.: arrangement, state, 2
consultō: on purpose, deliberately, 3
dēspērō (1): to have no hope, give up, 2
dīmittō, -ere, -mīsī, -missus: lose, send (away), 3
hiemō (1): spend the winter, 3
hortor, -ārī, hortātum: encourage, urge, 2
incertus, -a, -um: unreliable, doubtful, 2
iniūria, -ae f.: wrong, insult, injustice, 4
instituō, -ere, -uī, -ūtum: set, establish, 3
intereō, -īre, -īvī, -ītum: to die, perish, 3
intrā: within, among (+ acc.), 3

lābor, lābī, lapsum: glide, slide, slip, 1
līberō (1): free, liberate, 3
mōs, mōris m.: custom, manner, law, 4
negōtium, iī n.: business, task, 2
noctū: by night; abl. as adv. nox, noctis, 4
occāsio, -iōnis f.: opportunity, occasion, 2
occīdō, -ere, occidī, occīsus: kill, cut down 4
opprimō, -ere, -pressī, -pressum: crush,
　burden, overwhelm, 3
paucī, -ae, -a: little, few, scanty, 4
paulātim: gradually, little by little, 3
peditātus, -ūs m.: infantry, 3
perpetuus, -a, -um: constant, everlasting, 4
Petrosidius, -ī m.: Petrosidius, 1
posterus, -a, -um: next, following, 2
praesentia, -ae f.: presence, 2
profiteor, -ērī, -fessum: profess, declare, 1
proicio, -icere, -iēcī, -iectum: throw
　forward, project, 2
proprius: more closely, nearer, 3
sequor, -ī, secūtus: follow, pursue, 4

sermo, -mōnis m.: conversation, discourse, 3
silva, -ae f.: wood, forest, woodland, 4
statim: immediately, at once, 4
Titus, -ī m.: Titus, 4
tollō, ere, sustulī, sublātum: raise, destroy, 2

tribūnus, -ī m.: tribune, officer, 2
ulcīscor, -ī, ultum: avenge, take vengeance 1
ululātus, -ūs m.: howling, wailing, yelling, 1
unde: whence, from which source, 3
vērō: in truth, truly, in fact, to be sure, 3

---

1 **quōs...tribūnōs mīlitum...habēbat**: *those tribunes of the soldiers whom...*; tribūnōs is antecedent—not part of—quōs...habēbat
2 **sequī**: inf. sequor
  iubet: both tribūnōs, centuriōnēs are objects
3 **accessisset**: plpf. subjunctive accēdō
  iussus: PPP iubeō, iubēre
  imperātum facit: *carries out the command*; "the thing having been commanded" PPP
  suīs: *his own (men)*; dat. object of imperat
  ut...faciant: ind. command
  idem: *the same thing*; id-dem, neuter acc. sg.
4 **dē condiciōnibus...agunt**: *they talk about the conditions..*; common idiom employing agō and dē + ablative, here the conditions of surrender
  inter sē: *with one another*; 'among themselves'
  longior...īnstituitur sermō: *a longer conversation is arranged*
  cōnsultō: *deliberately*; ablative as an adverb
5 **circumventus**: the nom. subject is Sabīnus
6 **suō mōre**: *by their custom*; "from their custom"
  Victōriam: Latin exclamation take the acc.
7 **impetū...factō**: ablative absolute
  in nostrōs: *against our (soldiers)*
8 **Reliquī**: *the remaining (men)*; i.e. the survivors
  sē...recipiunt: *retreat*; "take themselves back"
9 **erant ēgressī**: plpf. deponent ēgredior
  ex quibus: *from these*; for transitions, English speakers prefer a demonstrative
10 **aquilam**: *the eagle*; i.e. the entire wooden standard which contained the golden image of an eagle on top; the aquilifer saves the eagle from capture as one today might save a flag
  vallum: i.e. the wall of the camp, which often consisted of mound of earth with a wooden palisade on top and a deep ditch below
  prō: *in front of*; + ablative
  pugnāns: pres. pple, pugnō
11 **aegrē...sustinent**: *with difficulty sustained*; "scarcely sustained"
  ad noctem: *till the night*
  noctū: *at night*; adverb
  ad ūnum: *to the man*
12 **dēspērātās salūte**: abl. abs.
  ipsī: *themselves*; nom. pl., intensive pronoun

lapsī: *having slipped*; pf. deponent pple labor
incertīs itineribus: *by uncertain routes*
13 **in hīberna**: *into winter-quarters*; a journey of about 100 miles at this time
14 **certiōrem faciunt**: *inform*; "make him more certain;" a common idiom in Caesar
  gestīs: *carried out*; PPP gerō
15 **sublātus**: *uplifted*; i.e. "elated," PPP tollō, as often, the prefix sub- means "from under up"
  in Aduatucōs: *to the Aduatuci*; or 'among...'
16 **regnō**: dative with the predicate adj. fīnītimī
17 **subsequī**: pres. deponent inf.
  Rē...concitātīs: two ablative absolutes
18 **posterō diē**: *on...*; ablative time when
  in Nerviōs: *to the Nervii, among the Nervii*
  nē...acceperint (et)...dīmittant: *that they not...*; negative ind. command governed by hortātur
  suī...liberandī: *of freeing themselves*; gen. sg. gerundive; when translating, employ a gerund-gerundive flip: make suī the gerund's object (sē), this genitive modifies occāsiōnem
19 **ulcīscendī Rōmānōs**: a gen. sg. gerund and acc. object (this construction is unusual since it is often expressed as a noun + modifying gerundive); parallel to liberandī and likewise modifying occāsiōnem
  prō eīs...iniūriīs: *(in return) for...*; eīs is a demonstrative modifying iniūriās
  quās acceperint: perfect subj. in a relative clause of characteristic; the antecedent is fem. plural iniūriīs
20 **interfectōs esse**: *that...*; pf. pass. infinitive interficiō with lēgātōs duōs as acc. subject
  lēgātōs duōs: i.e. Sabīnus and Cotta
21 **interīsse**: *to have perished*; interiisse, pf. inf. intereō with partem as acc. subject
  nihil esse negōtī: *that there is no trouble*; "nothing of business," negōtī is a partitive gen. the acc. + inf. is governed by profitētur below
  oppressam: *having been surprised*; opprimō
22 **hiemet**: pres. subj., verbs in subordinate clauses in ind. disc. are commonly subjunctive
  interficī: pres. passive inf., legiōnem is acc. subj.
  sē: *that he (was)*; ad esse; following profitētur

39.1 Itaque cōnfestim dīmissīs nuntiīs ad Ceutronēs, Grudiōs, Levācōs,   1
Pleumoxiōs, Geidumnōs, quī omnēs sub eōrum imperiō sunt, quam maximās
manūs possunt cōgunt et dē improvīsō ad Cicerōnis hīberna advolant
nōndum ad eum famā dē Titūrī morte perlātā. 2. Huic quoque accidit, quod
fuit necesse, ut nōnnūllī mīlitēs, quī lignātiōnis mūnītiōnisque causā in silvās   5
discessissent, repentīnō equitum adventū interciperentur. 3. Hīs circumventīs
magnā manū Eburōnēs, Nerviī, Aduatucī atque hōrum omnium sociī et
clientēs legiōnem oppugnāre incipiunt. Nostrī celeriter ad arma concurrunt,
vāllum conscendunt. 4. Aegrē is diēs sustentātur, quod omnem spem hostēs
in celeritāte pōnēbant atque hanc adeptī victōriam in perpetuum sē fore   10
victōrēs cōnfīdēbant.

40.1 Mittuntur ad Caesarem cōnfestim ab Cicerōne litterae magnīs
prōpositīs praemiīs, sī pertulissent: obsessīs omnibus viīs missī intercipiuntur.
2. Noctū ex materiā, quam mūnītiōnis causā comportāverant, turrēs
admodum CXX excitantur incrēdibilī celeritāte; quae dēesse operī vidēbantur,   15
perficiuntur. 3. Hostēs posterō diē, multō maiōribus coāctis copiīs, castra
oppugnant, fossam complent. Eādem ratiōne, quā prīdiē, ab nostrīs resistitur:
4. hoc idem reliquīs deinceps fit diēbus.

adipiscor, -ī, adeptum: get, obtain, reach, 1
admodum: completely, quite; just about, 2
advolō (1): to fly to, rush to, 1
aeger, -gra, -grum: sick, weary, 4
Ceutronēs, -um m.: Ceutrones (tribe) 1
cliens, -entis m.: client, dependent, 4
compleō, -ēre, -ēvī, -ētum: fill up, fill, 6
comportō (1): carry together, collect, 3
concurrō, -ere, -currī, -cursus: run eagerly, clash, 2
cōnfēstim: immediately, 4
cōnfīdō, -ere, cōnfīsus sum: trust, believe, rely upon, 4
conscendō, -ere, -ī, -ēnsus: climb, board, 1
deinceps: one after another, successively, 1
dīmittō, -ere, -mīsī, -missus: send (away), 3
excitō (1): excite, rouse up, raise, inspire, 3
fāma, -ae f.: rumor, story, hearsay, 2
fīō, fierī, factus: become, be made, 3
fossa, -ae f.: ditch, trench, 2
Geidumnī, -ōrum m.: Geidumnī, 1
Grudiī, -ōrum m.: Grudi, 1
improvīsus, -a, -um: unforeseen, unexpected, 1
incipiō, -ere, incēpī, inceptum: begin, 1
incrēdibilis, -e: unbelieveable, 1
intercipiō, -ere, -cēpī, -ceptum: catch, intercept, 3

Levācī, -ōrum m.: Levaci, 1
lignātio, -tiōnis f.: gathering of timber, 1
materia, -ae f.: timber, wood, material, 2
necesse: necessary; (it is) necessary, 4
noctū: by night; abl. as adv. nox, noctis, 4
nōndum: not yet, 3
nōnnullus, -a, -um: some, not none, 2
obsīdeō, -ēre, sēdī, sessum: besiege, beset, 2
opus, -eris n.: work, deed, toil, 2
perferō, -ferre, -tulī, -lātus: carry through, 2
perficiō, -ere: complete, accomplish, 3
perpetuus, -a, -um: constant, everlasting, 4
Pleumoxiī, -īorum m.: Pleumoxi, 1
posterus, -a, -um: next, following, 2
prīdiē: on the day before, the previous day, 1
prōpōnō, -ere, posuī, positum: to set forth, 1
quoque: also, 2
repentīnus, -a, -um: sudden, unexpected, 4
silva, -ae f.: wood, forest, woodland, 4
socius, -ī m.: comrade, ally, companion, 2
sustentō (1): to hold up, sustain, maintain, 1
via, -ae, f.: road, way, path, 2
victor, -ōris m.: conquerer, vanquisher, 1

2 **eōrum**: *their*; i.e. of the Nervii
quam maximās...possunt: *the largest groups (as) they are able*; quam + superl. = "as X as possible," possunt makes construction explicit
cōgunt: *they gather together*

3 **dē imprōvīsō**: *unexpectedly*; "from the unforeseen," often with preposition

4 **nōndum ad eum**: part of the abl. absolute from fāmā to perlātā
perlātā: PPP perferō
Titūrī: gen. sg., Quintus Titūrius Sabīnus

4 **Huic quoque**: *to this one also*; i.e. to Cicero
quod fuit necesse: *which was inevitable*

5 **ut...interciperentur**: *that...*; noun result clause governed by accidit
causā: *for the sake of...*; + preceding genitives

6 **discessissent**: *had gone out*; i.e. from the camp, plpf. subjunctive in a relative clause of characteristic

7 **Hīs circumventīs**: abl. absolute
magnā manū: *with a great band*; abl. of means with the ablative absolute

8 **Nostrī**: *our (soldiers)*

9 **conscendunt**: *(and) climb*; asyndeton, the lack of conjunctions suggests that the Romans were acting quickly and decisively
aegrē: *with difficulty*; adv. of aeger

10 **adeptī**: *having attained*; perfect deponent pple adipiscor
in perpetuum: *for ever*; "into perpetual (time)," supply neuter acc. tempus
fore: *would be*; alternative to futūrum esse, a fut. inf. in ind. discourse governed by cōnfīdēbant, sē is acc. subj.

12 **magnīs...praemiīs**: *...(to the messengers)*; abl. absolute; the offer is made to the messengers of the letters

13 **sī pertulissent**: *if (the messengers) had carried (the letters) through (to Caesar)*; protasis in a past contrary-to-fact condition
obsessīs...viīs: abl. absolute causal in force, the viae are likely paths or routes
missī: *(the messengers) sent*; PPP mittō

14 **noctū**: *at night*; ablative as adverb
causā: *for the sake of*; + preceding genitive

15 **incrēdibilī celeritāte**: *with...*; abl. of manner drops "cum" when there is an adjective, here i-stem 3rd declension
quae dēesse operī vidēbantur: *(the things) which seemed to be lacking for the work*; i.e. whatever seemed to be incomplete

16 **perficiuntur**: missing antecedent of the relative clause is subject
posterō diē: *on...*; time when
multō: *much...*; "by much," ablative of degree of difference with comparative maiōribus
maiōribus...copiīs: ablative absolute

17 **(et) fossam**: asyndeton
Eādem ratiōne: *by the same method*
quā (ratiōne) prīdīe: *in which (manner) (they resisted) the day before*; i.e. "as on the day before," relative clause, add ratiōne, resistitur
ab nostrīs resistitur: *our men resisted*; "it is resisted by our (men)," impers. pass. below

18 **hoc idem**: *this same thing*; id-dem, neuter singular nom. subject
fit: 3rd sg. pres. fiō; often passive for faciō
reliquīs...diēbus: *in...*; abl. time when

Impersonal Verb Constructions

Impersonal verbs are found in the 3rd sg. and translated with the subject "it." The passive of an intransitive verb (e.g. ventum est) is often used impersonally with dat. of agent but should be translated actively.

accidit	it happens + ut (noun result clause)	p. 18, 20, 28, 32, 48, 50, 56
constat	it is agreed	p. 18, 34
fās est	it is right + inf.	p. 28
fit	it happens/is done + ut (noun result clause)	p. 56
licet	it is allowed + inf.	p. 10, 32, 46, 52, 58
oportet	it is desirable/fitting/necessary + inf.	p. 6, 18
potest	it is possible	p. 10, 50
videtur	it seems +ut (noun result clause)	p. 52
cōnsurgitur	they rise (it is arisen)	p. 46
perventum est	they arrived (it was arrived)	p. 38
pugnārētur	they were fighting (it was fought)	p. 52, 64
pugnātum est	each side fought (it was fought by each side)	p. 14
resistitur	our men resisted (it was resisted by our men)	p. 56
ventum est	they came (it has been come)	p. 16, 38

40.5 Nūlla pars nocturnī temporis ad labōrem intermittitur; nōn aegrīs, nōn   1
vulnerātīs facultās quiētis dātur. 6. Quaecumque ad proximī dieī
oppugnātiōnem opus sunt, noctū comparantur; multae praeūstae sudēs,
magnus mūrālium pīlōrum numerus īnstituitur; turrēs contabulantur, pinnae
lorīcaeque ex crātibus attexuntur. 7. Ipse Cicerō cum tenuissimā valētūdine   5
esset, nē nocturnum quidem sibi tempus ad quiētem relinquēbat, ut ultrō
mīlitum concursū ac vōcibus sibi parcere cōgerētur.

41.1 Tunc ducēs prīncipēsque Nerviōrum quī aliquem sermōnis aditum
causamque amīcitiae cum Cicerōne habēbant colloquī sēsē velle dīcunt. 2.
Factā potestāte, eadem quae Ambiorīx cum Titūriō ēgerat commemorant: 10
omnem esse in armīs Galliam; 3. Germānōs Rhēnum trānsīsse; Caesaris
reliquōrumque hīberna oppugnārī. 4. Addunt etiam dē Sabīnī morte:
Ambiorīgem ostentant fideī faciendae causā. 5. Errāre eōs dīcunt, sī
quidquam ab hīs praesidī spērent, quī suīs rēbus diffīdant; sēsē tamen hōc esse
in Cicerōnem populumque Rōmānum animō, ut nihil nisi hīberna recūsent   15
atque hanc inveterāscere cōnsuētūdinem nōlint: 6. licēre illīs incolumibus per
sē ex hībernis discēdere et quāscumque in partēs velint sine metū proficīscī.

addō, -ere, -didī, -ditum: to bring to, add, 4
aditus, -ūs m.: approach, access, entrance, 2
aeger, -gra, -grum: sick, weary, 4
agō, agere, ēgī, āctum: drive, lead, do, 4
attexō, -ere, -texuī, textum: weave, add on 1
colloquium, -iī n.: conversation, talk, 1
commemorō (1): call to mind, recollect, 1
comparō (1): prepare, get ready, provide, 4
concursus, -ūs m.: running together, gathering, 1
contabulō (1): to equip with boarded platforms, 1
crātis, -is f.: (wicker) frame, fascines, 1
diffīdō, -ere, diffīsum: mistrust, despair (dat.), 1
dux, ducis m../f.: leader, guide, chief, 4
errō (1): to wander, rove, stray, 1
fīdēs, eī f.: faith, honor, 4
incolumis, -e: unscathed, uninjured, safe, 2
īnstituō, -ere, -uī, -ūtum: set, establish, 3
inveterāscō (1): to become old, 1
labor, -ōris m.: labor, hardship, task, 1
lorīca, -ae f.: parapet, breastwork, 1
metus, -ūs m.: dread, fear, 2
mūrālis, -e: of a wall, mural, 1
noctū: by night; abl. as adv. nox, noctis, 4

nocturnus, -a, -um: nocturnal, nightly, 3
nōlō, nolle, noluī: to refuse, be unwilling, 1
ostentō (1): show (off), display, point out, 1
parcō, -ere, pepercī: to spare, refrain (dat), 2
pīlum, -ī n.: pilum, javelin, 3
pinna, -ae f.: battlement on wall; feather, 1
potestās, -tātis f.: power, ability, capacity, 3
praesidium, -iī n.: guard, protection; assistance, 2
praeūstus, -a, -um: burned at the end, 1
princeps, -cipis m./f.: chief, leader, 4
quīcumque, quae-, quod-: whosoever, 4
quiēs, quiētis f.: rest, repose, sleep, 2
quisquam, quidquam: anyone, anything? 2
recūsō (1): to object to, refuse, reject, 1
sermo, -mōnis m.: conversation, discourse, 3
sudis, -is f.: stake, spike, 1
tenuis, -e: thin, slender, 1
tunc: then, at that time, 1
ultrō: voluntarily; moreover, beyond, 3
valētūdō, -dinis f.: state of health, health, 1
vōx, vōcis, f.: voice; utterance, word, 4
vulnerō (1): wound, injure, 3

1 **nocturnī temporis**: partitive genitive
ad labōrem: *for work*; expressing purpose it modifies the subject not the verb: the line reads "no part of the night time (devoted) for work is interrupted" whereas we would prefer "no part of the night time is interrupted from work"
aegrīs: *to the sick*; dat. indirect object

2 **vulnerātīs**: dat. indirect object
quiētis: gen. sg. quiēs
quaecumque...opus sunt: *whatsoever is the work (to be done)*; or "whatsoever is the need" opus est, "there is a need," often governs a dat. of interest and abl. of the object wanted; less frequently, as here, there is a subject and opus is the predicate
proximī diēī: gen. sg.

3 **noctū**: *at night*; abl. as adverb

4 **contabulantur**: *are equipped with boarded platforms*; the wooden towers are multi-storied with wood floors

5 **Ipse Cicerō**: nom. subj. within the cum-clause
cum..esset: *although he was*; impf. subjunctive in a cum-clause which is concessive in force
tenuissimā valētūdine: *of very weak health*; abl. of quality, predicate as esset

6 **nē...quidem**: *not even*; nē quidem emphasizes the intervening word
ad quiētum: *for...*; ad + acc. expresses purpose
ut...cōgerētur: *so that he was compelled*; impf. subj. in a result clause
ultrō: *voluntarily*

7 **parcere**: governs a dative

8 **aliquem...aditum**: *some (right of) entry into conversation*; the Nervii had previously established a rapport with the Romans that entitled them to approach and speak

9 **causamque amīcitiae**: *reason for friendship*
sēsē velle: *that they are willing*; i.e. Nervii, velle is a pres. inf. vōlō, colloquī is a deponent

complementary infinitive

10 **factā potestāte**: *permission having been given*; "opportunity having been made," idiom
ēgerat: *had discussed*; "had conducted"

11 **trānsīsse**: pf. inf. trānseō, Germānōs acc. subj.

12 **oppugnārī**: *are being assaulted*; pres. pass., hīberna, "winter-quarters" is acc. subject
Addunt: *they add*; i.e. "they say in addition"

13 **Ambiorīgem ostentant**: *they point to Ambiorix*
fīdeī faciendī: *of forming trust*; gen. sg. gerundive + noun; gerund-gerundive flip
eōs: *that they*; i.e. the Romans, acc. subject

14 **quidquam...praesidī**: *any protection*; "anything of protection," partitive gen.
spērent: *hoped*; impf. subj. in a subordinate clause in indirect discourse
quī...diffīdant: pres. subj. in a subordinate clause in indirect discourse
sēsē hōc esse...animō: *that they are of this mind toward...*; i.e. the Nerviī, abl. of quality as predicate

15 **in**: *toward...*
ut...recūset...nōlint: result clause, present subjunctive recūsō, nōlō
nihil nisi hīberna: *nothing except winter-quarters*; the Nerviī claim to be willing to be friends (see "amīcitiae" above) but will not allow the Romans to maintain a military camp in the territory of the Nervii

16 **licēre**: *that it is allowed for those...*; indirect disc., the infinitive represents an impersonal verb with governs a dat. of interest

17 **per sē**: *by themselves*
discēdere...proficīscī: infinitives, active and deponent, governed by licēre
quāscumque in partēs...velint: *in whatever directions they want/would want*; pres. subj. volō, in a relative clause of characteristic

---

Indicative Conditions In Secondary Sequence: Direct and Indirect Discourse

Simple Present (Pres., Pres.)
    dixī "sī credis, errās."   →   dixī sī haec crederēs, tē errāre
    I said, "if you believe this, you are wrong"   *I said that, if you believed this, you were wrong.*

Future More Vivid (fut. (pf.), fut.):
    dixī "sī credēs/credideris, errābis."   →   dixī sī haec crederēs, tē errātūrum esse
    I said, "if you believe this, you will be wrong"   *I said that, if you believed this, you would be wrong.*

Simple Past (past, past):
    dixī "sī credēbās/credidistī, errāvistī."   →   dixī sī haec crederēs/credidissēs, tē errāvisse.
    I said, "if you believed this, you were wrong"   *I said that, if you (had) believed this, you had been...*

for more, see p. 84

41.7 Cicerō ad haec ūnum modo respondit: nōn esse cōnsuētūdinem populī 1
Rōmānī accipere ab hoste armātō condiciōnem: 8. sī ab armīs discēdere velint,
sē adiūtōre ūtantur lēgātōsque ad Caesarem mittant; spērāre prō eius iūstitiā,
quae petierint, impertātūrōs.

42.1 Ab hāc spē repulsī Nerviī vallō pedum IX et fossā pedum XV hīberna 5
cingunt. 2. Haec et superiōrum annōrum cōnsuētūdine ab nōbīs cognōverant
et, quōs dē exercitū habēbant captīvōs, ab eīs docēbantur; 3. sed nūllā
ferramentōrum copiā, quae esset ad hunc ūsum idōnea, gladiīs caespitēs
circumcīdere, manibus sagulīsque terram exhaurīre vidēbantur. 4. Quā quidem
ex rē hominum multitūdō cognoscī potuit: nam minus hōrīs tribus mīlium 10
pedum XV in circuitū mūnītiōnem perfēcērunt 5. reliquīsque diēbus turrēs ad
altitūdinem vallī, falcēs testūdinēsque, quās īdem captīvī docuerant, parāre ac
facere coepērunt.

43.1 Septimō oppugnātiōnis diē, maximō coörtō ventō, ferventēs fusilī ex
argillā glandēs fundis et fervefacta iacula in casās, quae mōre Gallicō 15
strāmentīs erant tēctae, iacere coepērunt. 2. Hae celeriter ignem
comprehendērunt et ventī magnitūdine in omnem locum castrōrum
distulērunt.

adiūtor, -ōris m.: helper, assistant, 2
altitūdō, -inis f.: height, depth, altitude, 2
argilla, -ae f.: potter's clay, white clay, 1
armātus, -a, -um: armed, armor-clad, 2
caespes, -pitis m.: turf, sod, grass, 1
captīvus, -a, -um: prisoner, captive, 3
casa, casae f.: house, home, 1
cingō, -ere, cīnxī, cīnctus: surround, 1
circuitus, -ūs m.: circumference, circuit, 1
circumcīdō, -ere, -cīdī: cut around or off, 1
coepī, coepisse, coeptum: to begin, 9
comprehendō, -ere, -dī: seize, arrest; grasp 4
condiciō, -ciōnis f.: arrangement, state, 2
coörior, -īrī, coörtus: arise, break out, 2
discō, -ere, -didicī: learn, get to know, 2
differō, -ferre, distulī: carry different ways 2
doceō, -ēre, -uī, -ctus: teach, tell, 4
exhauriō, -īre, -īvī: take away, empty dry, 1
falx, falcis f.: grappling-hook; pruning-hook, 1
ferrāmenta, -ōrum n: iron tool, implement 1
fervefaciō, -ere, -fēcī: make hot, boil, melt, 1
ferveō, -ēre, ferbuī: glow hot; seethe, boil, 1
fossa, -ae f.: ditch, trench, 2
funda, ae f.: sling, 3
fusilis, -e: molten, liquid, soft, 1

Gallicus, -a, -um: Gallic, 1
gladius, -ī m.: sword, 3
glans, glandis m.: slug, bullet for sling, 1
hora, -ae f.: hour, 4
iaciō, iacere, iēcī, iactum: to throw, 4
iaculum, -ī n.: javelin, dart, 2
idōneus, -a, -um: suitable, appropriate, 1
ignis, ignis, m.: fire, 4
impetrō (1): obtain, accomplish, 3
iustitia, -ae f.: justice, fairness, equity, 1
modo: only, merely, simply; just now, 4
mōs, mōris m.: custom, manner, law, 4
nōs: we, 1
parō (1): prepare, make ready, 3
perficiō, -ere: complete, accomplish, 3
repellō, -ere, repulī, -pulsum: drive back, repulse, 1
respondeō, -ēre, -dī, -ōnsum: to answer, 3
sagulum, -ī n.: small military cloak, mantle 1
septimus, -a, -um: seventh, 1
strāmentum, -ī n.: straw; saddle, housing, 1
tegō, -ere, texī, tectum: to cover, 1
terra, -ae. f.: earth, ground, land, 2
testūdō, -tūdinis f.: tortoise, 2
ventus, ventī m.: wind, 3

1 **haec**: *these (things)*; neuter pl.
ūnum: *one (thing)*; neut. acc. sg., Caesar contrasts the multiple points of the Nervii with the single powerful point made by Cicero
modo: *just, only*; an adverb modifying ūnum

2 **nōn esse**: *it is not..*; ind. discourse; "accipere... condiciōnem" is the infinitive subject of esse and cōnsuētūdinem is the acc. predicate
ab armīs discēdere: *to lay down their weapons*; "to depart from their weapons"
sī...velint...ūtantur...mittant: *if they wish...let them employ...and send*; all pres. subj. in a mixed condition; in direct discourse the protasis velint is a fut. indicative and the apodosis verbs are imperatives or jussives, which in ind. discourse become jussives

3 **sē adiūtōre ūtantur**: *let them employ him (as) an advocate*; ūtor governs an ablative objects, adiūtōre is an abl. in the predicative position
spērāre: *(that) he hoped*; i.e. Cicero hoped
eius: *his*; i.e. Caesar's

4 **quae peti(v)erint**: *(the things) which*; pf. subj. of petō in a relative clause of characteristic, the missing antecedent is object of impertrātūrōs
impertātūrōs (esse): *that (they) would attain*; fut. infinitive; supply Nerviōs as acc. subject

5 **vallō...fossā**: ablative of means
pedum: *of feet*; gen. of measure

6 **haec**: *these things*; i.e. the vallum and fossa; object of cognōverant
et...et: *both...and*
superiōrum: *of previous*; comparative adj.
ab nōbīs: *from us*; abl. of source, the Nervii had learned their siege strategies from the Romans

7 **quōs...docēbantur...ab eīs**: *and by those, whom they were holding from our army as captives*; the antecedent of the relative quōs is the demonstrative eīs; capitīvōs is predicative

nūllā...copiā: *since there was...*; "(there being) no supply...", the construction is either an abl. of means or an abl. absolute, causal in force

8 **esset**: *was*; impf. sum in a relative clause of characteristic
ad hunc ūsum: *for...*; expressing purpose
gladiīs: abl. of means

9 **circumcīdere (et)...exhaurīre**: asyndeton, supply conjunction immediately after first inf., lack of conjunction suggests haste or speed
manibus sagulīsque: abl. of means
vidēbantur: they seemed; + complementary infs.; 'seem' is a common translation for videor
quā...ex rē: *from which matter*

10 **multitūdō**: i.e. the size of the population, the number of Nervii
cognōscī: pres. pass. inf.
minus hōrīs tribus: *in less than three hours*; comparative adv. + abl. of comparison; the time construction is abl. of time within

11 **mīlium pedum XV**: *15,000 feet*; "15 of thousands of feet" gen. of measure
reliquīs diēbus: *within...*; abl. time within

12 **ad altitūdinem vallī**: *(in proportion) to...*; the turrēs are as tall as the valla
īdem: eīdem, nom. pl. with captīvī; see line 7

14 **Septimō...diē**: *on...*; abl. time when
maximō coörtō ventō: abl. absolute
ferventēs: modifies glandēs; pres. pple acc. pl.
fusilī: modifies argillā; abl. sg., i-stem 3rd decl.

15 **glandēs**: *bullets*; "acorns," this is the projectile shot from a sling (funda)
fervefacta iacula: *heated javelins*; acc. d.o.

16 **erant tēctae**: tectae erant, plpf. pass. tegō
hae: *these (houses)*; supply casae

17 **comprehendērunt**: *caught*
ventī: nom. pl. subject
magnitūdine: *because of...*; abl. of cause

18 **distulērunt**: pf. 3rd pl. differō

Subjunctive Conditions In Secondary Sequence: Direct and Indirect Discourse

Fut. Less Vivid (pres. subj., pres. subj.)

dixī "sī credās, errēs."   →   dixī sī haec crederēs, tē errātūrum esse
I said, "if you should believe, you would be wrong"   *I said that, if you were to believe, you would be...*

Present Contrary-to-fact (impf. subj., impf. subj.)

dixī "sī crederēs, errārēs."   →   dixī sī haec crederēs, tē errātūrum esse
I said, "if you believed, you would be wrong"   *I said that, if you believed, , you would be wrong.**

Past Contrary-to-fact (plpf. subj. plpf. subj.)

dixī "sī credissēs, errāvissēs."   →   dixī sī haec credissēs, tē errātūrum fuisse.
I said, "if you had believed, you would have been..."   *I said that, if you had believed, you would have...*

for more, see p. 84

43.3 Hostēs maximō clāmōre, sīcutī partā iam atque explōrātā victōriā, turrēs   1
testudinēsque agere et scalīs vallum ascendere coepērunt. 4. At tanta mīlitum
virtūs atque ea praesentia animī fuit ut, cum undique flammā torrērentur
maximāque tēlōrum multitūdine premerentur suaque omnia impedīmenta
atque omnēs fortūnās cōnflagrāre intellegerent, nōn modo dēmigrandī causā   5
dē vallō dēcēderet nēmō, sed paene nē respiceret quidem quisquam, ac tum
omnēs ācerrimē fortissimēque pugnārent. 5. Hic diēs nostrīs longē
gravissimus fuit; sed tamen hunc habuit ēventum, ut eō diē maximus
numerus hostium vulnerārētur atque interficerētur, ut sē sub ipsō vallō
constīpāverant recessumque prīmīs ultimī nōn dabant. 6. Paulum quidem   10
intermissā flammā et quōdam locō turrī adactā et contingente vāllum tertiae
cohortis centuriōnēs ex eō, quō stābant, locō recessērunt suōsque omnēs
removērunt, nūtū vocibusque hostēs, sī introīre vellent, vocāre coepērunt;
quōrum prōgredī ausus est nēmō. 7. Tum ex omnī parte lapidibus coniectīs
dēturbātī, turrisque succēnsa est.   15

ācer, ācris, ācre: sharp, fierce, eager, bitter 2
adigō, -ere, -ēgī, -āctum: drive to, force to, 1
agō, agere, ēgī, āctum: drive, lead, do, 4
ascendō, -ere, -ī, -ēnsus: ascend, mount 2
audeō, -ēre, ausus sum: dare, venture, 4
centurio, -iōnis m.: centurion, 4
clāmor, clāmōris m.: shout, cry, 2
coepī, coepisse, coeptum: to begin, 9
cōnflagrō (1): be on fire, be consumed, 1
constīpō (1): to crowd together in, stuff, 1
contingō, -ere, tigī, tactum: touch, border, 1
dēcēdō, -ere, -cessī, -cessum: depart, die, 4
dēmigrō (1): to emigrate, depart, 1
dēturbō (1): dislodge, drive off, 1
ēventus, -ūs m.: consequence, result, issue, 2
explōrō (1): explore, search; gain, 1
flamma, ae f.: flame, 3
fortūna, -ae f.: fortune, chance, luck, 4
iam: now, already, soon, 4
intellegō, -ere, -lēxī, -lēctum: understand, 2
introeō, -īre, iī, -itum: go into, enter, 1
lapis, lapidis m.: stone, 1
modo: only, merely, simply; just now, 4

nēmō, nūllīus, nēminī, -em, nūllō: no one, 3
nūtus, -ūs m.: a nod, 1
paene: almost, nearly, 2
pariō, -ere, peperī, partum: produce, bear, 1
praesentia, -ae f.: presence, 2
prōgredior, -gredī, -gressus: step forward,
    go forth, advance, 2
quīdam, quaedam, quiddam: a certain, 4
quisquam, quidquam: anyone, anything? 2
recēdō, -ere, -cessī, -cessus: go back, 1
recessus, -ūs m.: retreat, recess, 1
removeō, -ēre, -mōvī, -mōtus: remove, 2
respiciō, -ere, -spexī, -spectum: look back to, 1
scāla, -ae f.: ladder; flight of stairs, stairs, 1
sicut: just as, so as, as if, 2
stō, -āre, stetī, stātum: stand still, stop, 3
succendō, -ere, -dī, censum: to set fire under, 2
testūdo, -tūdinis f.: tortoise, 2
torreō, -ēre, -ruī, tostum: burn, parch, 1
ultimus, -a, -um: farthest, extreme, last, 1
vōcō (1): call, name, address, summon, 1
vōx, vōcis, f.: voice; utterance, word, 4
vulnerō (1): wound, injure, 3

1 **maximō clāmōre**: *with a very loud shout*; abl. of manner, cum is dropped with the noun is modified by an adjective
sīcutī: *as if*...
partā...atque explōrātā: *produced and confirmed*; PPP in an ablative absolute; pariō is the verb "to give birth" and explōrō, in addition to the meaning "to search out" means "fixed," "established" or "confirmed" in Caesar

2 **agere**: *to drive forward*
mīlitum: *of (our) soldiers*; i.e. the Romans

3 **ea praesentia animī**: *and such was their presence of mind*; i.e. discipline and focus
ut...nōn modo...dēcēderet, sed...respiceret ...pugnārent: *(so) that*...; result clause; impf. subjunctives in secondary sequence
cum...: *although*...; cum-clause is concessive

4 **torrērentur...premerentur**: *were being scorched and...were being overwhelmed*; impf. subj. in the same cum-clause
sua: *their*; reflexive adjective

5 **impedīmenta atque...fortūnās**: acc. subj. of cōnflagāre, ind. disc. governed by intellegerent
fortūnās: *personal items*
nōn modo...sed: *not only...but (also)*

6 **dēmigrandī causā**: *for the sake of*...; gen. sg. gerund dēmigrō
nē...quidem: *not even*; this construction emphasizes the intervening word, in this case respiceret, which is part of the result clause that started with ut in line 3

7 **ācerrimē fortissimēque**: superlative adverbs

8 **nostrīs**: *for our (men)*; dat. of interest
longē: *far, by far*; adverb
gravissimus: *most grievous*; pred. adjective
hunc...ēventum, ut: *this result, (namely) that*...; ut introduces a noun result clause in

apposition to ēventum
eō diē: *on this day*; eō is a demonstrative

9 **ut...cōnstīpāverant...dabant**: *since*...; ut + indicative, "as" is causal in force
sub: *at the foot of*...; "beneath"

10 **prīmīs ultimī nōn dabant**: *the last (soldiers) were not giving (a means for) retreat to the first*; the rows of soldiers were crowded together on the battle line so that the soldiers on the front were pushed by those behind and could not retreat
paulum: *a little*; adverbial acc.

11 **intermissā flammā**: abl. absolute
quōdam locō: *in a certain place*; abl. place where; or "to..."dative with compound verb
turrī adactā et contingente: abl. abs., turrī is fem. i-stem abl.; PPP adigō; pres. pple contingō; the turrī is an enemy's tower

12 **tertiae cohortis**: gen. sg. modifies centuriōnēs
ex eō...locō: *from this place*; demonstrative
quō: *in which (place)*; abl. of place where

13 **suōsque omnēs**: *all their men*; acc. d.o.
nūtū vocibusque: *with a nod and words*; abl. of means
sī...vellent: *if they wished*; ind. discourse, impf. subjunctive; in direct discourse a pres. indicative: "if you wish to enter, (enter)!"

14 **quōrum...nēmō**: *none of whom*; partitive gen.
prōgredī: present deponent inf., prōgredior
ausus est: *dared*; pf. deponent, audeō is a semi-deponent verb, otherwise active, the perfect tenses are deponent
ex omnī parte: *from every direction*

15 **dēturbātī (sunt)**: *(the enemy) was dislodged*; pf. passive, add "sunt" parallel with succēnsa
turris: nom. sg. feminine

Purpose Constructions

There are a variety of ways to express purpose in Caesar's *Commentaries*. Notice how Caesar uses purpose clauses (adverbial and relative) in early books and other constructions in later ones. The dat. of purpose is often used with *sum* or with dat. interest in a double dative construction.

			examples
ut/nē + subj.	ut/nē audīret	*so that he might (not) hear*...	pp. 4, 6, 8, 10, 46, 70
quī + subj.	quī audīret	*who should hear*...	pp. 10
ad + gerund	ad haec audiendum	*for hearing*...	p. 10, 18
ad + noun + gerundive	ad haec audienda	*for these things to be heard*	pp. 2-8, 10, 18-20, 24
causā + gerund	audiendī causā	*for (the sake of) hearing*...	pp. 28, 40, 62
causā + gerundive	audiendī huius causā	*for the sake of this to be heard*	pp. 20, 58, 68
accusative supine	audītum	*to hear*...	pp. 22, 38, 52
dative of purpose	salūtī	*for safety*	p.12, 18-20, 38-44, 52, 64-6

44.1 Erant in eā legiōne fortissimī virī, centuriōnēs, quī prīmīs ōrdinibus   1
appropinquārent, Titus Pullō et Lucius Vorēnus. 2. Hī perpetuās inter sē
contrōversiās habēbant, quīnam anteferrētur, omnibusque annīs dē locīs
summīs simultātibus contendēbant. 3. Ex hīs Pullō, cum acerrimē ad
mūnitiōnēs pugnārētur, 'Quid dubitās,' inquit, 'Vorēne? aut quem locum   5
tuae probandae virtūtis exspectās? 4. Hic diēs dē nostrīs contrōversiīs
iudicābit.' Haec cum dīxisset, prōcēdit extrā mūnitiōnēs quaeque pars
hostium cōnfertissima est vīsa irrumpit. 5. Nē Vorēnus quidem tum sēsē vallō
continet, sed omnium veritus exīstimātiōnem subsequitur. 6. Mediocrī spatiō
relictō, Pullō pīlum in hostēs immittit atque ūnum ex multitudine   10
prōcurrentem trāicit; quō percussō et exanimātō hunc scūtīs prōtegunt, in
hostem tēla ūniversī coniciunt neque dant regrediendī facultātem. 7.
Trānsfīgitur scūtum Pullōnī et verūtum in balteō dēfīgitur. 8. Āvertit hic
casus vāgīnam, et gladium ēdūcere cōnantī dextram morātur manum,
impedītumque hostēs circumsistunt. 9. Succurrit inimīcus illī Vorēnus et   15
laborantī subvenit. 10. Ad hunc sē confestim ā Pullone omnis multitūdō
convertit: 11. illum verūto arbitrantur occīsum. Gladiō comminus rem gerit
Vorēnus atque ūnō interfectō reliquōs paulum prōpellit; 12. dum cupidius
īnstat, in locum dēiectus inferiōrem concidit. Huic rūrsus circumventō fert
subsidium Pullō, 13. atque ambō incolumēs, complūribus interfectīs, summā   20
cum laude sēsē intrā mūnitiōnēs recipiunt. 14. Sīc fortūna in contentiōne et
certāmine utrumque versāvit, ut alter alterī inimīcus auxiliō salūtīque esset,
neque dīiūdicārī posset, uter utrī virtūte anteferendus vidērētur.

ācer, ācris, ācre: sharp, fierce, eager, bitter 2
ambo: both, two together, 1
anteferō, -ferre, -tulī: prefer, carry before, 2
appropinquō (1): approach, draw near (dat), 3
auxilium, -ī n.: help, aid, assistance, 3
āvertō, -ēre, āvertī, āversum: turn away, 1
balteus, -ī m.: belt, baldric; girdle, 1
centurio, -iōnis m.: centurion, 4
certāmen, -minis n.: contest, conflict, 1
circumsistō, -ere, -stetī: to surround, 2
comminus: hand to hand, in close combat, 1
concidō, -ere, -cidī, -casum: to fall, 1
confertus, a, um: crowded together, dense, 3
cōnfēstim: immediately, 4
contendō, -ere, -ī, -ntus: strive; hasten, 4
contentio, -iōnis f.: struggle, effort, 1
convertō, -ere, -ī, -rsus: turn (about), 1
cupidus, -a, -um: desirous, eager, keen, 2
dēfīgō, -ere, -fixī, -fixum: fasten, stick fast, 1
dēiciō, -ere, -iēcī, -iectum: throw down 2
dexter, -tera, -terum: right, the right hand, 1

dīiūdicō (1): judge, decide (by fighting), 1
dubitō (1): waver, be uncertain, hestitate, 1
ēdūcō, -ere, -dūxī, -ductus: lead out, 3
exanimō (1): deprive of breath; kill, stun, 2
existimātio, -iōnis f.: judgment, opinion, 1
exspectō (1): look out for, wait for, await, 3
extrā: outside; beyond, outside of (acc), 1
fortūna, -ae f.: fortune, chance, luck, 4
gladius, -ī m.: sword, 3
immittō, -ere, -mīsī, -missum: launch into, 1
impeditus, -a, -um: hindered, impeded, 3
incolumis, -e: unscathed, uninjured, safe, 2
inferus, -a, -um: below, lower, 3
inimīcus, -a, -um: hostile, unfriendly, 4
inquam: say, 4
instō, -āre, -stitī, press on, take a position, 1
intrā: within, among (+ acc.), 3
irrumpō, -ere, -rupī, -ruptum: burst in, 1
iūdicō (1): judge, decide, assess, 2
labōrō (1): work, toil, labor, strive, 2
laus, laudis f.: praise, adulation, 1

mediocris, -e: moderate, ordinary, 1
moror, -ārī, -ātus: delay, linger; detain, 3
occīdō, -ere, occidī, occīsus: kill, cut down 4
percutiō, -ere, -cussī, cussum: strike hard, 1
perpetuus, -a, -um: constant, everlasting, 4
pīlum, -ī n.: pilum, javelin, 3
prōcēdō, -ere, -cessī, -cessum; proceed, 3
prōcurrō, ere, currī, cursum: run forward, 2
prōpellō, -ere, -pellī, -pulsum: drive forward
 or push away, 3
prōtegō, -ere, texī, tectum: to cover over, 1
quīnam quaenam quodnam: which, what, 1
regredior, -ī, regressus: step or go back 1
rursus: again, backward, back, 4
scūtum, -ī m.: shield, 2
sīc: thus, in this way, 3

simultās, -tātis f.: clash, feud, rivalry, 1
spatium, -iī n.: space, room, extent, 4
subveniō, -īre, -vēnī, -ventum: come up to,
 aid, relieve, 2
succurrō, -ere, : run under, undergo, occur, 1
Titus, -ī m.: Titus, 4
trāiciō, -icere, -iēcī, -iectum: pierce, cast across, 2
transfīgō, -ere, -fīxī, fixum: pierce, thrust, 1
tuus, -a, -um: your, yours, 1
ūniversus, -a, -um: all together, whole, 3
uter, utra, utrum: each or one (of two), 2
vāgīna, -ae f.: sheath, scabbard, 1
vereor, -ērī, -itus sum: be afraid, fear; revere, 4
versor (1): be engaged in, move about, deal with, 3
verūtum, -ī n.: javelin, 2
vir, virī m.: man, 4

---

1 **Erant**: *there were...*
 prīmīs ōrdinibus: *the front ranks*; in battle
 at regular intervals the front row was relieved
 by the second row and slipped to the rear; Pullo
 and Vorenus are about take over the first row
3 **quīnam anteferrētur**: *who was to be preferred*;
 "who was better," an ind. question in apposition
 to contrōversiās, likely impf. deliberative subj.
 omnibusque annīs: *every year*; abl. time when
 dē locīs summīs: *concerning the highest
 positions*; i.e. military promotions and honors
4 **simultātibus**: *in...*; abl. of respect
 ācerrimē: superlative adverb
 ad: *near*
5 **Quid**: *Why...?*
 pugnārētur: *they were fighting*; "it was fought
 (by them)," an impersonal impf. passive
 Vorēne: *Vorenus*; vocative direct address
 quem locum: *what (better) place*; i.e. "what
 better opportunity" relative adjective
6 **tuae probandae virtūtis**: *of proving your
 valor*; "of your valor going to be proven," a
 gerundive modifying virtūtis; through a gerund-
 gerundive flip a gerund with virtūtis as object
7 **haec**: *these things*; acc. obj. of plpf. subj. dīcō;
 Pullo is the subject of all the following verbs
 quaeque pars...est vīsa: *and what(ever) side
 seemed...*; videor, here pf. pass. is translated as
 the linking verb "seems," missing antecedent is
 the object of irrumpit
8 **cōnfertissima**: superlative pred. adj. governed
 by vīsa est and modifying the feminine sg. pars
 nē...quidem: *not even...*; this construction
 emphasizes the intervening word
 vallō: *within the wall*; abl. place where
9 **veritus**: *having come to fear...; pf. dep. pple

omnium exīstimātiōnem: object of veritus
mediocrī spatiō relictō: *a usual interval (of
 time) having been forsaken*; i.e. a short time,
 having intervened; abl. absolute, i-stem abl.
10 **in hostēs**: *against the enemy*
 ūnum: *one (enemy soldier)*
11 **prōcurrentem**: pres. pple. modifies ūnum
 quō percussō et exanimātō: *this one...*; abl.
 abs. with PPP percutiō, exanimō; a relative
 where English prefers a demonstrative
 hunc: *this one*; hunc refers to the same as quō
12 **regrediendī**: gerund, gen. sg. regredior
13 **Pullonī**: *Pullo's*; dat. poss. or dat. of interest
 hic casus: *this event*; the scabbard is turned in
 such a way that it is difficult to draw a sword
14 **gladium ēdūcere cōnantī**: *for the one
 trying...*; pres. pple cōnor
15 **illī, labōrantī**: dat. objects of compound verbs
17 **illum occīsum (esse)**: *that that one was killed*
18 **ūnō interfectō**: abl. absolute
 cupidius: comparative adverb, cupidus
19 **īnstat**: *presses on*; "takes a stand"
 dēiectus: *having slipped onto a lower ground*
 huic..circumventō: *to this one...; dat. i.o.
21 **sēsē...recipiunt**: *retreat*; common idiom
22 **utrumque versāvit**: *engaged in both men*
 ut...esset, posset, vidērētur: result clause
 alter alterī inimīcus: *one, hostile to the other,*
 auxiliō salūtīque esset: *would serve as help
 and refuge*; "for...," dat. purpose
23 **uter utrī**: *each one to the other*; dat. sg.
 virtūte: *in valor*; abl. of respect
 anteferendus: *to be preferred*; "going/worthy
 to be preferred" gerundive, a predicate of the
 linking verb vidērētur, "seemed" cf. line 3

45.1 Quantō erat in diēs gravior atque asperior oppugnātiō, et maximē quod   1
magnā parte mīlitum cōnfectā vulneribus, rēs ad paucitātem defensōrum
pervēnerat, tantō crebriōrēs litterae nūntiīque ad Caesarem mittēbantur;
quōrum pars dēprehēnsa in conspectū nostrōrum mīlitum cum cruciātū
necabātur. 2. Erat ūnus intus Nervius nōmine Verticō, locō nātus honestō,   5
quī ā prīmā obsidiōne ad Cicerōnem perfūgerat suamque eī fīdem
praestiterat. 3. Hic servō spē libertātis magnīsque persuādet praemiīs, ut
litterās ad Caesarem dēferat. 4. Hās ille in iaculō illigātās effert et Gallus inter
Gallōs sine ūllā suspiciōne versātus ad Caesarem pervenit. 5. Ab eō dē
periculīs Cicerōnis legiōnisque cognōscitur.   10

46.1 Caesar, acceptīs litterīs, hōrā circiter XI diēī statim nūntium in
Bellovacōs ad M. Crassum quaestōrem mittit, cuius hīberna aberant ab eō
milia passuum XXV; 2. iubet mediā nocte legiōnem proficīscī celeriterque ad
sē venīre. 3. Exit cum nūntiō Crassus. Alterum ad Gaium Fabium lēgātum
mittit, ut in Atrebātium fīnēs legiōnem adducat, quā sibi iter faciendum   15
sciēbat. 4. Scribit Labiēnō, sī reī pūblicae commodō facere posset, cum legiōne
ad fīnēs Nerviōrum veniat. Reliquam partem exercitūs, quod paulō aberat
longius, non putat exspectandam; equitēs circiter quadringentōs ex proximīs
hibernīs colligit.

addūcō, -ere, duxī, ductum: draw/lead to, 4
asper, aspera, asperum: rough, harsh, violent, 1
Atrebas, Atrebātis, m.: Atrebates, 3
Bellovacī, -ōrum m.: Bellovaci (in Belgīs), 1
colligō, -ere, -lēgī, -lēctum: gather, collect, 1
commodum, -ī n.: convenience, advantage, interest, 1
conficiō, -ere: to exhaust, finish, 4
conspectus, -ūs, m.: look, sight, view, 2
creber, -bra, -bum: crowded, frequent, 1
cruciātus, -ūs m.: torture, torment, 2
dēfensor, -ōris m.: defender, protector, 1
dēprehendō, -ere, -dī, -ēnsus: seize, catch, 1
efferō, -ferre, -tulī, ēlātus: raise, lift up 4
exeō, -īre, -iī (īvī), -itus: go out, 4
exspectō (1): look out for, wait for, await, 3
Fabius, -ī m.: Fabius, 3
fīdēs, eī f.: faith, honor, 4
Gaius, -ī m.: Gaius, 4
honestus, -a, -um: respectable, honorable, 1
hora, -ae f.: hour, 4
iaculum, -ī n.: javelin, dart, 2
inligō, -āre, -āvī, illigātum: tie or bind on, 1

intus: within, inside, 1
lībertās, -tātis f.: freedom, liberation, 2
M.: Marcus, 3
medius -a –um: in the middle of, 3
nascor, nascī, nātus sum: be born, grow, 3
necō (1): kill, slay, destroy, 1
nōmen, nōminis n.: name, 2
obsidio, -iōnis f.: siege, blockade, 2
paucitās, -tātis f. (1): fewness, scarcity, 3
perfugiō, -ere, -fūgī: flee, take refuge, 1
putō (1): to think, imagine, 3
quadringentī: four hundred, 2
quaestor, -oris m.: quaestor, 3
sciō, -īre, -īvī (iī), -ītus: know (how), 2
scrībō, -ere, -scripsī, scriptum: write, 2
servus, -ī, m.: slave, 1
statim: immediately, at once, 4
suspīcio, -ciōnis f.: mistrust, suspicion, 4
versor (1): be engaged in, move about, deal with, 3
Verticō, -ōnis m.: Vertico, 1
vulnus, -eris n.: wound, blow, 3

1 **Quantō...gravior...tantō crēbriōrēs**: *the more grievous...the more frequent*; "by as much...by so much," correlatives, ablative of the degree of difference with comparative adjective
  in diēs: *daily*
  maximē: *especially*; "very greatly"
  magnā...vulneribus: ablative absolute
3 **pervēnerat**: *had arrived at*; rēs is subject
  nuntiī: *messengers*
  quōrum pars: *some of which (messengers)*; partitive gen.,
4 **dēprehēnsa**: *taken*; modifies fem. sg. pars
5 **Erat**: *there was*
  intus: *within*; i.e. within Cicero's camp
  nōmine: *by name*; "in name," abl. of respect
  locō...honestō: *in an honorable station*; status
  eī: *to him*; i.e. to Cicero, dat. sg.
6 **praestiterat**: *had shown, had performed*
7 **Hic**: *this one*; i.e. Vertico
  servō: *slave*; dat. i.o. of persuādeō
  spē, praemiīs: abl. means
  ut...dēferat: *that...;* ind. command with present subj. governed by persuādet
8 **ille**: *that one*; i.e. the slave
  hās: *these*; fem. pl. antecedent litterae
  Gallus...versātus: *as a Gaul engaged...*
9 **ab eō**: *by him*; by the slave, abl. of agent
10 **cognōscitur**: *he learned*; "it is known by him"
11 **acceptīs litterīs**: abl. absolute
  hōrā...XI: *at around the 11th hour*; time when, approximately 5 p.m.
  diēī: partitive genitive
12 **cuius**: gen. relative pronoun quī, quae, quod
  aberant ab eō: *were...away from him*; i.e.

from Caesar
13 **milia passuum XXV**: *25 miles*; "thousands of paces," acc. of extent of space
  mediā nocte: abl. of time when
  proficiscī: pres. deponent inf.
14 **cum nūntiō**: *with the messenger*; or "with (the arrival of) the message"
  Alterum: *another*; modifies lēgātum
15 **ut...adducat**: *that...;* ind. command with pres. subj.
  fīnēs: *territory*
  quā: *where*
  sibi iter faciendum (esse): *that a journey had to be made by him*; "a journey was going to be made by him" ind. discourse, a passive periphrastic (gerundive + form of sum) with dat. of agent expressing necessity or obligation
16 **Labiēnō**: dat. i.o.
  sī...posset: *if*; impf. subj. possum
  reī pūblicae commodō: *for the interest of the republic*; dat. purpose or, if reī is dat. not gen., double dative (dat. of interest & dat. purpose)
  (ut) cum legiōne veniat: *that..;* ind. command with pres. subj. governed by scribit
  fīnēs: *territory*
17 **exercitūs**: gen. sg.
  paulō: *a little*; "by a little," abl. degree of difference with comparative longius
18 **longius**: *farther*; comparative adverb
  exspectandam (esse): *must be waited for*; "is going to be waited for," passive periphrastic (gerundive + esse) expresses obligation or necessity; add esse, in indirect disc. governed by putat; fem. sg. partem is acc. subject

---

Compound Verbs: the Importance of Prefixes

Notice how the spelling of many prefixes, especially ad- and con-, change through assimilation and assume the consonant at the begins of the verb. Compounds often govern a dative instead of an accusative object.

		mittō, -ere: send, 20		**cēdō, ere**: withdraw, move, 2
a/ab-	away from	**āmittō**: lose, let go away, 2		
ad-	to, toward	**admittō**: admit, allow, 2		**accēdō**: approach, 5
con-	together with	**committō**: begin, entrust, 4		**concēdō**: withdraw, yield, 2
dē-	from, down from	**dēmittō**: send down, sink, 1		**dēcēdō**: depart, withdraw, 4
dis-	different directions	**dīmittō**: send away, 3		**discēdō**: go away, depart, 9
ē/ex-	out from	**ēmittō**: send off, 1		**excēdō**: go out, depart, 3
in-	in, on, into	**immittō**: launch into, 1		**incēdō**: walk, march, 0
inter-	between	**intermittō**: interrupt, leave off, 5		**intercēdō**: come between, 1
per-	through	**permittō**: let through, allow, 0		
prae-	before, ahead	**praemittō**: send ahead, 2		**praecēdō**: surpass, go ahead, 1
pro-	forth, in advance	**prōmittō**: send forth, untertake, 0		**prōcēdō**: go forth, 3
re-	back, again	**remittō**: send back, 4		**recēdō**: go back, withdraw, 1
sub-	(up from) under	**submittō**: send up, 1		**succēdō**: go up, approach, 3

47.1 Hōrā circiter tertiā ab antecursōribus dē Crassī adventū certior factus eō   1
diē milia passuum XX procēdit. 2. Crassum Samarobrīvae praeficit
legiōnemque attribuit, quod ibi impedīmenta exercitūs, obsidēs cīvitātum,
litterās pūblicās frūmentumque omne quod eō tolerandae hiemis causā
dēvexerat relinquebat. 3. Fabius, ut imperātum erat, nōn ita multum morātus   5
in itinere cum legiōne occurrit. 4. Labiēnus, interitū Sabīnī et caede
cohortium cognitā, cum omnēs ad eum Treverōrum cōpiae vēnissent,
veritus, sī ex hībernīs fugae similem profectiōnem fēcisset, ut hostium
impetum sustinēre posset, praesertim quōs recentī victōriā efferrī scīret,
litterās Caesarī remittit, quantō cum perīculō legiōnem ex hībernīs ēductūrus   10
esset; rem gestam in Eburiōnibus perscrībit; docet omnēs equitātūs
peditātūsque cōpiās Treverōrum tria milia passuum longē ab suīs castrīs
cōnsēdisse.

antecursor, -ōris m.: scout, advanced guard, 1
attribuō, -ere, -uī, -utum: allot, assign to, add, 1
caedēs, caedis f.: murder, slaughter, killing 2
consīdeō, -ēre, -sēdī: to sit down, settle, 2
dēvehō, -ere, -vēxī, -vectum: carry away, 1
doceō, -ēre, -uī, -ctus: teach, tell, 4
ēdūcō, -ere, -dūxī, -ductus: lead out, 3
efferō, -ferre, -tulī, ēlātus: raise, lift up 4
Fabius, -ī m.: Fabius, 3
fuga, -ae f.: flight, haste, exile, speed, 3
hiems, hiemis f.: winter, storm, 4
hora, -ae f.: hour, 4
impetus, -ūs m.: attack, onset, assault, 7
interitus, -ūs m.: destruction, annihilation, 1
ita: so, thus, 7
moror, -ārī, -ātus: delay, linger; detain, 3

occurrō, -ere: run to meet, attack, 2
peditātus, -ūs m.: infantry, 3
perscrībō, -ere, -scripsī: describe thoroughly, 1
praeficiō, -ere, -fēcī, -fectum: set (acc) over (dat),
   put (acc) in charge over (dat), 2
praesertim: especially, particularly, 2
prōcēdō, -ere, -cessī, -cessum; proceed, 3
recens, recentis adj.: new, fresh, recent, 1
remittō, -ere, -mīsī, -missum: send back, 4
Samarobrīva, -ae f.: Samarobriva, 1
sciō, -īre, -īvī (iī), -ītus: know (how), 2
similis, simile: similar to, like (dat.), 1
tolerō (1): endure, sustain, bear, support, 1
Trēveri , -ōrum m.: Treveri (Germanic), 4
vereor, -ērī, -itus: be afraid, fear; revere, 4

1 **Hōrā...tertiā**: *at...*; abl. of time when
ab antecursōribus: abl. of agent
certior factus: *having been informed*; "having been made more certain," a common idiom in Caesar, certior is a comparative adj., here a predicate of PPP of faciō

2 **eō diē**: *on that day*; time when, demonstrative
milia passuum XX: *for 20 miles*; "twenty thousands of paces," acc. of extent of space
praeficit: *put (acc) in charge over (dat.)*

3 **quod**: *because...*

4 **quod...dēvexerat**: *which...*; relative pronoun, frūmentum is the antecedent
eō: *to there*; "to that place," adverb
tolerandae hiemis: gerund-gerundive flip, translate the gerundive as a gerund and gen. hiemis as an acc. object of tolerandae; the entire construction is an obj. of the preposition causā

5 **ut**: *as*; ut + indicative, as often "as" or "when"
imperātum erat: *it...*; impersonal plpf. pass.
multum: *much*; inner acc. or adverbial acc.

6 **interitū...cognitā**: abl. absolute

7 **cum...vēnisset**: *when...*; plpf. subjunctive
cōpiae: *troops*; modified by omnēs

8 **veritus...ut...posset**: *having begun to fear that he would not be able*; inceptive pf. dep. pple

vereor governs a fearing clause (nē - that, ut - that not) with impf. subj. in secondary seq.
fugae: *to flight*; governed by similem

8 **sī...fēcisset**: *if he had made*; plpf. subjunctive, introducing a mixed contrafactual condition

9 **quōs...scīret**: *since he knew that those were elated by their recent victory*; quōs + impf. subjunctive is a relative clause causal in sense, equivalent to a cum-clause (quōs = cum eōs) causal in sense; cf. quī in V.33; pass. inf. efferō
recentī: i-stem ablative with victōriā

10 **quantō...perīculō**: *(stating) with how much danger....*; introducing an ind. question with an implicit verb of speaking in "litterās... remittit"
ēductūrus esset: *would lead out*; "was going to lead out," fut. periphrastic (future pple + sum) in primary sequence which in dir. disc would be "ēductūrus erat"

11 **gestam**: *carried out*; PPP gerō
in Eburiōnibus: *among the Eburiones*
omnēs...copiās: *that all....*; acc. subject of pf. infinitive cōnsēdisse in ind. discourse

12 **tria milia passuum**: *three miles*; "three thousand paces," acc. of extent of space
longē: *far*; adverb

Deponent Verbs in the Readings

adgredior, -ī, aggressus sum: attack, 1
  ēgredior, -ī, -gressum: go out, disembark, 5
  regredior, -ī, regressum: step or go back 1
adipiscor, -ī, adeptum: get, obtain, reach, 1
arbitror, arbitrārī, arbitrātum: to judge, 10
auxilior, -ārī, auxiliātum: to help, assist, 1
confiteor, -ērī, -fessum: admit, reveal, 1
cōnor, cōnārī, cōnātum: to try, 6
cunctor, -ārī, -ātum: to delay, hesitate 1
frūmentor, -ārī: to forage, fetch corn, 1
hortor, -ārī, hortātum: encourage, urge, 2
  adhortor, -ārī, -ātum: encourage, urge on, 1
  cohortor, -ārī, cohortātum: encourage, incite, 3
lābor, lābī, lapsum: glide, slide, slip, 1
loquor, -ī, locūtum: speak, say, 2
  colloquor, -quī, -locūtum: to converse, 4
medeor, -ērī: heal, cure; assist, alleviate, 1
mercor, -ārī, mercātum: to trade, traffic, 1
moderor, -ārī, -ātum: restrain, regulate, 1
molior, -īrī, molītum: set into motion, stir, 1
moror, -ārī, -ātum: delay, linger; detain, 3
nanciscor, nanciscī, nactum: obtain, meet, 1
nascor, nascī, nātum: be born, grow, 3

nītor, nītī, nīsus sum: to struggle, lean on, 1
contestor, -ārī, -ātum: to call as witness, 1
orior, -īrī, ortum: arise, rise, spring, 3
  adorior, -īrī, -ortus sum: rise up, attack, 2
  coōrior, -īrī, coōrtum: arise, break out, 2
patior, -ī, passum: suffer, endure; allow, 2
polliceor, -cērī, -citum: promise, offer, 2
potior, -īrī, -ītum: gain, win (*abl.*), 2
proelior, -ārī, -ātum: to give battle, fight, 1
proficīscor, -ī, -fectum: set out, depart, 23
profiteor, -ērī, -fessum: profess, declare, 1
prosequor, sequī, secūtum: follow, pursue 1
queror, querī, questum: complain, lament, 1
sequor, -ī, secūtum: follow, pursue, 4
  consequor, -ī, secūtum: follow; pursue 1
  exsequor, sequī, secūtum: follow/carry out 1
  insequor, -sequī, -secūtum: follow, ensue, 1
  subsequor, -ī, secūtum: follow after, behind 7
suspicior, -ārī, suspicātum: to suspect, 3
ulciscor, -ī, ultum: avenge, take vengeance 1
ūtor, -ī, ūsus sum: use, employ (*abl.*), 5
vagor, -ārī, -ātum: wander, roam to and fro, 1
vereor, -ērī, -itum: be afraid, fear; revere, 4

48.1 Caesar, cōnsiliō eius probātō, etsī opiniōne trium legiōnum dēiectus ad   1
duās redierat, tamen ūnum commūnis salūtis auxilium in celeritāte ponēbat.
Vēnit magnīs itineribus in Nerviōrum fīnēs. 2. Ibi ex captīvīs cognoscit, quae
apud Cicerōnem gerantur, quantōque in periculō rēs sit. 3. Tum cuidam ex
equitibus Gallīs magnīs praemiīs persuādet utī ad Cicerōnem epistolam   5
dēferat. 4. Hanc Graecīs conscriptam litterīs mittit, nē, interceptā epistolā,
nostra ab hostibus cōnsilia cognōscantur. 5. Sī adīre non possit, monet ut
trāgulam cum epistolā ad āmentum deligātā intrā mūnītiōnem castrōrum
abiciat. 6. In litterīs scribit sē cum legiōnibus profectum celeriter adfore;
hortātur ut pristīnam virtūtem retineat. 7. Gallus perīculum veritus, ut erat   10
praeceptum, trāgulam mittit. 8. Haec cāsū ad turrim adhaesit neque ab nostrīs
bīduō animadversa tertiō diē ā quōdam mīlite cōnspicitur, dempta ad
Cicerōnem dēfertur. 9. Ille perlectam in conventū mīlitum recitat
maximāque omnēs laetitiā adficit. 10. Tum fūmī incendiōrum procul
vidēbantur; quae rēs omnem dubitātiōnem adventūs legiōnum expulit.   15

abiciō, -ere, -iēcī, -iectum: throw away, 2
adeō, -īre, ī(v(ī, itus: approach, encounter, 2
adficiō, -ere, -fēcī, -fectum: affect, afflict, 3
adhaereō, -ēre, -haesī: cling to, stick to, 1
adsum, -esse, -fuī: be present, assist, (dat.), 3
āmentum, -ī n.: strap, leather thong, 1
auxilium, -ī n.: help, aid, assistance, 3
biduum, -ī n.: a period of two days, 2
captīvus, -a, -um: prisoner, captive, 3
conscrībō, -ere, -scrīpsī: enlist, enroll, 2
conspiciō, -īre: catch sight of, perceive, behold 1
conventus, -ūs m.: meeting, assembly, 1
dēficiō, -ere, -fēcī, -fectum: fail, give out, 3
dēiciō, -ere, -iēcī, -iectum: throw down, dislodge, 1
dēligō (1): to tie down, fasten, 2
dēmō, -ere, dempsī, demptum: take down, 1
dubitātio, -tiōnis f.: wavering, uncertainty, 1
epistula, -ae f.: letter, missive, 3
expellō, ere, pulī, pulsum: drive out, expel 2
fūmus, -ī m.: smoke, vapor, steam, 1

Graecus, -a, -um: Greek, 2
hortor, -ārī, hortātum: encourage, urge, 2
incendium, -iī n.: fire, conflagration, 1
incipiō, -ere, incēpī, inceptum: begin, 1
intrā: within, among (+ acc.), 3
laetitia, -ae f.: gladness, joy, delight, 1
moneō, -ēre, -uī, -itum: to warn, advise, 2
opīniō, -niōnis f.: opinion, thought, belief, 2
perlegō, -ere, -lēgī, -lectum: survey, scan, 1
praecipiō, -ere, -cēpī, -ceptum: receive in
    advance, instruct, admonish, 2
pristinus, -a, -um: former, previous, earlier 2
procul: far, from a distance, from afar, 3
quīdam, quaedam, quiddam: a certain, 4
recitō (1): recite, read aloud, 1
redeō, -īre, -īvī: go back, return, 1
retineō, -ēre, -uī, tentum: hold back, keep, 2
scrībō, -ere, -scrīpsī, scriptum: write, 2
trāgula, -ae f.: tragula (a Gallic javelin) 3
vereor, -ērī, -itus: be afraid, fear; revere, 4

1 **cōnsiliō...probātō**: abl. absolute
etsī: *even if...*; i.e. although
opiniōne: *from the hope for...*; "from the thought," abl. of separation; Caesar had hoped for three legions but received only two
dēiectus: *disappointed*; i.e. dejected, dispirited

2 **duās**: duās legiōnēs
redierat: plpf. redeō
ūnum...auxilium: *a single source*

3 **magnīs itineribus**: *in long marches*; i.e. forced marches; 25-30 miles per day
fīnēs: *borders*
quae...gerantur: *what (things) are carried on*; ind. question with pres. subjunctive

4 **apud Cicerōnem**: *in Cicero's camp*
quantō in...: *in how great...*; cf. p. 68, (V.47.4) ind. question with pres. subj. of sum
cuidam: *a certain...*; cui-dam, dat. indirect obj. quīdam of persuādet

5 **utī...dēferat**: *that...*; utī is an alternative to ut, here in an indirect command governed by persuādeō; pres. subj. dēferō

6 **hanc**: *this (letter)*
Graecīs...litterīs: *with Greek letters*; in Greek or perhaps Latin in Greek script
nē...cognōscantur: *that...may not...*; negative purpose clause; pres. subj. in primary sequence

7 **possit**: *he is able*; a subordinate clause in ind. discourse, replacing indicative with pres. subj.
ut...abiciat: *that...*; ind. command governed by monet; pres. subj. in primary sequence

8 **āmentum**: a leather loop on a javelin that allows for better aim and distance when the javelin is thrown

9 **sē...adfore**: *that he will be present...*; adfore is an alternative for adfutūrum esse, fut. inf. of adsum
profectum: PPP proficīscor

10 **ut...retineat**: *that...*; ind. command
veritus: *having begun to fear*; inceptive pf. dep. pple vereor governs perīculum as object
ut erat praeceptum: *as it had been instructed*; ut + indicative

11 **mittit**: *launches*; i.e. throws
haec: *this (javelin)*; supply nom. sg. trāgula
cāsū: *by chance*
ab nostrīs: *by our (men)*; abl. agent

12 **bīduō**: *in...*; abl. time when or within
animadversa: PPP modifying haec (trāgula)
tertiō diē: abl. time when

13 **perlectam (epistulam)...recitat**: *that one recites the letter, once read through,...*; English prefers two main verbs where Latin often prefers to make the first of two actions into a PPP: "that one read through the letter and then recited it..."

14 **adficit**: *affects (acc) with (abl.)*; abl. means

15 **quae rēs**: *a matter which...*; quae modifies fem. sg. rēs, the antecedent of the relative clause, in apposition to fūmī (or the entire clause)

The Remainder of Book V

Cicero and his camp are hopeful when they see the fires as a sign of Caesar's approach. Confronted with 60,000 Gauls, Caesar forms a camp. After a brief skirmish, he pretends to retreat into his fortifications, and when the Gauls follow him, he orders his cavalry and then his foot soldiers to rush out of the gates and attack the enemy. The Gauls are taken by surprise, and those who are not immediately killed flee into the nearby swamps and forests.

Caesar hastens to Cicero's camp, where he learns that nine of every ten soldiers has been wounded in the siege. Caesar praises both Cicero and the legion and informs Cicero about the fate of Sabinus and Cotta's legion and in particular the recklessness of Sabinus.

When Labienus, encamped 60 miles away, learns of Caesar's victory, Indutiomarus, leader of the Treveri, initially decides to stop preparations to attack Labienus and to withdraw. But as other Gauls learn about Sabinus' defeat and begin to make preparations to fight, Indutiomarus returns with a much larger force. With the aid of cavalry, Labienus is able to surprise the Gauls and kill Indutiomarus. After this episode the Gauls return to their homes, and the uprising comes to an end.

	1st Declension		2nd Declension (m.)		2nd Declension (n.)	
Nom.	copia	copiae	legatus	legatī	proelium	proelia
Gen.	copiae	copiārum	legatī	legatōrum	proeliī	proeliōrum
Dat.	copiae	copiīs	legatō	legatīs	proeliō	proeliīs
Acc.	copiam	copiās	legatum	legatōs	proelium	proelia
Abl.	copiā	copiīs	legatō	legatīs	proeliō	proeliīs

	3rd Declension (m/f)		3rd Declension (n.)	
Nom.	mīles	mīlites	iter	itinera
Gen.	mīlitis	mīlitum	itineris	itinerum
Dat.	mīlitī	mīlitibus	itinerī	itineribus
Acc.	mīlitem	mīlitēs	iter	itinera
Abl.	mīlite	mīlitibus	itinere	itineribus

	4th Declension (m/f)		4th Declension (n.)	
Nom.	manus	manūs	cornū	cornua
Gen.	manūs	manuum	cornūs	cornuum
Dat.	manuī	manibus	cornū	cornuibus
Acc.	manum	manūs	cornū	cornua
Abl.	manū	manibus	cornū	cornuibus

	5th Declension (m/f)	
Nom.	rēs	rēs
Gen.	reī	rērum
Dat.	reī	rēbus
Acc.	rem	rēs
Abl.	rē	rēbus

Selected Pronouns

	is	*he*	ea	*she*	id	*it*
Nom.	is	*he*	ea	*she*	id	*it*
Gen.	eius	*his*	eius	*her*	eius	*its*
Dat.	eī	*to/for him*	eī	*to/for her*	eī	*to/for it*
Acc.	eum	*him*	eam	*her*	id	*it*
Abl.	eō	*with/from him*	eā	*with/from her*	eō	*with/from it*

	eī	*they*	eae	*they*	ea	*they*
Nom.	eī	*they*	eae	*they*	ea	*they*
Gen .	eōrum	*their*	eārum	*their*	eōrum	*their*
Dat.	eīs	*to/for them*	eīs	*to/for them*	eīs	*to/for them*
Acc.	eōs	*them*	eās	*them*	ea	*them*
Abl.	eīs	*with/from them*	eīs	*with/from them*	eīs	*with/from them*

*is, ea, id is a demonstrative and in Caesar is often translated as "this/that" in the singular and "these/those" in the plural.

	quī	quae	quod	quī	quae	quae	*who, which, that*
Nom.	quī	quae	quod	quī	quae	quae	*who, which, that*
Gen.	cuius	cuius	cuius	quōrum	quārum	quōrum	*whose, of whom/which*
Dat.	cuī	cuī	cuī	quibus	quibus	quibus	*to whom/which*
Acc.	quem	quam	quod	quōs	quās	quae	*whom, which, that*
Abl.	quō	quā	quō	quibus	quibus	quibus	*by/with/from whom/which*

Nom.	ille	illa	illud	*that*	hic	haec	hoc	*this*
Gen.	illīus	illīus	illīus	*of that*	huius	huius	huius	*of this*
Dat.	illī	illī	illī	*to/for that*	huic	huic	huic	*to/for this*
Acc.	illum	illam	illud	*that*	hunc	hanc	hoc	*this*
Abl.	illō	illā	illō	*with/from that*	hōc	hāc	hōc	*b/w/f this*

Nom.	illī	illae	illa	*those*	hī	hae	haec	*these*
Gen.	illōrum	illārum	illōrum	*of those*	hōrum	hārum	hōrum	*of these*
Dat.	illīs	illīs	illīs	*to those*	hīs	hīs	hīs	*to these*
Acc.	illōs	illās	illa	*those*	hōs	hās	haec	*these*
Abl.	illīs	illīs	illīs	*with/from those*	hīs	hīs	hīs	*with/from these*

	reflexive pronoun		possessive reflexive adjective					
Nom.	---		suus	sua	suum	suī	suae	sua
Gen.	suī		suī	suae	suī	suōrum	suārum	suōrum
Dat.	sibi		suō	suae	suō	suīs	suīs	suīs
Acc.	sē		suum	suam	suum	suōs	suās	sua
Abl.	sē		suō	suā	suō	suīs	suīs	suīs

Adjectives and Adverbs

Decl.	Positive	Comparative	Superlative
1st/2nd	altus, -a, -um *high (deep)*	altior, altius *higher (deeper)*	altissimus, -a, -um *highest, very high (deepest)*
3rd	fortis, forte *brave*	fortior, fortius *braver, more brave*	fortissimus, -a, -um *bravest, most brave, very brave*
1st/2nd	altē *deeply*	altius *more deeply*	altissimē *very deeply*
3rd	fortiter *bravely*	fortius *more bravely*	fortissimē *very bravely*

Irregular Adjectives and Adverbs

Positive	Comparative	Superlative
bonus, -a, -um *good*	melior, melius *better*	optimus, -a, -um *best*
magnus, -a, -um *great*	maior, maius *greater*	maximus, -a, -um *greatest*
parvus, -a, -um *small*	minor, minus *smaller*	minimus, -a, -um *smallest*
multus, -a, -um	---, plus	plurimus, -a, -um

amō, amāre, amāvī, amātum: to love

	active		translation	passive		translation
Indicative						
Pres.	amō	amāmus	*I love*	amor	amāmur	*I am (being) loved*
	amās	amātis		amāris	amāminī	
	amat	amant		amātur	amantur	
Impf.	amābam	amābāmus	*I was loving*	amābar	amābāmur	*I was (being) loved*
	amābās	amābātis		amābāris	amābāminī	
	amābat	amābant		amābātur	amābantur	
Fut.	amābō	amābimus	*I will love*	amābor	amābimur	*I will be loved*
	amābis	amābitis		amāberis	amābiminī	
	amābit	amābunt		amābitur	amābuntur	
Perf.	amāvī	amāvimus	*I have loved*	amāta sum	amātae sumus	*I have been loved*
	amāvistī	amāvistis		amāta es	amātae estis	*was loved*
	amāvit	amāvērunt		amāta est	amātae sunt	
Plpf.	amāveram	amāverāmus	*I had loved*	amāta eram	amātae erāmus	*I had been loved*
	amāverās	amāverātis		amāta erās	amātae erātis	
	amāverat	amāverant		amāta erat	amātae erant	
Fut. Pf	amāverō	amāverimus	*I will have*	amāta erō	amātae erimus	*I will have been*
	amāveris	amāveritis	*loved*	amāta eris	amātae eritis	*loved*
	amāverit	amāverint		amāta erit	amātae erunt	
Subjunctive						
Pres.	amem	amēmus	same as	amer	amēmur	same as
	amēs	amētis	indicative	amēris	amēminī	indicative
	amet	ament		ametur	amentur	
Impf.	amārem	amārēmus		amārer	amārēmur	
	amārēs	amārētis		amārēris	amārēminī	
	amāret	amārent		amāretur	amārentur	
Perf.	amāverim	amāverīmus		amāta sim	amātae sīmus	
	amāverīs	amāverītis		amāta sīs	amātae sītis	
	amāverit	amāverint		amāta sit	amātae sint	
Plpf.	amāvissem	amāvissēmus		amāta essem	amātae essēmus	
	amāvissēs	amāvissētis		amāta essēs	amātae essētis	
	amāvisset	amāvissent		amāta esset	amātae essent	

Imperative

amā	amāte	*love!*

Participle

Pres.	amāns (*gen.* amantis)	*loving*		
Perf.			amātus, -a, -um	*having been loved*
Fut.	amātūrus, -a, -um	*going to love*	amandus, -a, -um	*going to be loved*

Infinitive

Pres.	amāre	*to love*	amārī	*to be love*
Perf.	amāvisse	*to have loved*	amātum esse	*to have been loved*
Fut.	amātūrum esse	*to be going to love*		

teneō, tenēre, tenuī, tentum: to hold

	active		translation	passive		translation
Indicative						
Pres.	teneō	tenēmus	*I hold*	teneor	tenēmur	*I am (being) held*
	tenēs	tenētis		tenēris	tenēminī	
	tenet	tenent		tenētur	tenentur	
Impf.	tenēbam	tenēbāmus	*I was holding*	tenēbar	tenēbāmur	*I was (being) held*
	tenēbās	tenēbātis		tenēbāris	tenēbāminī	
	tenēbat	tenēbant		tenēbātur	tenēbantur	
Fut.	tenēbō	tenēbimus	*I will hold*	tenēbor	tenēbimur	*I will be held*
	tenēbis	tenēbitis		tenēberis	tenēbiminī	
	tenēbit	tenēbunt		tenēbitur	tenēbuntur	
Perf.	tenuī	tenuimus	*I have held*	tenta sum	tentae sumus	*I have been held*
	tenuistī	tenuistis		tenta es	tentae estis	*was held*
	tenuit	tenuērunt		tenta est	tentae sunt	
Plpf.	tenueram	tenuerāmus	*I had held*	tenta eram	tentae erāmus	*I had been held*
	tenuerās	tenuerātis		tenta erās	tentae erātis	
	tenuerat	tenuerant		tenta erat	tentae erant	
Fut. Pf.	tenuerō	tenuerimus	*I will have held*	tenta erō	tentae erimus	*I will have been held*
	tenueris	tenueritis		tenta eris	tentae eritis	
	tenuerit	tenuerint		tenta erit	tentae erunt	
Subjunctive						
Pres.	teneam	teneāmus	same as	tenear	teneāmur	same as indicative
	teneās	teneātis		teneāris	teneāminī	
	teneat	teneant		teneatur	teneantur	
Impf.	tenērem	tenērēmus		tenērer	tenērēmur	
	tenērēs	tenērētis		tenērēris	tenērēminī	
	tenēret	tenērent		tenērētur	tenērentur	
Perf.	tenuerim	tenuerīmus		tenta sim	tentae sīmus	
	tenuerīs	tenuerītis		tenta sīs	tentae sītis	
	tenuerit	tenuerint		tenta sit	tentae sint	
Plpf.	tenuissem	tenuissēmus		tenta essem	tentae essēmus	
	tenuissēs	tenuissētis		tenta essēs	tentae essētis	
	tenuisset	tenuissent		tenta esset	tentae essent	

Imperative

	tenē	tenēte	*hold!*

Participle

	active		translation	passive	translation
Pres.	tenēns (*gen.* tenentis)		*holding*		
Perf.				tentus, -a, -um	*having been held*
Fut.	tentūrus, -a, -um		*going to hold*	tenendus, -a, -um	*going to be held*

Infinitive

	active	translation	passive	translation
Pres.	tenēre	*to hold*	tenērī	*to be held*
Perf.	tenuisse	*to have held*	tentum esse	*to have been held*
Fut.	tentūrum esse	*to be going to hold*		

dūcō, dūcere, dūxī, ductum: to lead

	active		translation	passive		translation
Indicative						
Pres.	dūcō	dūcimus	*I lead*	dūcor	dūcimur	*I am (being) led*
	dūcis	dūcitis		dūceris	dūciminī	
	dūcit	dūcunt		dūcitur	dūcuntur	
Impf.	dūcēbam	dūcēbāmus	*I was leading*	dūcēbar	dūcēbāmur	*I was (being) led*
	dūcēbās	dūcēbātis		dūcēbāris	dūcēbāminī	
	dūcēbat	dūcēbant		dūcēbātur	dūcēbantur	
Fut.	dūcam	dūcēmus	*I will lead*	dūcar	dūcēmur	*I will be led*
	dūcēs	dūcētis		dūcēris	dūcēminī	
	dūcet	dūcent		dūcētur	dūcentur	
Perf.	dūxī	dūximus	*I have led*	ducta sum	ductae sumus	*I have been led*
	dūxistī	dūxistis		ducta es	ductae estis	
	dūxit	dūxērunt		ducta est	ductae sunt	
Plpf.	dūxeram	dūxerāmus	*I had led*	ducta eram	ductae erāmus	*I had been led*
	dūxerās	dūxerātis		ducta erās	ductae erātis	
	dūxerat	dūxerant		ducta erat	ductae erant	
Fut.. Pf.	dūxerō	dūxerimus	*I will have led*	ducta erō	ductae erimus	*I will have been led*
	dūxeris	dūxeritis		ducta eris	ductae eritis	
	dūxerit	dūxerint		ducta erit	ductae erunt	
Subjunctive						
Pres.	dūcam	dūcāmus	same as	dūcar	dūcāmur	same as indicative
	dūcās	dūcātis	indicative	dūcāris	dūcāminī	
	dūcat	dūcant		dūcātur	dūcantur	
Impf.	dūcerem	dūcerēmus		dūcerer	dūcerēmur	
	dūcerēs	dūcerētis		dūcerēris	dūcerēminī	
	dūceret	dūcerent		dūcerētur	dūcerentur	
Perf.	dūxerim	dūxerīmus		ducta sim	ductae sīmus	
	dūxerīs	dūxerītis		ducta sīs	ductae sītis	
	dūxerit	dūxerint		ducta sit	ductae sint	
Plpf.	dūxissem	dūxissēmus		ducta essem	ductae essēmus	
	dūxissēs	dūxissētis		ducta essēs	ductae essētis	
	dūxisset	dūxissent		ducta esset	ductae essent	
Imperative						
	dūc(e)	dūcite	*lead!*			
Participle						
Pres.	dūcēns (*gen.* dūcentis)		*leading*			
Perf.				ductus, -a, -um		*having been led*
Fut.	ductūrus, -a, -um		*going to lead*	dūcendus, -a, -um		*going to be led*
Infinitive						
Pres.	dūcere		*to lead*	dūcī		*to be led*
Perf.	dūxisse		*to have led*	ductum esse		*to have been led*
Fut.	ductūrum esse		*to be going to lead*			

capiō, capere, cēpī, captum: to take, seize

	active		translation	passive		translation
Indicative						
Pres.	capiō	capimus	*I take*	capior	capimur	*I am (being) taken*
	capis	capitis		caperis	capiminī	
	capit	capiunt		capitur	capiuntur	
Impf.	capiēbam	capēbāmus	*I was taking*	capiēbar	capiēbāmur	*I was (being) taken*
	capiēbās	capiēbātis		capiēbāris	capiēbāminī	
	capiēbat	capiēbant		capiēbātur	capiēbantur	
Fut.	capiam	capiēmus	*I will take*	capiar	capiēmur	*I will be taken*
	capiēs	capiētis		capiēris	capiēminī	
	capiet	capient		capiētur	capientur	
Perf.	cēpī	cēpimus	*I have taken*	capta sum	captae sumus	*I have been taken*
	cēpistī	cēpistis		capta es	captae estis	*was taken*
	cēpit	cēpērunt		capta est	captae sunt	
Plpf.	cēperam	cēperāmus	*I had taken*	capta eram	captae erāmus	*I had been taken*
	cēperās	cēperātis		capta erās	captae erātis	
	cēperat	cēperant		capta erat	captae erant	
Fut. Pf.	cēperō	cēperimus	*I will have taken*	capta erō	captae erimus	*I will have been*
	cēperis	cēperitis		capta eris	captae eritis	*taken*
	cēperit	cēperint		capta erit	captae erunt	

Subjunctive						
Pres.	capiam	capāmus	same as	capiar	capiāmur	same as indicative
	capiās	capiātis		capiāris	capiāminī	
	capiat	capiant		capiātur	capiantur	
Impf.	caperem	caperēmus		caperer	caperēmur	
	caperēs	caperētis		caperēris	caperēminī	
	caperet	caperent		caperētur	caperentur	
Perf.	cēperim	cēperīmus		capta sim	captae sīmus	
	cēperīs	cēperītis		capta sīs	captae sītis	
	cēperit	cēperint		capta sit	captae sint	
Plpf.	cēpissem	cēpissēmus		capta essem	captae essēmus	
	cēpissēs	cēpissētis		capta essēs	captae essētis	
	cēpisset	cēpissent		capta esset	captae essent	

Imperative

cape	capite	*take!*

Participle

Pres.	capiēns (*gen.* capientis)	*taking*	
Perf.		captus, -a, -um	*having been taken*
Fut.	captūrus, -a, -um	*going to take*	capiendus, -a, -um	*going to be taken*

Infinitive

Pres.	capere	*to take*	capī	*to be taken*
Perf.	cēpisse	*to have taken*	captum esse	*to have been taken*
Fut.	captūrum esse	*to be going to take*		

sciō, scīre, scīvī, scītum: to know

	active		translation	passive		translation
Indicative						
Pres.	sciō	scīmus	*I know*	scior	scīmur	*I am (being) known*
	scīs	scītis		scīris	scīminī	
	scit	sciunt		scītur	sciuntur	
Impf.	sciēbam	sciēbāmus	*I was knowing*	sciēbar	sciēbāmur	*I was (being) known*
	sciēbās	sciēbātis		sciēbāris	sciēbāminī	
	sciēbat	sciēbant		sciēbātur	sciēbantur	
Fut.	sciam	sciēmus	*I will know*	sciar	sciēmur	*I will be known*
	sciēs	sciētis		sciēris	sciēminī	
	sciet	scient		sciētur	scientur	
Perf.	scīvi	scīvimus	*I have known*	scīta sum	scītae sumus	*I have been known*
	scīvistī	scīvistis		scīta es	scītae estis	
	scīvit	scīvērunt		scīta est	scītae sunt	
Plpf.	scīveram	scīverāmus	*I had known*	scīta eram	scītae erāmus	*I had been known*
	scīverās	scīverātis		scīta erās	scītae erātis	
	scīverat	scīverant		scīta erat	scītae erant	
Fut. Pf.	scīverō	scīverimus	*I will have*	scīta erō	scītae erimus	*I will have been*
	scīveris	scīveritis	*known*	scīta eris	scītae eritis	*known*
	scīverit	scīverint		scīta erit	scītae erunt	
Subjunctive						
Pres.	sciam	sciāmus	same as	sciar	sciāmur	same as indicative
	sciās	sciātis	indicative	sciāris	sciāminī	
	sciat	sciant		sciātur	sciantur	
Impf.	scīrem	scīrēmus		scīrer	scīrēmur	
	scīrēs	scīrētis		scīrēris	scīrēminī	
	scīret	scīrent		scīrētur	scīrentur	
Perf.	scīverim	scīverīmus		scīta sim	scītae sīmus	
	scīverīs	scīverītis		scīta sīs	scītae sītis	
	scīverit	scīverint		scīta sit	scītae sint	
Plpf.	scīvissem	scīvissēmus		scīta essem	scītae essēmus	
	scīvissēs	scīvissētis		scīta essēs	scītae essētis	
	scīvisset	scīvissent		scīta esset	scītae essent	
Imperative						
	scī	scīte	*know!*			

Participle

Pres.	sciēns (gen. scientis)	*knowing*		
Perf.			scītus, -a, -um	*having been known*
Fut.	scītūrus, -a, -um	*going to know*	sciendus, -a, -um	*going to be known*

Infinitive

Pres.	scīre	*to know*	scīrī	*to be known*
Perf.	scīvisse	*to have known*	scītum esse	*to have been known*
Fut.	scītūrum esse	to *be going to know*		

Sum, esse, fuī, futūrum: to be			**possum, posse, potuī, -- : to be able, can**		
		translation			translation
Indicative					
Pres.	sum	sumus	*I am*	possum	possumus	*I am able, can*
	es	estis		potes	potestis	
	est	sunt		potest	possunt	
Impf.	eram	erāmus	*I was*	poteram	poterāmus	*I was able, could*
	erās	erātis		poterās	poterātis	
	erat	erant		poterat	poterant	
Fut.	erō	erimus	*I will be*	poterō	poterimus	*I will be able*
	eris	eritis		poteris	poteritis	
	erit	erunt		poterit	poterunt	
Perf.	fuī	fuimus	*I have been,*	potuī	potuimus	*I have been able,*
	fuistī	fuistis	*I was*	potuistī	potuistis	*I was able, could*
	fuit	fuērunt		potuit	potuērunt	
Plpf.	fueram	fuerāmus	*I had been*	potueram	potuerāmus	*I had been able*
	fuerās	fuerātis		potuerās	potuerātis	
	fuerat	fuerant		potuerat	potuerant	
Fut. Pf.	fuerō	fuerimus	*I will have been*	potuerō	potuerimus	*I will have been able*
	fueris	fueritis		potueris	potueritis	
	fuerit	fuerint		potuerit	potuerint	
Subjunctive					
Pres.	sim	sīmus	same as	possim	possīmus	same as
	sīs	sītis	indicative	possīs	possītis	indicative
	sit	sint		possit	possint	
Impf.	essem	essēmus		possem	possēmus	
	essēs	essētis		possēs	possētis	
	esset	essent		posset	possent	
Perf.	fuerim	fuerīmus		potuerim	potuerīmus	
	fuerīs	fuerītis		potuerīs	potuerītis	
	fuerit	fuerint		potuerit	potuerint	
Plpf.	fuissem	fuissēmus		potuissem	potuissēmus	
	fuissēs	fuissētis		potuissēs	potuissētis	
	fuisset	fuissent		potuisset	potuissent	

Imperative

xxx   xxx

Infinitive

Pres.	esse	*to be*	posse	*to be able*
Perf.	fuisse	*to have been*	potuisse	*to have been heard*
Fut.	futūrum esse*	*to be going to be*	----	

* alternative = fore

sum, esse, fuī, futūrum: to be, 165
   adsum, -esse, -fuī: be present, assist, 3
   dēsum, -esse, -fuī: be lacking, lack, fail, 6
   intersum, -esse, -fuī: take part in, engage in, 1

possum, posse, potuī: be able, can, avail, 40
praesum, -esse, -fuī: be over, preside over, 2
subsum, -esse, -fuī: be near, close at hand, 1

eō, īre, i(v)ī, itūrum: to go

	active		translation
Indicative			
Pres.	eō	īmus	*I go*
	īs	ītis	
	it	eunt	
Impf.	ībam	ībāmus	*I was going*
	ībās	ībātis	
	ībat	ībant	
Fut.	ībō	ībimus	*I will go*
	ībis	ībitis	
	ībit	ībunt	
Perf.	iī	iimus	*I went, have gone*
	īstī	īstis	
	iit	iērunt	
Plpf.	ieram	ierāmus	*I had gone*
	ierās	ierātis	
	ierat	ierant	
Fut. Pf.	ierō	ierimus	*I will have gone*
	ieris	ieritis	
	ierit	ierint	
Subjunctive			
Pres.	eam	eāmus	same as indicative
	eās	eātis	
	eat	eant	
Impf.	īrem	īrēmus	
	īrēs	īrētis	
	īret	īrent	
Perf.	ierim	ierimus	
	ieris	ieritis	
	ierit	ierunt	
Plpf.	īssem	īssēmus	
	īssēs	īssētis	
	īsset	īssent	

Imperative

	ī	īte

Participle

Pres.	iēns (euntis)	*going*
Perf.	---	
Fut.	itūrus, -a, -um	*going to go*

Infinitive

Pres.	īre	*to go*
Perf.	īsse	*to have gone*
Fut.	itūrum esse	*to be going to go*

Compound verbs

adeō, -īre, i(v)ī, itus: approach, encounter, 2
eō, īre, īvī, itum: to go, come, 4
exeō, -īre, -iī (īvī), -itus: go out, 4
ineō, -īre, iī, -itum: go into, enter, 1
intereō, -īre, -īvī, -ītum: to die, perish, 3
introeō, -īre, iī, -itum: go into, enter, 1
obeō, -īre, -īvī, -ītum: go to meet, oppose 1
prōdeō, -īre, -iī, -itum: advance, go forth, 1
redeō, -īre, -īvī: go back, return, 1
subeō, -īre, -iī, -itum: go up to, approach, 1
trānseō, -īre, -iī (īvī), itus: go across, pass, 6

volō, velle, voluī: to wish, want

	active		translation

Indicative

Pres.	volō	volumus	*I wish*	← irregular present tense
	vīs	vultis[1]		[1]pg. 14, 46 [2]pg. 28
	vult	volunt[2]		

Impf.	volēbam	volēbāmus	*I was wishing*
	volēbās	volēbātis	
	volēbat	volēbant	

Fut.	volam	volēmus	*I will wish*
	volēs	volētis	
	volet	volent	

Perf.	voluī	voluimus	*I have wished*
	voluistī	voluistis	
	voluit	voluērunt	

Plpf.	volueram	voluerāmus	*I had wished*
	voluerās	voluerātis	
	voluerat	voluerant	

Fut. Pf.	voluerō	voluerimus	*I will have wished*
	volueris	volueritis	
	voluerit	voluerint	

Subjunctive

Pres.	velim	velimus	same as indicative	← irregular present tense (not volam)
	velis	velitis		[3]pg. 52 [4]pg. 28, 42, 58, 60
	velit[3]	velint[4]		

Impf.	vellem	vellēmus		← irregular imperfect tense (irreg. velle)
	vellēs	vellētis		[5]pg. 10, 40, 52, 58, 62
	vellet	vellent[5]		

Perf.	voluerim	voluerīmus
	voluerīs	voluerītis
	voluerit	voluerint

Plpf.	voluissem	voluissēmus
	voluissēs	voluissētis
	voluisset	voluissent

Imperative

	xxxx	xxxx	*wish!*

Participle

Pres.	volēns (gen. volentis)	*wishing*
Perf.	xxxx	
Fut.	xxxx	

Infinitive

Pres.	velle	*to wish*	← irregular infinitive
Perf.	voluisse	*to have wished*	
Fut.	xxxx		

sequō, sequī, secūtus-a-um sum: to follow

	deponent		translation
Indicative			
Pres.	sequor	sequimur	*I follow*
	sequeris	sequiminī	
	sequitur	sequuntur	
Impf.	sequēbar	sequēbāmur	*I was following*
	sequēbāris	sequēbāminī	
	sequēbātur	sequēbantur	
Fut.	sequar	sequēmur	*I will follow*
	sequēris	sequēminī	
	sequētur	sequentur	
Perf.	secūta sum	secūtae sumus	*I have followed*
	secūta es	secūtae estis	
	secūta est	secūtae sunt	
Plpf.	secūta eram	secūtae erāmus	*I had followed*
	secūta erās	secūtae erātis	
	secūta erat	secūtae erant	
Fut.. Pf.	secūta erō	secūtae erimus	*I will have followed*
	secūta eris	secūtae eritis	
	secūta erit	secūtae erunt	
Subjunctive			
Pres.	sequar	sequāmur	same as indicative
	sequāris	sequāminī	
	sequātur	sequantur	
Impf.	sequerer	sequerēmur	
	sequerēris	sequerēminī	
	sequerētur	sequerentur	
Perf.	secūta sim	secūtae sīmus	
	secūta sīs	secūtae sītis	
	secūta sit	secūtae sint	
Plpf.	secūta essem	secūtae essēmus	
	secūta essēs	secūtae essētis	
	secūta esset	secūtae essent	

Imperative

	sequere	sequitor	*follow!*

Participle

Pres.	sequēns (gen. sequentis)	*following*	
Perf.	secūtus, -a, -um	*having followed*	
Fut.	secūtūrus, -a, -um	*going to follow*	sequendus,-a -um *going to be followed*

Infinitive

Pres.	sequī	*to follow*
Perf.	secūtum esse	*to have followed*
Fut.	secūtūrum esse	*to be going to follow*

1. Relative Clause of Purpose

There are two different types of purpose (final) clauses: adverbial and relative. Adverbial purpose clauses are introduced by *ut/nē* and are regularly translated with the modal verbs *may* and *might*. Relative clauses of purpose behave in the same way as adverbial purpose clauses—employing present subjunctive in primary sequence and imperfect subjunctive in secondary sequence—but they are introduced by a relative pronoun.

There are only two examples of relative clauses of purpose in this commentary. When you translate these clauses, use the modal verbs *may/might* or *would/should* depending on the context:

legātōs....mittunt quī dīcerent...	*they sent envoys who would/should say...*	p. 11
	= so that they might say...	
nāvēs...quibus reportārī possent	*ships by which they might be able to be carried back*	p. 19
	= so that they might be able to be carried back	

2. Relative Clause of Characteristic (Generic Relative Clause)

The function of a relative clause of characteristic is is to clarify *what sort of person* or *what sort of thing* the antecedent is. This clause governs a subjunctive verb and very often modifies a general or indefinite antecedent (e.g. he is a man who flees from danger). The indicative mood, by contrast, suggests that the antecedent is a particular someone doing something (e.g. he is the man who fled from danger).

e.g. Is est quī ā perīculō fugat.	*He is (the sort of) one who flees from danger.*
or	*He is (the sort of) one who **would** flee from danger.*

This type of relative clause can be causal, concessive, or consecutive (result) in sense depending on the context. While you should translate pf. and plpf. subjunctives as you would an indicative, you may translate pres. and impf. subjunctives two different ways: (a) as an indicative or (b) as a potential subjunctive with the modal verb *would* (see above). Caesar frequently uses this clause when the antecedent is (a) missing, as in the example above, (b) a generic noun, or (c) an indefinite pronoun (e.g. *is, ea, id*).

ea quae...pertinērent	*those (sort of) things which pertained/would pertain to setting out*	p. 4
regnum...quod pater ante habuerit	*(the sort of) kingdom which his father held before*	p. 6
id quod fēcerit	*that (sort of thing) which he did*	p. 40
neque is sum quī...terrear	*I am not (such a) one who am terrified/would be terrified*	p. 46

3. Relative Clause in Indirect Discourse

In indirect discourse, the verbs of subordinate clauses—including including relative clauses—become subjunctive. Caesar frequently uses quod-clauses and conditional clauses (sī-clauses) in this way, but his use of relative clauses in indirect discourse is surprisingly rare:

quod imperium obtentūrus esset	*because he was about to obtain the command*	p. 6
quod...pendere cōnsuēsset	*which he had been accustomed to pay*	p. 40
quōrum alter mīlia...absit	*one of whom is about fifty miles away*	p. 42

In most instances, these subjunctives do not require a special translation and therefore should be translated in the tense in which you find them. If the relative clause was originally a relative clause of purpose or a relative clause of characteristic, however, you should translate it accordingly.

Conditional sentences in indirect discourse undergo a number of changes that make them more difficult to identify and translate than their counterparts in direct discourse.

I. Identifying conditions in direct discourse:

If-then clauses are called **conditions** or **conditional sentences**. All conditions have two parts: (a) the **protasis** (premise, if-clause, or conditional) and (b) the **apodosis** (result, then-clause, or consequent). In order to identify one of the six main types of conditions below, you must identify the tense and mood of the verbs in both the *protasis* and *apodosis*. If the tense and moods of the verbs do no fit one of the six types, we call such a sentence a **mixed condition**.

name	protasis	apodosis	example in translation
simple present	pres.	pres.	If you believe, you are mistaken.
simple past	past	past	If you believed, you were mistaken.
future more vivid	fut./fut. pf.	fut.	If you believe, you will be mistaken.
future less vivid	pres. subj.	pres. subj.	If you should believe, you would be mistaken.
present contrafactual	impf. subj.	impf. subj.	If you were believing, you would be mistaken.
past contrafactual	plpf. subj.	plpf. subj.	If you had believed, you would have been mistaken.

II. Identifying conditions in indirect discourse

In indirect discourse, every apodosis becomes an infinitive and every protasis—whether originally indicative or subjunctive—becomes subjunctive. In secondary sequence, the infinitive remains the same, but the protasis undergoes more changes (often becoming impf. subj.), which makes the condition difficult to identify. Below is a summary of those changes.

Indicative Conditions		
direct discourse		indirect discourse
Simple Present: *If you believe, you are wrong.*		
primary	dīcō "sī crēdis, errās."	dīcō sī haec crēdās, tē errāre
secondary	dixī "sī crēdis, errās."	dixī sī haec crēderēs, tē errāre
Simple Past: *If you believed, you were wrong.*		
primary	dīcō "sī crēdēbās/crēdidistī, errāvistī."	dīcō sī haec crēderēs/crēdideris, tē errāvisse.
secondary	dixī "sī crēdēbās/crēdidistī, errāvistī."	dixī sī haec crēderēs/crēdidissēs, tē errāvisse.
Future More Vivid: *If you believe, you will be wrong.*		
primary	dīcō "sī crēdēs, errābis."	dīcō sī haec crēdās, tē errātūrum esse
secondary	dixī "sī crēdēs, errābis."	dixī sī haec crēderēs, tē errātūrum esse

Subjunctive Conditions		
direct discourse		indirect discourse
Future Less Vivid: *If you should believe, you would be wrong.*		
primary	dīcō "sī crēdās, errēs."	dīcō sī haec crēdās, tē errātūrum esse
secondary	dixī "sī crēdās, errēs."	dixī sī haec crēderēs, tē errātūrum esse
Present Contrafactual: *If you were believing, you would be wrong.*		
primary	dīcō "sī crēderēs, errārēs."	dīcō sī haec crēderēs, tē errātūrum esse
secondary	dixī "sī crēderēs, errārēs."	dixī sī haec crēderēs, tē errātūrum esse
Past Contrafactual: *If you had believed, you would have been wrong.*		
primary	dīcō "sī crēdissēs, errāvissēs."	dīcō sī haec crēdissēs, tē errātūrum fuisse.
secondary	dixī "sī crēdissēs, errāvissēs."	dixī sī haec crēdissēs, tē errātūrum fuisse.

Caesar Alphabetized Core Vocabulary (5 or more times)

The following seven pages includes all words in the Caesar selections that occur five or more times arranged in an alphabetized vocabulary list. The author tabulated the frequency lists by collating all of Caesars' words in the selections and counting them. Digital flashcards are available online.

ā, ab: (away) from, by, 80
absum, -esse, āfuī: be absent, lack, 6
ac: and, and also, and even, 24
accēdō, -ere, -cessī, -cessus: approach, 5
accidō, -ere, accidī: to happen, fall to, 13
accipiō: to take without effort, receive, get, accept, 10
ad: to, toward; near, at 110
Aduātucī, -ōrum m.: Aduatuci (in Belgae), 5
adventus, -ūs m.: arrival, approach, 7
ager, agrī m.: field, land; farm, 8
aliquī, -qua, -quod: some, any, definite, 8
alius, -a, -ud: other, another, else, 13
alter, -era, -erum: other (of two), 12
altus, -a, -um: high, lofty, tall, 5
Ambiorix, -rigis m.: Ambiorix, 15
amīcitia, -ae, f.: friendship, 12
animadvertō, -ere, -vertī, -versum: turn mind to, notice 5
animus, -ī m: mind, spirit; pl. courage, 6
annus, -ī m.: year, 11
appellō (1): call, call by name, 5
apud: among, at the house of (acc.), 7
arbitror, arbitrārī, arbitrātus sum: to judge, think, 10
arma, -ōrum n.: arms, equipment, tools, 7
ascendō, -ere, -ī, -ēnsus: ascend, mount 2
at: but; mind you; but, you say, 7
atque: and, and also, and even, 60
aut: or (aut...aut – either...or), 32
autem: however, moreover, 5

barbarus, -a, -um: foreign, savage, 5
Belgae, -ārum m.: Belgians, 6
bellum, -ī, n.: war, 16
Britannia, -ae f.: Britain, 6

Caesar, -aris m.: Caesar, 40
calamitās, -tātis f.: loss, misfortune, calamity, disaster, 5
capiō, -ere, cēpī, captum: to take, capture, seize, 11
castra, -ōrum n.: camp, encampment, 23
casus, -ūs m.: misfortune, mishap; fall 5
causa, -ae f.: reason, cause; case, 21
celeritās, -tātis f.: quickness, swiftness, speed, 5
celeriter: quickly, swiftly, speedily, 6
certus, -a, -um: definite, sure, certain, reliable, 8
Cicero, Cicerōnis m.: Cicero 14

circiter: (round) about, not far from, 7
circumveniō, -īre: to come around, encircle, 6
cīvitās cīvitātis, f.: state, citizenship, 20
coepī, coepisse, coeptum: to begin, 9
cognōscō, -ere, -nōvī, -nitum: to learn, come to know, pf. know, 14
cōgō, cōgere, coēgī, coāctum: to collect; compel, 11
cohors, cohortis f.: cohort, company, troop 14
commūnis, -e: common, 6
compleō, -ēre, -ēvī, -ētum: fill up, fill, 6
complūrēs n.: several, 5
concilium, -iī n.: meeting, rendezvous, 6
confirmō (1): make strong, confirm strengthen, 5
co(n)iciō, -ere, -iēcī: throw together, throw, take oneself, 10
cōnor, cōnārī, cōnātus sum: to try, 6
cōnsilium, -iī n.: plan, counsel, 12
conspiciō, -ere, -spexī, -spectus: see, behold, 5
constituō, -ere, -uī, -ūtus: decide, establish, resolve, 14
cōnsuescō, -ere, cōnsuē(v)ī, -suētum: to be accustomed, 8
consuētūdo, -inis f.: custom, habit, 5
contineō, -ēre, -nuī, -tentum: hold or keep together, 6
contrōversia, -ae f.: dispute, debate, 7
conveniō, -īre, -vēnī, -ventus: come together, assemble, 9
copia, -ae f.: abundance, supply; troops, 12
Cotta, -ae m.: Cotta, 10
Crassus, -ī m.: Crassus, 5
cum: with (+ abl.); when, since, although, 86

dē: (down) from; about, concerning, 41
dēferō, -ferre, -tulī, -lātum: report, offer 8
dēmonstrō (1): to show, demonstrate, 5
dēsum, -esse, -fuī, -futūrum: be lacking, lack, fail, 6
dīcō, -ere, dīxī, dictus: say, speak, tell, call, name, 18
diēs, -ēī m./f.: day, time, season, 33
discēdō, -ere, -cessī, -cessum: to go away, depart, 9
disciplīna, -ae f.: training, instruction, 5
dō, dare, dedī, datum: give; grant, 18
Druidēs, -um m.: Druids, 6
dūcō, -ere, dūxī, ductus: lead, draw; consider, 7
dum: while, as long as, until, 6
duo, duae, duo: two, 8

ē, ex: out from, from, out of (+ abl.), 72
Eburōnēs, -um m.: Eburones (German), 5
efficiō, -ere, -fēcī, -fectus: make, form, 5
ēgredior, -ī, -gressus: go out, disembark, 5
eques, equitis m.: horseman, rider, 12
equitātus, -ūs m.: cavalry, 5
et: and, also, even, 167
etiam: also, even, besides, 8

etsī: even if, although, though, 5
exercitus, -ūs m.: (trained) army, 9
existimō (1): judge, consider, think, 9

facilis, -e: easy; adv. facile, easily, 10
faciō, -ere, fēcī, factum: do, make, perform; grant, 40
facultās, -tātis f.: opportunity, power, skill, ability, 5
ferē: almost, nearly, closely, 7
ferō, ferre, tulī, lātus: carry, bear, endure, 7
fīlius, -iī m.: son, 5
fīnis, -is m./f.: end, border; territory, 17
fīnitimus, -a, -um: neighboring; subst. neighbors, 6
flūmen, -inis n.: river, stream, 9
fortis, -e: strong, brave, valiant, 7
frūmentum, -ī n.: grain, 10

Gallia, -ae f.: Gaul, 17
Gallus, -a, -um: Gallic; subst. a Gaul, 15
genus, generis, n.: origin, kind, sort, 10
Germānus, -a, -um: German, 9
gerō, -ere, gessī, gestus: carry (on), wage, 8
gravis, -e: heavy, serious, severe; venerable, 9

habeō, -ēre, habuī, -itus: have, hold; consider, 32
Helvētius, -a, -um: Helvetian; subst. a Helvetian 16
hīberna, -ōrum n.: winter-quarters, 26
hic, haec, hoc: this, these, 92
homō, -inis m./f.: man, mortal, human, 15
hostis, -is m./f.: stranger, enemy, foe, 43

ibi: there, in that place, 5
īdem, eadem, idem: the same, 14
ille, illa, illud: that, those, 22
impedīmentum, -ī n.: baggage, impediment, 6
imperium, -ī n.: command, power, 7
imperō (1): command, order, bid, 7
impetus, -ūs m.: attack, assault, onset, 7
in: in, on (abl.), into, to (acc.) 173
incitō (1): put into motion, urge on, 5
inferō, -ferre, -tulī, illātum: wage, carry on, 7
initium, -ī n.: beginning, entrance, 6
inter: between, among (+ acc.), 15
interim: meanwhile, in the meantime, 5
interficiō, -ere, -fēcī, -fectum: kill, slay, destroy, 14
intermittō, -ere: interrupt, discontinue, leave off, 5
ipse, ipsa, ipsum: -self; the very, 17
is, ea, id: this, that; he, she, it, 133
ita: so, thus, 7
itaque: and so, 6
iter, itineris n.: way, road, route, journey, 17
iubeō, iubēre, iussī, iussum: to order, command, 17

Labiēnus, ī m.: Labienus, 5
lēgātus, -ī m.: an envoy, legate, 16
legio, -ōnis f.: legion, (~4200 soldiers), 32
licet: impersonal, it is allowed or permitted, 5
littera, -ae f.: letter of the alphabet, letter, literature, 12
locus, -ī m.: place, region, location, 31
longē: far, at a distant, 6
longus -a, -um: long, 8
Lucius, -ī m.: Lucius, 10

magnitūdo, -inis f.: greatness, size, 5
magnus, -a, -um: great, large; mighty, important, 29
maior, maius: greater, 6
manus, manūs, f.: hand; group, 9
maximē: exceedingly, especially, 6
maximus, -a, -um: greatest, largest, 15
mīles, mīlitis, m.: soldier, 33
mīlle pl. mīlia, ium n.: thousand, 9
minor, minus: less, smaller, 7
mittō, -ere, mīsī, missus: send, hurl, dismiss, 20
mors, mortis, f.: death, 9
multitūdo, inis f.: multitude, population, people, 11
multus, -a, -um: much, many, 11
mūnītio, -iōnis f.: fortification, paving, 7

nam: for, 9
nāvis, nāvis, f.: ship, boat, 23
nē: lest, that not, no, not, 13
neque: and not, nor (neque…neque = neither…nor), 27
Nerviī, -iōrum m.: Nervii (Belgic Gauls) 9
nihil: nothing, 10
nisi: if not, unless 6
nōn: not, by no means, not at all, 36
noster, nostra, nostrum: our, 36
nox, noctis, f.: night, 9
nūllus, -a, -um: none, no, no one, 9
numerus, -ī m.: number, multitude, 13
nuntius, -iī m.: messenger, 6

ob: on account of, because of (acc.), 5
obsēs, obsidis m./f.: hostage, 5
obtineō, -ēre, -uī, -tentum: hold, maintain, 6
omnis, omne: every, all, 72
oppugnātio, -tiōnis f.: an assault, 6
oppugnō (1): capture by assault, attack, 6
ōrātio, -ionis f.: speaking, speech, language, 8
ordō, -inis m.: order, line, array; status, 6
Orgetorix, -is m.: Orgetorix, 6

pars, partis, f.: part, side, direction, 43

passus, -ūs: pace, step, 7
paulus, -a, -um: little, small, 9
pāx, pācis f.: peace, quiet, rest, 6
per: through, across (acc) 18
perīculum, -ī n.: risk, danger, peril, 14
permoveō, -ēre: to move deeply, trouble, excite, agitate, 5
persuādeō, -ēre, -suāsī, -suāsum: persuade, convince, 12
pertineō, -ēre, -tinuī: to pertain to, reach, stretch to, 7
perturbō (1): confuse, disturb, throw into confusion, 6
perveniō, -īre, -vēnī, -ventum: arrive, 8
pēs, pedis m.: foot, 5
petō, petere, petīvī, petītum: seek, aim at, 7
plērumque: for the most part, mostly, commonly, 5
ponō, ponere, posuī, positum: to put, place, 6
populus, -ī m.: people, nation, 9
possum, posse, potuī: be able, can, avail, 40
post: after, behind (+ acc.); afterward, next, 5
praemium, -ī n.: reward, prize, 5
praestō, -āre, -stitī, -stitus: perform, show, be better, 6
premō, -ere, pressī, pressus: check, pursue, control, 7
prīmus -a -um: first, 15
prīvō (1): deprive of, rob, strip from (abl), 5
prō: before, for, in behalf of (abl.), 16
probō (1): approve, commend, 5
proelium, -iī n.: battle, combat, 15
profectio, -ōnis f.: departure, 5
proficīscor, -ī, -fectus: set out, depart, 23
prohibeō, -ēre, -uī, -itus: keep off, prohibit, 6
propter: on account of, because of, 5
prōvincia, -ae f.: province, 7
proximus, -a, -um: nearest, very close, 12
pūblicus, -a, -um: public, common, 11
pugna, -ae f.: battle, fight, 7
pugnō (1): to fight, 9
Pullo, Pullōnis, m.: Pullo, 6

quantus, -a, -um: how great, much, many, 6
-que: and, 109
quī, quae, quod (quis? quid?): who, which, that, 226
quidem: indeed, in fact, certainly, 6
Quintus, -ī m.: Quintus, 6
quisque, quidque: each one, each person, 9

ratio, ratiōnis, f.: calculation, account, method, 5
recipiō, -ere, -cēpī, -ceptum: take back, recover, 10
regnum, -ī n.: royal power, kingdom, realm, 8
relinquō, -ere, -līquī, -lictum: to leave behind, 7
reliquus, -a, um: remaining, the rest of, 28

rēs, reī, f.: thing, matter, affair, business, 64
resistō, -ere, -stitī: stand still, halt; oppose, 5
Rhēnus, -ī m.: Rhine River, 9
Rhodanus, -a, -um: Rhone, 5
Rōmānus, -a, -um: of Rome, Roman, 15

Sabīnus, ī m.: Sabinus, 7
salūs, -ūtis f.: safety, refuge; health, 10
sē: himself, herself, itself, themselves, 74
sed: but, moreover, however, 13
Sēquanus, -a, -um: Sequanian, 5
sēsē: emphatic form of reflexive sē, 14
sī: if (only), whether, in case that, 30
signum -ī, n.: sign, signal; gesture, seal, 5
sine: without (abl.), 8
singulus, -a, -um: one by one, separate, 5
spērō (1): hope (for), expect, 6
spēs, -ēī f.: hope, expectation, 6
sub: under, below, beneath, underneath, 5
subitō: suddenly, 5
subsequor, -ī, secūtus sum: to follow after or behind, 7
subsidium, iī n.: reserve troops; third line of battle, 5
sum, esse, fuī, futūrum: to be, 165
summus, -a, -um: top of, highest (part of) 10
superō (1): surpass, overcome, 6
superus, -a, -um: upper, higher, above, 9
sustineō, -ēre, -uī: hold up, sustain, 8
suus, -a, -um: his, her, its, their own, 54

tamen: however, nevertheless, 14
tantus, -a, -um: so great, so large, 10
telum, -ī n.: projective, weapon, blow, 9
tempus, temporis, n.: time, occasion, 11
teneō, tenēre, tenuī, tentum: to hold, keep, 6
tertius, -a, -um: third, 8
Titurius, -ī m.: Titurius, 8
tōtus -a, -um: whole, entire, 7
trānseō, -īre, -iī (īvī), itus: pass (by), 6
trēs, tria: three, 7
tum: then, at that time, 12
turris, turris f.: tower, walled tower, 7
tūtus, -a, -um: safe, secure, guarded, 7

ūllus, -a, -um: any, 5
undique: (from) everywhere, from or on all sides, 5
ūnus, -a, -um: one, 29
ūsus, -ūs m.: use, practice, application, 10
ut: as, just as, when (+ ind.); (so) that, in order that, 59
uterque, utraque, utrumque: each (of two) 8
ūtor, -ī, ūsus sum: use, employ (abl.), 5

vallum, -ī n.: wall, fortification, palisade, 11
veniō, -īre, vēnī, ventus: come, go, 14
victoria, -ae f.: victory, 7
videō, vidēre, vīdī, vīsum: to see, 14
virtūs, -ūtis f.: valor, manhood, excellence, 11
vīta, -ae, f.: life, 5
volō, velle, voluī: will, wish, be willing, 13
Vorēnus, -ī m.: Vorenus, 5

Notes